Music Endangerment

MUSIC ENDANGERMENT
How Language Maintenance Can Help

Catherine Grant

OXFORD
UNIVERSITY PRESS

Oxford University Press is a department of the University of
Oxford. It furthers the University's objective of excellence in research,
scholarship, and education by publishing worldwide.

Oxford   New York
Auckland   Cape Town   Dar es Salaam   Hong Kong   Karachi
Kuala Lumpur   Madrid   Melbourne   Mexico City   Nairobi
New Delhi   Shanghai   Taipei   Toronto

With offices in
Argentina   Austria   Brazil   Chile   Czech Republic   France   Greece
Guatemala   Hungary   Italy   Japan   Poland   Portugal   Singapore
South Korea   Switzerland   Thailand   Turkey   Ukraine   Vietnam

Oxford is a registered trademark of Oxford University Press
in the UK and certain other countries.

Published in the United States of America by
Oxford University Press
198 Madison Avenue, New York, NY 10016

© Oxford University Press 2014

All rights reserved. No part of this publication may be reproduced, stored in
a retrieval system, or transmitted, in any form or by any means, without the prior
permission in writing of Oxford University Press, or as expressly permitted by law,
by license, or under terms agreed with the appropriate reproduction rights organization.
Inquiries concerning reproduction outside the scope of the above should be sent to the
Rights Department, Oxford University Press, at the address above.

You must not circulate this work in any other form
and you must impose this same condition on any acquirer.

Library of Congress Cataloging-in-Publication Data
Grant, Catherine, 1977–
Music endangerment: how language maintenance can help / Catherine Grant.
  pages cm
Includes bibliographical references and index.
ISBN 978-0-19-935217-3 (hardback : alk. paper) — ISBN 978-0-19-935218-0
(pbk. : alk. paper)   1. Applied ethnomusicology.   2. Sustainability.   3. Language
maintenance.   I. Title.
ML3799.2.G73 2014
781.6—dc23   2013036298

Publication of this book has been financially supported by an AMS 75 PAYS Endowment
awarded to the author by the American Musicological Society, funded in part by the National
Endowment for the Humanities and the Andrew W. Mellon Foundation.

9 8 7 6 5 4 3 2 1
Printed in the United States of America
on acid-free paper

CONTENTS

Foreword by Anthony Seeger   vii
Preface   xi
   A Note on Terminology   xiii
About the Companion Website   xv

Introduction   1
    The Problem of Music Endangerment   1
    Bringing Languages Into the Picture   4
    Why Music Endangerment Matters   7
    Troublesome Terminology   10
    Some Ethical Considerations   12
1. What We Know and What We've Done   15
    1.1 Theoretical Foundations   17
    1.2 Documentation and Preservation   23
    1.3 Recognition and Celebration   28
    1.4 Transmission and Dissemination   31
    1.5 Policy and Enterprise   35
    1.6 Coordination and Evaluation Mechanisms   39
    1.7 Conclusions   44
2. Language and Music Vitality: A Comparative Framework   47
    2.1 Systems of Learning Music   48
    2.2 Musicians and Communities   52
    2.3 Contexts and Constructs   56
    2.4 Infrastructure and Regulations   62
    2.5 Media and the Music Industry   64
    2.6 Conclusions   69
3. Learning From Language Maintenance   73
    3.1 Dead or Alive? Identifying and Assessing Music
        Endangerment   74
    3.2 Developing Advocacy for Music Sustainability   79

    3.3 Developing Maintenance and Revitalization Strategies   84
    3.4 Reflecting on Aims and Outcomes of Strategies   93
    3.5 Developing Coordinating Mechanisms   97
    3.6 Conclusions   102
4. How to Identify and Assess Endangerment: The Music Vitality and Endangerment Framework   105
    4.1 Modifying the Language Framework   106
    4.2 Building a New Framework for Music   111
    4.3 Conclusions   125
5. Measuring Up: Putting the Framework to Work   127
    5.1 A Short History of *Ca Trù*   127
    5.2 Carrying Out the Vitality Assessment   130
    5.3 A Vitality Assessment of *Ca Trù*   132
    5.4 Conclusions   161
6. Where to From Here?   164
    6.1 Taking Stock: A Brief Summary   166
    6.2 Next Steps in Practical Terms   170
    6.3 Next Steps in Research Terms   174
    6.4 Closing Words   176

Bibliography   178
Index   197

FOREWORD

> Lost, lost forever!
> No more music and dance.
> No one can do them 'cause no one has learned them
> And so we have lost them for good.
> (words by Anthony Seeger)

Narratives of loss and examples of disappearing languages and musical traditions assail us at every turn. By some estimates a half of the world's languages will no longer be spoken by the end of this century. Local musicians in many countries struggle to find students to learn their craft and audiences willing to listen to them. National governments and international agencies express concern about the rapid loss of local traditions and try to address the problem with legislation and programs. At the same time humans have never been able to listen to as much music or access as many words as they now can using both old and new media, from historic recordings and manuscripts to today's blog posts and mobile phone videos. In most places we are also composing more music and creating more mash-ups that reach beyond the limits of local traditions than ever before. Some people attribute the gains and losses to the globalization of media and emergence of ever-faster communications technology along with the inevitable spread of a global economic system. But musical change is neither that universal, inevitable, or unidirectional. The world today looks nothing like that in which Mozart composed, yet his music continues to be popular and a search on YouTube yields over six million videos, of which one version of a piece has had more than eight million viewers. Latin hasn't disappeared; Gregorian chant in Europe and the Vedic chanting in India continue to this day. But the last speakers of several American Indian languages have died since 2000 and complete knowledge of many other musical forms may have been lost forever.

How are we to understand this confusing diversity of outcomes? What should musicians, audiences, and local communities do to help ensure future performances of traditions they value? Can scholars and the interested public play a role in sustaining human cultural diversity? Should they? Is every situation unique, or is it possible to generalize? This book addresses these questions and many more. Catherine Grant brings an impressive array of skills and thinking to her systematic examination of the sustainability of language and music in the complex social, political, and economic environments of the 21st century. It is a pleasure to see its publication and an honor to be invited to write its foreword.

Grant makes a very important contribution to the emergent field of applied ethnomusicology here. This book is divided into two parts, the first of which provides an exceedingly thorough, thoughtful, and useful review of literature from two different academic disciplines, language maintenance and ethnomusicology, and considers how the first may help inform the second on issues of sustainability. The second part develops a measure of the vitality of musical traditions that Grant applies to the specific case of *ca trù* in Vietnam using documents, interviews, and firsthand knowledge.

I believe the linguists concerned with the widespread disappearance of languages around the world have been more systematic than ethnomusicologists in their approaches to the problem and quicker to employ new technologies, in collaboration with communities, to counteract the trends. They moved earlier to develop measures of language vitality, and they established digital resources for teaching that provide local communities with access to recordings and lesson plans. There are probably several reasons why these efforts have been more comprehensive than those of ethnomusicologists, among them the absoluteness of language disappearance—when the last speakers of a language die, it is very difficult to re-establish that language in living form—and the greater willingness or urgency among some ethnic groups to support steps to retain their languages, more so than the sounds of a particular musical form. Music itself is not so clearly and completely endangered; when the last performers of one musical genre die, some other kind of music related to it and associated with a form of community identity is often still performed.

Ethnomusicologists and folklorists have long wondered why certain musical traditions thrive or revive and others disappear. Linguists studying what they call "endangered languages" have somewhat more systematically sought to create replicable measures to determine the vitality of language. Grant critically reviews an impressive amount of literature in both fields and constructs a Music Vitality and Endangerment Framework (MVEF) that she suggests can be used to gauge the vitality of musical genres anywhere in the world. The twelve factors in the MVEF that affect the vitality of music genres are (1) intergenerational transmission, (2) change in the number of proficient musicians, (3) change in the number of people engaged with the genre, (4) change in the music and music practices, (5) change in performance contexts and functions, (6) responses to mass media and the music industry, (7) infrastructure and resources for music practices, (8) knowledge and skills for music practices, (9) governmental policies affecting music practices, (10) community members' attitudes toward the genre, (11) relevant outsiders' opinions toward the genre, and (12) amount and quality of documentation. These variables recognize that musical traditions depend on transmission, continuity, change, and interested audiences, but also that these take place in a context of emerging mass media, the involvement of outsiders, and the often unpredictable actions of local and national governments. The measures allow for the charismatic actions of an individual passionate actor and also for the results of media attention, national cultural policies, and tourism.

Nothing like this has been attempted in such a systematic way in ethnomusicology. While a somewhat similar measure was initially developed for endangered languages and some earlier attempts were made to apply those to music, Grant carefully constructs the MVEF based on her insightful discussion of the differences between language and musical genres and a review of the debates within the linguistics community, with healthy attention paid to ethical issues. Her twelve different measures of vitality are a great improvement over impressionistic labeling or classifications that rely only on a few variables. I think something based on the MVEF will be widely adopted (as well as debated) in the fields of ethnomusicology, musicology, folklore, and performance studies. The framework is convincing partly because of the extremely careful and extensive analysis Grant has conducted of the existing literature in ethnomusicology and her use of a case study of the Vietnamese *ca trù* to illustrate it. The history and current situation of that genre demonstrate how complex the situation for any given musical tradition can be.

Readers are fortunate that the author has taken great pains to make this book approachable and its topics easy to find. It is a model for applied ethnomusicology—Grant has made it delightfully simple to navigate and read. Her arguments proceed logically from topic to topic. Her discussions of the literature go far beyond citations and summaries: she discloses disagreements among specialists and raises important concerns of her own. She has also constructed many extremely helpful tables—don't ignore them—and she has documented her work with a rich and extensive bibliography. While it may disappoint mystery fans who want everything to be revealed only at the very end, Grant's approach to ideas makes it easy to find where specific topics are raised, to use the tables for overviews, and to consult the text on subsequent occasions.

While I am certain that the coming decades will see rapid growth in our understanding of the impact of global processes, local policies, and individual initiatives on intangible cultural heritage of all kinds, this book should contribute significantly to our conversations, our understandings, and to our policies for years to come.

Anthony Seeger
Distinguished Professor of Ethnomusicology, Emeritus, UCLA
Director Emeritus, Smithsonian Folkways Recordings

PREFACE

In recent decades, communities across the world have been impacted by a raft of deep economic, social, and political changes, both local and global. For some communities, these changes have strengthened the vitality of their cultural expressions, or at least have had little adverse effect on them. For others, though—especially indigenous and minority communities—the shifts have led to the endangerment and even the loss of cultural expressions, against the will of the communities concerned. Music is among the many kinds of performance expressions that have been affected in this way. The endangerment or loss of musical traditions within a culture may have repercussions for individual and social identity, social cohesion, and the strength of other forms of cultural expression within those communities. It also has wider consequences for the diversity of human heritage.

This book responds to an increasing sense of international urgency to better understand the wide-scale endangerment and loss of intangible expressions of culture, including music. Despite international awareness of the need for action, and also despite the long-term (sometimes uneasy) relationship the discipline of ethnomusicology has had with "dying" music cultures, our understanding of music endangerment is relatively weak. In exploring the phenomenon and possible ways to engage with it, this book draws in particular on experience from the field of language maintenance, which has blossomed since the early 1990s and has gone some way to increasing understanding of how endangered cultural heritage may best be supported.

Although the topic of music endangerment may be of particular interest to music researchers, wider awareness and understanding of the consequences of cultural endangerment will be important in order to address it. For that reason, my intended reader is anyone with an interest in, or concern for, promoting a diversity of cultures in an increasingly globalized world. Particularly, I hope this book might act as a point of reference and departure for policy makers, community-based cultural workers, and culture bearers themselves. My aim is to open (or perhaps reopen) the conversation on endangered musics, and ultimately to benefit those communities whose musical expressions are endangered against their will.

My interest in the topic of music endangerment was ignited by my involvement with a project run by Queensland Conservatorium Research Centre at Griffith University (Brisbane, Australia). *Sustainable Futures for Music Cultures: Towards an Ecology of Musical Diversity* (2009–2013) aimed to understand the dynamics of vibrant and sustainable music genres and to offer communities pathways to supporting the viability of their music. My work on that project excited me enough to pursue the topic further and to explore the similarities I observed between the endangerment of music genres and that of languages. In this way, my long-term interest in language as an aspect of culture also finds expression in this book.

My sincere thanks goes to all those who generously agreed to participate in my research as interviewees; to Phạm Thị Huệ and the *ca trù* community of Hanoi for their rich contribution to the case study chapter of this book; to those friends, colleagues, and anonymous referees who offered helpful critical feedback on the manuscript; to Anthony Seeger for so graciously writing the foreword; and to Adam Cohen, Suzanne Ryan, and the team at Oxford University Press for their wonderful support in preparing the manuscript for publication. Special thanks to Professor Huib Schippers, formerly my doctoral supervisor and now my senior colleague, without whose encouragement and guidance this book would not have been written.

This book is in seven parts. The Introduction presents the concept of music endangerment and argues why it is an issue of concern (see A Note on Terminology). Chapter 1 describes what we already know about the topic and presents a range of practical initiatives that have been employed to support endangered genres, pointing to some key gaps and weaknesses in our understanding about how best to help them. Chapter 2 examines the similarities and differences between language and music in relation to their vitality. The resulting comparative framework, as well as the gaps in understanding music endangerment that were identified in Chapter 1, guide the discussion in Chapter 3. This chapter suggests five key ways in which language maintenance may inform ways to support endangered music genres. The next two chapters implement one of these suggestions. Chapter 4 develops and presents a tool (the Music Vitality and Endangerment Framework, or MVEF) for identifying and measuring music endangerment. To exemplify how this might work in practice, Chapter 5 uses that tool to assess the level of endangerment of one genre with a checkered history. Finally, Chapter 6 reflects upon the implications of the book, and recommends next steps for supporting endangered music genres.

A NOTE ON TERMINOLOGY

Throughout this book, I use the term *music genre* to refer to a discrete musical tradition, a defined or in some way unified set or subset of repertory (notwithstanding the fact that boundaries between one genre and another can be difficult to define). Three (random) examples are Javanese *gamelan gong kebyar*, Andalusian flamenco music, and Vietnamese *ca trù*. In the literature, a common term for music genre is *musical tradition*, which I have chosen to avoid for its uncertain relationship to change and innovation.

I sometimes refer loosely to "small" music genres—genres that by virtue of their nondominance (culturally, socially, demographically, or otherwise) may face particular challenges to their viability. Several music genres collectively contribute to making up a *music culture*: a group of people's total involvement with music, including concepts, practices, beliefs, institutions, and materials (after Titon, 2009d). Members of a music culture may or may not share a language, nationality, or ethnic origin.

Music culture has overlap with the concept of a *community*, a term I use broadly to refer to either a group of people who share their language or music culture by virtue of their common geographical, cultural or ethnic background, or to denote a "community of practice" (Wood & Judikis, 2002, p. 12): a group of people bound together first and foremost by their linguistic or musical practice and interests. This is consistent with the more general concept of a *community* as "any group of individuals who share something, anything, in common, and consider themselves to have some allegiance to each other as a result" (Graves, 2005, p. 25).

Terminology relating to music endangerment itself warrants a close critique, and is discussed at some length in the Introduction.

ABOUT THE COMPANION WEBSITE

www.oup.com/us/musicendangerment

Oxford has created a password-protected website to accompany *Music Endangerment: How Language Maintenance Can Help*. We encourage readers to visit the site to accesses audio and video tracks, photos, and supplementary materials that illustrate and elucidate points made in the book. Audio and video examples are signaled in the text by Oxford's symbol ◉, and images and text are signaled by ◉. Further information and resources relating to the endangerment, vitality, and viability of languages and music genres are also available on the site.

Readers may access the site using username Music2 and password Book4416. Please note that these are case sensitive.

Music Endangerment

Introduction

Arguably more than at any other period in history, recent decades have seen massive change to our world. Economic and industrial development, urbanization, increased international tourism and migration, and the advance of technology and global information networks are just a few of the factors that have led to deep and rapid socioeconomic transformations at both local and global levels. There are certainly positive upshots, including wide-scale access to information, increased intellectual exchange, and access to and appreciation of other values and cultures. At the same time though, these transformations are taking their toll on the planet. The threat they pose to biodiversity is no longer contested, and addressing that as a matter of urgency is high on the public agenda.

While global environmental concerns are widely profiled, somewhat less so are the repercussions that these transformations have on cultural expressions, particularly those of indigenous and minority peoples. Tangible manifestations of cultures, such as buildings, temples, historic sites, and artworks, have been placed in physical peril for a number of reasons, including encroaching industrialization and tourism. Also in jeopardy are intangible expressions of culture—what the United Nations Education, Scientific, and Cultural Organization (UNESCO) calls "intangible cultural heritage." This heritage includes, among other things, the theatre, dance, music, language, and rituals of a people, as well as the spiritual and philosophical systems that inform them.

THE PROBLEM OF MUSIC ENDANGERMENT

In the case of music, the many and complex local and global changes of recent decades have a range of effects on the vitality and viability of genres.

In some cases, the cultural shifts that happen in response to external forces can represent the successful adaptation of a music genre to the changing environment. Those shifts may even result in new forms of creativity that invigorate a music genre or the music practices of a community at large. At a general level, the state of music is arguably as strong and diverse as it has ever been. It is even feasible that musical diversity has *increased* in past decades, as a result of the interconnections and influences between genres brought about especially by the rise of communications technology.

This possibility does not, however, contradict the conviction expressed in UNESCO's 2003 *Convention for the Safeguarding of Intangible Cultural Heritage* that cultural (including musical) expressions are being lost at an unprecedented rate. Sometimes the loss is by the free choice of the communities concerned, who no longer see a need for a certain cultural practice in a changing environment. In other instances it is against their will, such as when a population disperses or is decimated by poverty, disease, or war, or in situations of political and/or economic imbalances of power. A glance to many indigenous cultures illustrates the point. For example, more than 98% of all Australian Indigenous performance traditions present in the country at the beginning of British occupation (1788) have been lost, and all those remaining are in danger, according to one estimate (Corn, 2012, p. 240). When people and their cultural practices come under pressure from cultural, socioeconomic, or political shifts, the viability of music genres may be placed in jeopardy. Performance contexts may disappear, the social function of the genre may become redundant, and intergenerational transmission processes may weaken.

Specific threats to the viability of music genres take various forms. Opening international borders means that small, local music cultures—those "belonging to the weak end of power distribution" (Nettl, 2005, p. 168)—may be forced to contend with more dominant external ones. Cultural hegemony adds to the likelihood of displacement by larger powers (most saliently, perhaps, by western pop music). Trade liberalization agreements affect the right of governments to specifically support local music genres. The increasingly widespread use of the Internet facilitates the dissemination of music, but it also raises complex issues with regard to copyright, intellectual property, artists' rights, and fair trade.

In addition to external forces, threats to the viability of music may also surface within a community. As local peoples move away from their rural ways of life, or as a population drifts to urban centers, the cultural function and context of music may be forced to adapt. Former modes of music transmission (such as through families) may be disrupted, and changes in ways of learning and teaching, for example when a traditional genre begins to be taught in a formal institution, may prove unviable. Community attitudes to music may change (driven by either internal or external factors), leading to traditional music genres falling out of favor, especially with young people. Although these shifts take place within a community, they are often intimately linked with wider processes of change, and the community is not always able to exercise control over them.

An estimate of the number of music genres in the world is difficult to find in the literature. Baumann refers to an extant 15,000 cultures (5,000 of them indigenous or aboriginal; 1992, p. 162). If each culture is steward of more than one music genre, the total number of genres will probably be significantly larger than this, setting aside, for the moment, the complexities of defining *genre*. How many of these genres are endangered is unknown, but qualitative research indicates that many "small" music genres are under considerable threat. In 2003, UNESCO's *Convention for the Safeguarding of Intangible Cultural Heritage* articulated the urgent need to address the precarious situation of much of the world's intangible cultural heritage, including music. A subsequent International Music Council report underscored this imperative, declaring that the homogenization of music at an international level is a real risk (Letts, 2006).

When considering global musical diversity, though, it is important to remember that the endangerment or loss of any given musical expression happens at the local level. In the words of Anthony Seeger, "We can talk about cultural grey-out, but it's actually light by light that it's greying out" (personal interview, March 22, 2011). Arguably it is at the community level that the loss of musical expressions is most keenly felt, and here too that counteractive measures are likely to be most effective. It may be, then, that the best way to take action against music endangerment is at the grassroots. Yet it may be helpful to remember that each specific situation of musical endangerment is positioned in a wider context too, and that the threat to musical expressions exists across the world.

Ethnomusicologists have a long-standing engagement with the ethnographic documentation of musical traditions seen as doomed to extinction; the concern has persisted almost throughout the history of the discipline. In the mid-twentieth century, it found resonance and validation through certain movements in linguistics and anthropology, like the so-called "urgent anthropology" of the 1950s that concerned itself with "the imminent destruction of societies, cultures, and artifacts by modernization" and that argued for the need to focus anthropological resources on preserving them (Nettl, 2005, p. 167). By the early 1990s, however, there was a general perception among ethnomusicologists that earlier "salvage" or "white knight" efforts to save dying music genres were overly romanticized and neocolonial, and music preservation interests had fallen out of favor with researchers.

Current ethnomusicological approaches to musics in decline tend to be more pragmatic than those earlier ones. They typically acknowledge the natural processes of the emergence, change, and decay of musical expressions, while showing an awareness of the many powerful global and local forces acting upon "small" music genres. Yet our understanding of the possibilities for supporting endangered genres is incipient compared with the knowledge and experience gained through the concerted, international effort that has taken place to try to keep endangered languages strong.

BRINGING LANGUAGES INTO THE PICTURE

Academic investigation into the relationship of language and music has a deep and long history (neatly outlined by Feld and Fox, 1994). Up to the mid-1970s, research mostly centered on the possibility of applying linguistic models to musical analysis, and the overlap of musical and linguistic phenomena: the musical properties of speech, for example, or the relationships between song structure, texts, and poetics (Feld, 1974). These fields of investigation have continued to develop, but since the 1980s they have expanded to include broader aspects of the language–music relationship, like the biological origins of language and music and their relative functions in the survival of our species. In these later studies, research from other disciplines, such as anthropology, psychology, and neuroscience, has significantly contributed to our understanding of the language–music equation.

In relation to the links between language and music within their social and ecological environments, the relatively new field of *biocultural diversity* investigates the intricate links between natural ecosystems and human cultures (Grant, 2012a). It is founded on the principle that biological, cultural, and linguistic diversity are interrelated and codependent within a socio-ecological system. The connection between linguistic and musical (and environmental) vitality and viability within a society is neither direct nor simple, however. One thing at least is clear: Language and music do not exist in separate, parallel spheres, and the vitality of one can affect the vitality of the other. Campbell (2012) writes of the "profound" ramifications of language shift on song practice among the people of the Tiwi Islands, for example, and several projects have employed music as a vehicle to help strengthen endangered languages (see Green, 2010, in relation to Australian Aboriginal Dharug; and Johnson, 2013, on the interconnections between song and endangered language on the island of Guernsey). While I acknowledge these links between the vitality and viability of language and music, in this book I am more concerned with the *parallels* between language and music in relation to their vitality and viability: that is, I wish to examine first and foremost the conceptual, not actual, links between the sustainability of languages and music genres.

As intangible manifestations and expressions of culture, music and language are affected by many of the same forces within the global and local environment. Like music genres, languages (particularly those of indigenous and minority peoples) may be adversely affected by cultural dominance, loss of traditional ways of life, unsustainable tourism and travel, the homogenizing influence of the mass media, hegemonic governmental policies, and the impact of technology, among other things. The scale of the threat is egregious: of the six to seven thousand languages worldwide, the figure usually quoted by linguists is that around half may be lost by the end of the twenty-first century. A lower-end estimate of the percentage of languages at risk is that of Vakhtin (2013), who places it at just 29%, but as Vakhtin himself concedes, 29% is "also bad enough" (p. 260).

Although languages seen to be in danger of disappearing have long been a topic of research for linguists (indeed, much early anthropological linguistics was devoted to documenting "dying" languages), it was the early 1990s when sociolinguists began to perceive the severity and urgency of the situation and take coordinated action. In 1995, the opening statement of the Endangered Languages Fund had a ring of desperation:

> Languages have died off throughout history, but never have we faced the massive extinction that is threatening the world right now.... The cultural heritage of many peoples is crumbling while we look on. Are we willing to shoulder the blame for having stood by and done nothing? (Foundation for Endangered Languages, 1995, para. 1)

Five years later, Crystal estimated that in the time it took to write his book *Language Death*, another six or so languages "died"; he implored linguists to act quickly "using as many means as possible to confront the situation and influence the outcome.... [T]ime is running out" (2000, p. 166).

Agitated by several landmark articles about the world's language crisis in the journal *Language* (foremost among them Hale et al., 1992), academic research into language endangerment quickly gave rise to practical initiatives directed toward maintaining and reviving languages under threat. In 1993, UNESCO adopted its *Endangered Languages Project* and launched the *Red Book of Endangered Languages of the World* (now supplanted by

UNESCO's *Atlas of the World's Languages in Danger*); within a couple of years, the International Clearing House for Endangered Languages had been established at the University of Tokyo, and the UK-based Foundation for Endangered Languages was inaugurated.

Since that time, despite the range of practical approaches to maintaining and revitalizing threatened languages, the sense of urgency has remained. In 2009, the Indigenous Language Institute (ILI) in New Mexico issued the following statement:

> ILI is driven by the urgency of the work to revitalize indigenous languages. We believe that there is a ten-year window of opportunity to make a difference, and to turn the tide of language decline.... There is a race against time to save the precious human heritage and to maintain diversity. (Heritage Languages in America, 2009, "Insights" section, para. 1)

Three years later, the Alliance for Linguistic Diversity (supported by Google) launched the Endangered Languages Project with the following pronouncement:

> Humanity today is facing a massive extinction: languages are disappearing at an unprecedented pace.... Languages are entities that are alive and in constant flux, and their extinction is not new; however, the pace at which languages are disappearing today has no precedent and is alarming. (Alliance for Linguistic Diversity, 2012)

Recognizing the "race against time," global efforts to support endangered languages are ongoing, and strong.

In contrast, comparatively little international effort has focused on implementing practical initiatives to help protect or promote endangered music genres. This suggests a need for effective systems to support those genres, whether through new policies, documentation, practical initiatives, or other means. To this end, language maintenance and revitalization efforts represent comparatively well-trodden pathways to supporting intangible cultural heritage. Moreover, the parallels between the predicaments of language and music in the local and global environment suggest that there may be parallels in ways to help them survive. It seems the field of language maintenance holds potential to inform our understanding of the best ways to support the vitality and viability of music genres.

The central question I set out to answer in this book, then, is this: *How can approaches relating to the maintenance of endangered languages inform ways to support endangered music genres?* As stepping-stones along the way,

I identify and appraise the range of current theory and practice relating to the vitality and viability of music genres; identify the similarities and differences between music and languages in relation to their vitality and viability; propose some ways in which theoretical and practical approaches to language maintenance and revitalization may help repair the key gaps and weaknesses of current approaches for music; and provide a concrete example of how theory from the field of language maintenance could be adapted for use with music.

WHY MUSIC ENDANGERMENT MATTERS

Despite some complexities surrounding the ethics of cultural maintenance (explored later in this book), researchers, cultural activists, and national and international agencies are generally strongly in favor of making efforts to protect and promote intangible expressions of culture, including music. Decades ago, Alan Lomax argued that scholars are "impelled to a defense of the musics of the world" (1977, p. 137); for Baumann, "the protection of music as living tradition is not only an academic postulate but a cultural and political necessity" (1992, p. 15). The international nongovernmental organization Terralingua professes that resilient and vibrant cultures in general are a matter of social justice and basic human rights (2013). There are many reasons for views like these; the five most salient serve as a rationale for this book.

For Humanity's Sake

The first reason to support endangered music genres is applicable to intangible expressions of culture at large, and is eloquently expressed in the literature on language maintenance. Languages, the argument goes, often contain instances of intellectual genius (Hale, 1998); they also offer a direct glimpse at the creativity of the human mind (Mithun, 1998). The loss of a language therefore means an intellectual and creative loss for humanity. According to the *Universal Declaration on Cultural Diversity*, "heritage in all its forms must be preserved, enhanced and handed on to future generations as a record of human experience and aspirations" (UNESCO, 2001, Article 7). The disappearance of a music genre arguably also represents the loss of a manifestation of human intellect and creativity. Music serves functions beyond language, holding the potential to express aspects of culture and cultural identity that are incommunicable through words. Because each music genre manifests a unique expression of what it is to be human, often displaying a continuum of human creativity and imagination through generations, the loss of a music genre is a loss to human heritage.

For Diversity's Sake

A second reason we should care about the vitality and viability of music genres is that they contribute to the rich diversity of the planet, and of humankind. As with biodiversity, the greater the diversity of cultural practices and music genres (the "richer the gene pool"; Letts, 2006, p. 9), the better the chances that new combinations and permutations will permit cultures to successfully adapt to changing contexts. Existing cultural expressions are informed by past expressions, and will inform future ones; emerging cultural expressions are almost always nourished by older traditions, which form a point of departure for invention and transformation. Cultural diversity, therefore, "widens the range of options open to everyone" (UNESCO, 2001, Article 3). The corollary is that the loss of cultural (including musical) diversity holds "dramatic consequences" for humankind (Maffi, 2005, p. 599). Marett even believes that "vanishing songs" will have consequences for the whole of humanity, since songs represent ways of being in the world, and their extinctions could "potentially compromise our ability to adapt to as yet unforeseen changes" (2010, p. 251).

For Culture's Sake

Third is the consideration that intangible cultural expressions like language, music, visual art, dance, theatre, ritual, and ceremony are often interdependent within a culture. The loss of a music genre, for example, may mean the loss of the unique language embedded within it, or the loss of an associated dance or ritual. By the same token, efforts to maintain or revitalize endangered music genres may strengthen the vitality of other forms of cultural expression, like language (through song) or rituals. Importantly too, songs are sometimes the unique vehicles of the transmission of local knowledge, culture, and history. Songs may encode knowledge of genealogies and mythologies, records of ancestors and clan names, knowledge of the universe and the land, medicinal and culinary knowledge, social norms, taboos, histories, and cultural skills and practices, among other things.

Wachsmann once called this "the intimate link between music, speech, and the entire experience of ourselves" (1982, p. 211), and it creates a powerful motive to ensure the vitality and viability of music genres.

For People's Sake

A fourth rationale for supporting endangered music genres relates to the role music can play in building individual and collective identity. Music is a means by which identity can be expressed, and in most cultures, music's core function in social events, ceremony, and daily life means that it plays a crucial role in defining and strengthening personal, social, and cultural identity. Music reaffirms our membership of a community, and our sense of being and belonging. Consider the words of senior Tiwi woman Lenie Tipiloura: "If all the old songs are lost, then we don't remember who we are" (Campbell, 2012, p. 3); or those of the Amazonian Suyá: "When we stop singing, we will really be finished" (Seeger, 2004, p. xix). Like languages, music can be used to express who we are, individually and collectively, and to distinguish ourselves from other groups of people. Particularly among indigenous and minority peoples, music can provide a sense of continuity with the past, with cultural traditions and ancestral heritage. Maintaining the music genres of these peoples may strengthen their sense of identity for future generations.

For Society's Sake

Finally, in addition to helping strengthening individual and collective identity, vital and viable music genres can also strengthen social cohesion and individual well-being, both within and between cultures. It is well established that music can be important for expressing emotion, for entertainment, communication, aesthetic pleasure, and to validate social institutions and religious rituals. There are indications across cultures that participation in music assists fuller participation in wider society, and can increase the likelihood of children and adults being well-adjusted members of society. Furthermore, as a marker of culture, music has the ability to promote cross-cultural understanding, exchange, co-operation, reconciliation, and peace.

These five reasons are certainly not the only reasons we should make efforts toward vital and viable music genres. Cultural revitalization can contribute to cultural tourism, community capacity building, and positive health outcomes. Cultures and cultural diversity contribute to economic growth and the development of a knowledge-based economy. The cultural dimension is important in enabling and driving sustainable development and in achieving the Millennium Development Goals, as the United Nations has increasingly recognized. It might be argued too that there are quite simply musicological grounds to keep music genres strong: having access to a wide diversity of musics, for example, may help us better understand the nature of music itself. Together, these reasons form a compelling rationale for taking steps to support endangered music genres.

TROUBLESOME TERMINOLOGY

The concept of *intangible cultural heritage*, encompassing both language and music, provides a useful starting point for considering the terminology relevant to the topic of this book. UNESCO's *Convention for the Safeguarding of Intangible Cultural Heritage* describes *intangible cultural heritage* as "practices, representations, expressions, knowledge, skills—as well as the instruments, objects, artifacts and cultural spaces associated therewith—that communities, groups and, in some cases, individuals recognize as part of their cultural heritage" (2003a, Article 2.1). This includes oral traditions and expressions (language, poetics, storytelling), performing arts (music, theatre/drama, dance), social practices, rituals, festive events, traditional craftsmanship, traditional medicine, and knowledge and practices about nature and the universe. According to that same convention, *safeguarding* refers to

> measures aimed at ensuring the viability of the intangible cultural heritage, including the identification, documentation, research, preservation, protection, promotion, enhancement, transmission, particularly through formal and non-formal education, as well as the revitalization of the various aspects of such heritage. (Article 2.3)

By these definitions, the topic of this book explicitly concerns the *safeguarding* of *intangible cultural* (musical) *heritage*. Yet, by and large, I do not employ these terms. My reservations about them are closely aligned with (and indebted to) those of Titon, who suggests that by thinking of music in terms of heritage, a thing of the past, it immediately puts us in "a defensive posture of collecting, preserving, safeguarding, protecting, and mediating music, through proclamations and set-asides, special spaces and sanctuaries" (2009b, p. 135). He offers an alternative:

> But if we think of a music culture as something here, living, a renewable daily resource among us, we move into a discourse of sustainability, people in partnership, taking on the privilege and excitement and reaping the rewards of stewardship. (p. 135)

Titon's partiality toward the notion of *sustainability* (over *safeguarding*) is reflected by—or reflective of—an increasing occurrence of that term and concept within ethnomusicological discourse, and more broadly in relation to culture (particularly within the United States), in the past decade or so.

Yet the term *sustainability* is contentious too. In relation to culture at large, economist Sen argues it harbors a similar preservationist stance to that which Titon believes is inherent in the term *heritage*: "The rhetoric of 'sustaining'—as opposed to having the freedom to grow and develop—frames the cultural debate in prematurely conservationist terms" (in Graves, 2005, p. 107). At the second meeting of the Applied Ethnomusicology Study Group of the International Council of Traditional Music (in Hanoi, Vietnam, July 2010), where *sustainability* was a theme, participants voiced reservations about whether the term reflects desirable aims and approaches in relation to music. Without consensus, a host of other possible terms were proposed, including *revitalization, transformation, creative regeneration, cultivation*, and—delightfully playfully—*safe-gardening*. Other terms found in the literature include *preservation* and *conservation*. *Revival* is its own discrete subfield of ethnomusicological investigation, but refers to something other than explicit efforts aimed at strengthening the viability of music genres in decline (a point I return to in the next chapter).

Evidently, ethnomusicological research on music vitality and viability has not yet developed standardized terminology, even to refer to itself. The risk is of reaching deadlock: no term, perhaps, is perfect. Precedent from the sociolinguistic literature is not fully helpful: meanings of terms are often more clearly defined than in the ethnomusicological discourse, but the lack of consistency across the discipline is bewildering. Definitions of *revival, revitalization, maintenance, renewal, reclamation*, and *restoration*, while often well-articulated, fluctuate according to researcher, country, and context. Even the most common umbrella term for efforts supporting language vitality and viability—*language maintenance*—is sometimes used more narrowly, to refer only to efforts directed toward a language still spoken by all or most members of a community (in that case contrasting with *language revitalization*, which is used in relation to "weaker" languages). *Sustainability* and *safeguarding* are terms rarely found in research on endangered languages, though exceptions exist.

Taking all these factors into consideration, in this book I use the term *language maintenance* to refer to the field of study that encompasses efforts to maintain and revitalize languages. I frequently use the phrase *vitality and viability* in relation to both music and language: notwithstanding some limited academic use (e.g. Coulter, 2007) it harbors no heavily-laden meaning, and avoids unwanted implications of either a static tradition or a preservationist bearing. Despite the lack of consensus among ethnomusicologists, I employ the term *sustainability* to refer to the ability of a music genre to endure, without in any way implying that it should be preserved unchanging. In an attempt to avoid some of the charges—which I believe are reasonable—raised against the rhetoric of *safeguarding*, I reserve my use of the terms *musical heritage*, *(intangible) cultural heritage* and *safeguarding* for specific cases where the context warrants their use, or in direct reference to literature that itself employs these terms.

In many ways, the term *endangerment* is problematic too: it arguably falsely implies a simple dichotomy between *safe* and *endangered*, and may be redolent of the "romanticized" view of dying cultures characterized by scholarship of earlier decades. Labeling a music genre or language "endangered" may also imply too strongly, wrongly, that it is on the inexorable path to extinction. I return to these philosophical concerns in later chapters. Despite its inadequacies, I have chosen to use the term: in part for lack of a better alternative, since *endangerment* seems the clearest and simplest term for the state I wish to describe; but also because the term is employed constantly and consistently in the language maintenance literature, and is not foreign within ethnomusicological discourse either. When I define *endangerment*, then, as "under threat of extinction" (as UNESCO does; 2003b, p. 2), I do so with the understanding that endangerment is best conceived as a continuum, and without intending to imply the irreversible decline of the language or music genre in question.

SOME ETHICAL CONSIDERATIONS

There are some complex ethical considerations to sustaining endangered music genres. Perhaps not least of the concerns of the researcher of endangered cultures is that of a self-fulfilling prophecy—redolent, as Myers would say, of the geologist who yells "avalanche" on a snowy mountain (1992, p. 23). This may be a particular risk in contexts where "outsider" researchers are held in high esteem by a community. Conversely, the attention of outsiders may act as a mechanism that aids musical vitality and viability—for example when it stimulates a community to recognize the decline, or the inherent value, of a genre, and thus take steps to strengthen it.

Perhaps even more fundamental to the topic of music endangerment is the question of whether (or when) it is "right" for outsiders—or even for communities themselves—to engage in endeavors to maintain or revitalize endangered music genres. In the field of language maintenance, it has generally been considered an ethical *responsibility* for researchers of endangered languages to actively support efforts to maintain them. On the other hand, it is far from clear that endeavors to maintain endangered cultural expressions are always ethically sound. Almost certainly in some cases they are not: for example, in repressive regimes where musicians or language speakers may be persecuted for their expression of culture. The sociolinguistic literature is racked by internal dissent about the ethics of language maintenance efforts, both with regard to specific cases and on general principle: Arguably, those efforts intervene and interfere with natural evolutionary processes of the rise and decay of cultures; they emphasize ideologies of purism, disallowing change in tradition; they are too often driven by neocolonial and authoritarian outsider involvement; and not least, time and time again they have been ineffective or have brought unanticipated or unwanted consequences (Grant, 2012b, provides a more in-depth analysis of these issues).

In relation to music too, these are important and complex ethical considerations, and I raise them again at various points later in this book. In general, though, I believe it wholly possible for a researcher to ethically engage with a community that is trying to create a viable future for its music. In some cases, this may even be an obligation. While I was carrying out fieldwork in Cambodia in early 2013, Seng Norn, a 72-year old master-artist of the highly endangered funeral music genre *kantaoming*, requested my help to fund a new set of instruments for his teaching. As a privileged Western visitor to his country, where the average wage is well under $100 a month (meaning that my budget airfares alone were roughly equal to the average annual income), I felt in no position to refuse his request. (The instruments were delivered later that year; see Example I.1🟢.)

Possible avenues of engagement for researchers are many. One aim could be to empower the community, for example by helping to improve the understanding and awareness of outsiders in relation to it. Other potential roles include documenting the genre, raising funds, building the capacity of the community, generating community leadership, offering support and advice, creating educational resources, supporting education and transmission processes, alerting communities to the possibilities for revitalization, engaging in advocacy and lobbying, increasing public or scholarly awareness of the local or global situation, and helping to implement revitalization projects or strategies. The nature of researcher engagement will vary widely according to the situation at hand. Variables include the nature of the community's concern at the predicament, the cohesiveness of its attitudes and ideas about the future of its music, the factors contributing to endangerment, and the resources at hand. In all cases, the notion of the "First Voice" should be paramount (Galla, 2008), with communities in full control of making their own informed choices about the future of their cultural expressions.

An ideology of preserving anything and everything endangered, or of top–down prescriptions about what should be maintained, is far from my conception of what it is to sustain music genres. Most contemporary ethnomusicologists would recoil at the early twentieth-century attitude to preserving music, whereby "the collector would intrude, trying to persuade people not to change their ways, insisting that it was incumbent on them to retain preindustrial practices" (Nettl, 2005, p. 167). A given community may sense little or no loss at the impending extinction of a certain music genre; perhaps that genre no longer serves a purpose, or the community decides it would rather the genre die out than be given artificial life support, or be kept alive in "corrupt" form. I make no value judgments on these matters; those decisions are to be made by the community concerned. When in this book I refer to the importance of keeping music genres strong, then, I either mean it only in a general sense (for the kinds of reasons given earlier in this Introduction) or in relation specifically to those genres whose communities wish for their ongoing viability.

I hope that this book stimulates further ethnomusicological discourse on the issue of musical sustainability, as well as the development of approaches to support vibrant and viable music genres. In that way, I wish to ultimately help communities in their efforts toward the vitality and viability of their musical and wider cultural expressions. In keeping with the spirit of applied ethnomusicology—and social research in general, which commonly involves some intent to positively impact upon people's lives—the overarching motive of this book is to help communities reap the benefits that flow from vibrant music cultures. In this way, I hope it holds a small place within a larger system of contributions to a better world.

CHAPTER 1

What We Know and What We've Done

Researchers have proposed and developed various theories that directly or indirectly inform our understanding of music endangerment and sustainability, and an array of practical initiatives also exist to support vibrant and viable music genres. By surveying these theoretical foundations and practical initiatives, I aim to identify some of their strengths and weaknesses, as well as possible deficiencies in current knowledge and common approaches to supporting music genres under threat. In this way, this chapter lays the groundwork for identifying which language maintenance approaches may represent pathways to better practice.

Efforts to support music viability defy neat classification. The five-part taxonomy of practical initiatives presented in this chapter takes its loose inspiration from a minor but well-constructed strategy of the government of Newfoundland and Labrador to safeguard the intangible cultural heritage of that region (Heritage Foundation of Newfoundland and Labrador, n.d.). Admittedly, some initiatives really have a foot in two or more of the five "clusters," but I hope the taxonomy nevertheless provides a useful, if imperfect, framework for thinking about them. Theory underpins (or could, or should, underpin) all practical initiatives supporting music genres. Figure 1.1, a representation of the taxonomy, includes a few examples for each cluster of the practical initiatives that will be discussed.

I begin this chapter with an overview of theoretical foundations for understanding music vitality and viability, and then turn to each of the five clusters: documentation and preservation; recognition and celebration; transmission and dissemination; policy and enterprise; and coordinating mechanisms.

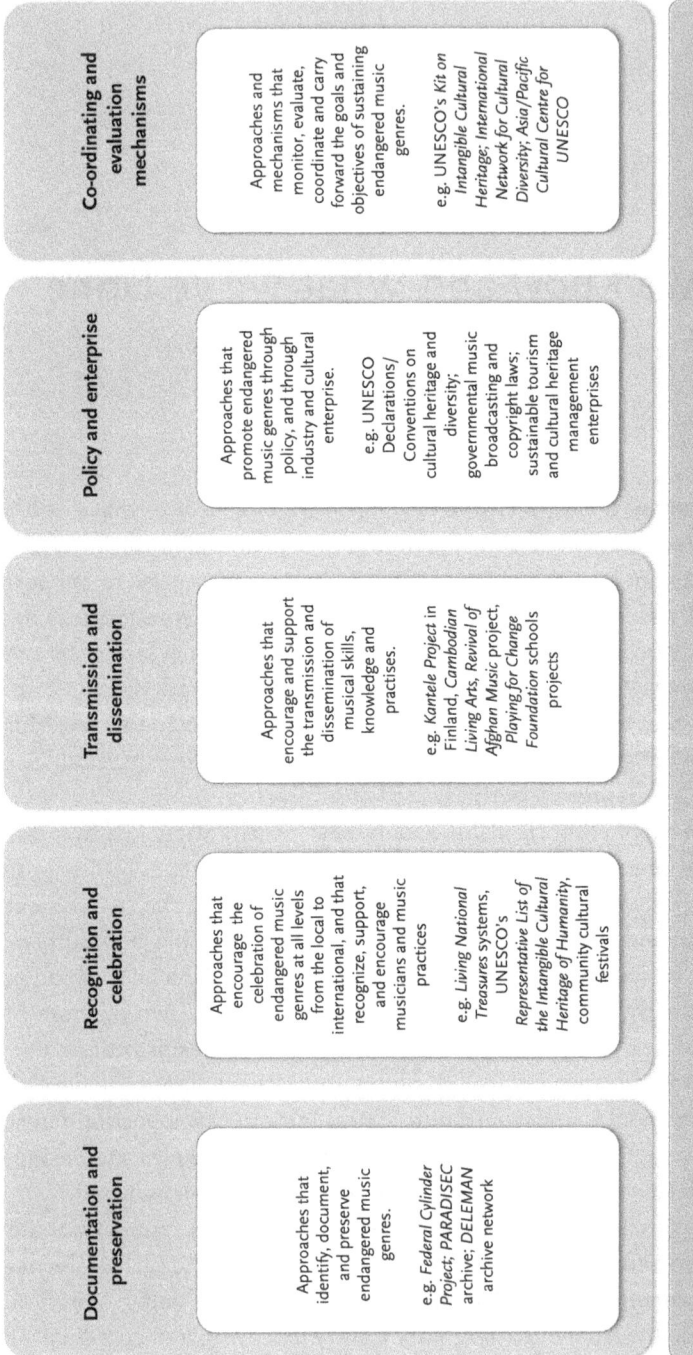

Figure 1.1 Taxonomy of approaches to supporting music

1.1 THEORETICAL FOUNDATIONS

Our current understanding of the dynamics of music endangerment and viability is informed by knowledge from a vast range of subject areas and disciplines, including anthropology, sociology, area studies, media studies, development studies, cultural studies, and more. It would be an impossible task to detail all the thinking that contributes to our current understanding of the issue. I have chosen to focus on only four theoretical areas, which I believe represent keystones for understanding music endangerment and what can be done about it: globalization and musical diversity; ecological models for sustainability; musical transculturation and change; and music revivals.

At the heart of discourse on music sustainability is the question of whether an increasingly globalized world is bringing about "a musical life of wonderful flexibility and intellectual breadth" (Mundy, 2001, p. 14) or is expediting the atrophy of music genres that do not find a ready place in the contemporary global environment. The phenomenon of globalization has been described and defined in myriad ways, most often referring to its political and economic dimensions but also to its technological, environmental, and cultural aspects. A useful starting point is Giddens's definition of globalization: "the intensification of worldwide social relations which link distant localities in such a way that local happenings are shaped by events occurring many miles away and vice versa" (1990, p. 64). This "linking of distant localities" has generated many complex processes and outcomes, some of which may be seen as beneficial to the viability of music genres, others adverse, and some both at once.

One of the most obvious upsides to globalization in relation to music is the vastly increased access to local music genres, at least among those individuals with access to modern technology. These days, a teenager in Jakarta can listen to a Peruvian folk song or Azerbaijani *mugam* at whim. Another benefit is the resultant greater cross-fertilization of music genres and music cultures, which has arguably *increased* musical diversity at a global level. Nettl writes:

> It's hard to overstate the harm done to most of the world's peoples by colonialism, capitalism, and globalization, but difficult to make a case for a pejorative evaluation of the musical results. The musical experience of the average individual is much broader today than in the past. The hybrids and mixes resulting from intercultural contact could be interpreted as enrichment as easily as pollution, and old traditions as a class have not simply disappeared. (2005, p. 434)

Yet globalization can bring with it commoditization, exploitation, and cultural homogenization that inhibits the vitality of some music genres, and Nettl's statement that "old traditions as a class have not simply disappeared" is true only in general; specific genres have certainly been lost, such as many of indigenous communities around the world. In the 1960s, Wiora wrote of an era of "global industrial culture" and the convergence of music cultures (1965, pp. 147–197). Soon after, Alan Lomax warned of mass cultural "grey-out" (1968, p. 4) and later published a call-to-arms to his colleagues to act against the "threat of extinction" to cultural diversity (1977, p. 125). Nettl believes that these kinds of perspectives that view the twentieth century as a period of musical homogenization are rather pessimistic (2005, p. 434), yet he too seems to concede that "distinctions among musical cultures seems to be receding—are we coming to Lomax's feared 'cultural grey-out'?—and musical variegation is maybe declining" (2010, p. 106). Concerns about the impact of globalization on cultures resonate within anthropology and environmental sciences too, where some perspectives are somber (see for example Davis, 2003).

Like broader processes of globalization, the commodification of music can be both beneficial and detrimental to the viability of music genres. Already in the 1990s, the colossal presence of the mass media was implicit in what seemed to some to be "the undisputable fact of a complete commodification and industrialization of musical production in areas hitherto untouched by capitalist transformation" (Erlmann, 1993, p. 4). Ethnomusicological research into the music industry (Cottrell, 2010, gives an overview) has illuminated the potential for the mass media to benefit musicians, communities, and the viability of "small" music genres—for example, by serving as a valuable vehicle for promoting and celebrating them and encouraging local pride in a genre. But it also points to complexity of issues of piracy, misappropriation, and exploitation, and in the worst instance to the potential for the mass media to act "as the ultimate factor in cultural disintegration" (Romero, 1992, p. 195).

Mass media dissemination shapes music genres in various ways, such as when musicians begin to incorporate technology encountered in the recording studio into their musical practice, or when song texts are changed to comply with the non-localized, non-politicized demands of an international audience. The term *mediaization* was coined to describe these and the many other processes of change undergone by *mediated* (mass media distributed) music (see Malm, 1993). For "small" music genres, mediaization (like globalization) is a double-edged sword: it enables the genres to compete and perhaps survive in the media environment, but it also means that they run the risk of "being sucked into the transculturation process and losing their specific properties, ending up as a component in some "'world music' style" (Malm, 1993, p. 347).

Based on understandings of the impact on music genres of commodification, industry, and the mass media, as well as wider theories on the cultural dimensions of globalization (like that of Appadurai, 1996), several researchers have attempted to develop frameworks to ensure continued musical diversity, or at least to counteract perceived homogenization. Malm proposes that musical diversity might be supported by helping genres to transition into contemporary society—for example by creating new venues and live performance contexts, by subsidizing records and videos with local forms of music, by ensuring national radio and TV stations can produce their own music programs, and by using cost-effective mass media technology to produce educational materials (1992, pp. 225–226). While Mundy's three-tiered approach to protecting and promoting musical diversity centers on the international, transnational, and national levels (2001), Slobin (1993) serves to remind us that the roles of the subnational, local, and "subcultural" levels (neighborhoods, family, and other microunits of belonging and bonding) are sure to play a role as well.

Research into the effects of globalization on cultures and cultural diversity was preceded by investigations into the effects of globalization on biological species, biodiversity, and the natural environment. The analogy between these two issues has limitations (humans can be "bi-musical," for example, but not "bi-species," and they acquire music culturally and not genetically). Yet the parallels that do exist are brought into relief by the frequency with which ecology, ecosystems, and the environment are metaphorically invoked in the ethnomusicological literature (quite aside from the substantial and growing body of work on the very real connections between the sustainability and preservation of cultural and ecological heritage; see Grant 2012a). An early example is Archer's 1964 piece "On the ecology of music," in which he suggests that music is "especially amenable to an ecological approach in which a mobile, fluid, dynamic interrelationship with every other social aspect exists" (p. 28). Stubington (1987) draws on an environmental analogy to distinguish between the "preservation" (documentation) and "conservation" (revitalization) of music genres; Letts mentions the ecosystem analogy in passing with regard to musical diversity (2006, pp. 9–10); Hayward perceives parallels between applied ethnomusicological research and his own work as a "kind of low-scale green activist" (QCRC, 2008b; see Example 1.1🔊); Schippers (2010, pp. 180–181) describes five broad sets of factors that affect "sustainable ecologies" for music; and Cottrell refers to the risk of ethnomusicologists "upsetting the delicate eco-systems that sustain fragile traditions," and even of effecting a kind of "mass-mediated musical Darwinism" (2011, p. 231). Further examples are easy to find.

The very discipline of ethnomusicology has largely comprised investigation of the interaction between music and its environment, particularly since the 1970s. In his study of the vicissitudes of Hindustani music in a fast-changing modern India, Neuman (1980) offered a conceptual foundation for considering musical vitality and viability that takes into account the range of local and global sociological, economic, and political factors impacting upon each and every genre. Various other descriptive studies provide more recent insight into specific cases of musical endangerment in their wider contexts. Sanyal and Widdess (2004) examine the atrophy and subsequent recontextualization of Indian *dhrupad*; Norton (2005, 2008) does the same for north Vietnamese *ca trù*; and within his musical ethnography, Moyle (2007) gauges the future of the music of Takū. But while the likenesses between musical and ecological frameworks have clearly not gone unnoticed, ethnomusicological research into musical diversity and sustainability has only recently begun to draw more extensively upon ecology-based models. Only recently have studies explored more generalized ecological theories of musical change, diversity, vitality, and viability that take into account the complex interplay between music genres, cultures at large, and broader sociopolitical and socioeconomic circumstances in the globalized world described by Malm, Appadurai, and others.

The benefits of taking ecological models into account when thinking about issues of music endangerment and sustainability appear substantial. Ecology frameworks might inform further development of a model of musical diversity that defines with greater clarity what constitutes sustainable musical environments, indicates how to gauge their health, helps identify the broader socioeconomic challenges faced by endangered music genres, points to methods that may resolve those challenges, and helps anticipate future outcomes of actions (and inactions). A specific example of a potentially useful concept comes from the "deep ecology" movement, which moves away from notions of environmental management in favor of stewardship, since arguably, a firmer concept of stewardship in relation to musical ecosystems "offers the most promising path toward sustainability in musical cultures today" (Titon, 2009a, p. 11). The principles of applied ethnomusicology (Harrison & Pettan, 2010) seem to lend weight to this view, with equality and reciprocity being paramount, and decisions in relation to cultural expressions being made in integral connection with the needs and wishes of their custodians. Stewardship is only one of several principles from the "new conservation ecology" that may find resonance with approaches to musical sustainability (for others, see Titon, 2009b and 2009c).

Another area of study that may inform our understanding of music endangerment and vitality is musical transculturation, as well as the synergetic oppositions between tradition and innovation, purism and syncretism, and continuity and change. These issues have featured prominently in ethnomusicological research over the past several decades. Conceptual models relating to them can inform our understanding of the dynamics of music endangerment in various ways—for example, by elucidating the impact on music cultures of the complex forces of globalization described above.

Rather than *acculturation* (see Merriam, 1964, p. 303), the term *transculturation* is arguably preferable to describe the transformational processes resulting from contact between music cultures, for a variety of reasons; not least, the moot implication by the term *acculturation* that there exists such a thing as an "unacculturated" or untainted music (Kartomi, 1981, pp. 230–233). This is especially true in the current global environment, in which local identities are typically complex and hybridity is the norm rather than the exception. In the last decades, the concept of transculturation has brought a new perspective to the ethnomusicological understanding of musical change, in some ways legitimizing in the eyes of scholars the emergence of new from old in music genres. Yet so far, arguably, ethnomusicologists have largely brought only their own perceptions of change to the research table, "learning little and not having much to say about the perception of musical change in the various societies of the world" (Nettl, 2005, p. 289).

Several music researchers have explored and explained the myriad potential outcomes of, and responses to, the processes of transculturation, particularly non-Western responses to Western music. Nettl (2005, 2010) describes a number of possible reactions to cross-cultural contact, ranging from abandonment of a music culture through to syncretism (hybridization) and modernization. Malm's typology of the processes and effects of cross-cultural contact on musical genres (1993), which takes into greater account the mechanisms of the music industry, identifies four possible situations that affect viability of local music genres in different ways—both advantageously (which is perhaps most likely in the case of what he terms *cultural exchange*) and detrimentally (e.g. *cultural imperialism*). In Kartomi's theory too (1981), some possible outcomes of transculturation appear potentially favorable to the viability of one or even both the cultures in contact, such as *nativistic revival*, where a subordinate culture becomes aware of its own neglect of its music and makes an effort to revitalize it. It is often hard to argue in black and white that any given response to transculturation is wholly good or bad for cultural vitality or viability.

If cultural traditions should and do naturally change, approaches to supporting music genres need not only to take into account what are often referred to as "authentic" and "traditional" musical practices, but also how those practices are situated within changing, contemporary contexts. In Erlmann's words, "How do we account for the fact that we can no longer meaningfully talk about the music of a West African village without taking into consideration the corporate strategies of Sony, U.S. domestic policy and the price of oil?" (1993, p. 4). One possible approach is to explore possibilities for recontextualization and innovation, if the community should wish. The *Culturally Engaged Research and Facilitation* approach to applied research, for example, advocates "preserv[ing] and promot[ing] traditional cultures *simultaneously* with their development. The emphasis here is not so much on a purist 'freezing' and protection of traditional cultures as a maintenance of the old along with the new" (Hayward, 2005, pp. 55–56).

These complex issues of change, purism, and authenticity are often at the crux of theories of music revivals, which therefore offer further insights into issues central to music endangerment, vitality, and viability. Revivals may be defined as "social movements which strive to 'restore' a musical system believed to be disappearing or completely relegated to the past for the benefit of contemporary society... [with an] overt cultural and political agenda expressed by the revivalists themselves" (Livingston, 1999, p. 66). If authenticity as a construct is a keystone of revivals, as Livingston and others suggest, it is paradoxical that revival movements characteristically incorporate the continuous transformation of the tradition (however *tradition* is defined, which is problematic in itself). Many revivalists "assert that they're bolstering a declining musical tradition. But rather than encourage continuity, musical revivals recast the music—and culture—they refer to" (Feintuch, 1993, p. 184). In asserting that revivals are "actually musical transformations, a kind of reinvention" (p. 184), Feintuch invokes the concept of *invented tradition* (Hobsbawm & Ranger, 1983), which surfaces regularly in discussions about authenticity and change in cultural heritage.

These concepts and constructs hold considerable potential to inform theory on music endangerment and sustainability, by providing insights into the complex dynamics of continuity, change, and renewal of music genres in the contemporary global environment. Particular case studies of music revivals may also be useful in this regard, such as research on folk revival movements of the 1960s to 1980s, including those in Hungary (Frigyesi, 1996) and Finland (Ramnarine, 2003), as well as the revivals of Mexican mariachi (Sheehy, 2006), Afroperuvian music (León, 2007), and Serbian folk music (Jovanović, 2005). Some of these revivals draw attention to the difficulty of making judgments about the likely trajectory of a music genre; others feature the influence of outsiders on the revival process (a phenomenon noted by a number of researchers). The differences between these cases underscore the difficulty of constructing a general theory of revivals that embrace complex and diverse musical worlds. In Feintuch's words, "musical revivals are not one thing" (2006, p. 1).

One final comment might be made here, relating to a dearth of focused research on the role of notation and transcription in music revivals, or in music vitality and viability in general. Like recordings, transcriptions can act as a form of preservation, but they undergo far more filtering than recordings, and also require musicianship, whereas recordings might be made without any scholarly intent or musical knowledge. Notation is sometimes given passing reference in research on music revivals (for example by Feintuch, 1993, p. 188, in relation to how two Northumbrian piping tune books, published in 1936 and 1970, had the effect of "centering the revival's repertoire" and defining the tradition). General scholarship on transcription and notation (like Ellingson, 1992a, 1992b) provides a good starting point for understanding the potential relationship between these phenomena and the trajectory of music genres, but that relationship itself remains a relatively under-researched domain.

1.2 DOCUMENTATION AND PRESERVATION

> ...identifying, documenting and preserving endangered music genres...

Of all practical approaches supporting sustainable endangered music genres, documentation is almost certainly the most extensive—perhaps a result of the ethnomusicological emphasis on that activity throughout the history of the discipline. Hundreds of organizations and projects are centrally involved with documenting and archiving local music genres, some of them with a specific goal to preserve these cultural expressions for posterity. By documenting, researchers can play an important role in helping perpetuate music genres. To draw on one example: several early–twentieth-century researchers recorded and notated Sámi joik traditions, believing they were recording something that was disappearing; around a century later, their work is being consulted by musicians seeking to reconstruct some aspects of these traditions (T. Ramnarine, personal interview, March 16, 2011).

Some scholars harbor equivocal views about the benefit of documentation for the vitality of endangered traditions, or about the role of documentation in "preservation" efforts. Nettl argues that it is not enough to preserve "the musical artifact" alone: "If I am justified in being generally critical of the role of preservation in the ethnomusicology of the past," he says, "it is because it has often failed to recognize that there is much more to music than the piece" (2005, p. 171). Echoing these concerns and adding others besides, Ellis argued in the early 1990s that for the continued transmission of seriously endangered Central Australian songs, documentation is one of the most potentially dangerous activities:

> Documentation of present-day performances can enable us to learn *about* the music and mythic map of the Dreaming but cannot record the spiritual essence of it. Further than this, these documents often create serious intercultural conflicts because the ownership of the songs can no longer be maintained in the traditional way, and their documented form can actually cause cultural disintegration. Such documents are useless in terms of regenerating the traditions in areas where breakdown of old practices has caused loss of music and language. (1992, p. 259)

A further concern with audio or video documentation is that recordings have sometimes come to be regarded by communities as definitive representations of a genre, precluding scope for creativity and reinterpretation (e.g. Livingston, 1999, p. 75). With regard to documentation in written form, Aubert cites the case of the once-banned Ottoman genre *fasıl*, which survived largely due to musicological transcriptions made in the late nineteenth and early twentieth centuries; but observes that "having the writing as an exclusive recourse is not sufficient to preserve all the flavour and fluidity of an aesthetics so intimately connected with principles of an oral tradition" (2007, pp. 72–73).

Most researchers agree that documentation alone is not sufficient for the continuation of a vibrant, living tradition. Yet as already described in relation to music revivals, there sometimes exists a direct link between the documentation of a music genre and its continuity in living form, suggesting an important role for documentation in both preservation and revitalization (Grant, 2010). Documentation, for example, can play a role in promoting both public and community knowledge and awareness of the significance of a music genre. Thus, although the vision of the *National Recording Project for Indigenous Performance in Australia* is to "systematically record and document the unique and endangered performance traditions of Indigenous Australia" (Corn, 2011, "Vision" section, para. 1), it ultimately hopes to catalyze cultural survival through these means (Corn, 2012).

In music revivals, historical recordings are often used as the basis for formulating repertoire, stylistic features, and the history of a tradition (Livingston, 1999, p. 71); notated music may serve some of the same roles, as in the case of the Northumbrian piping revival mentioned in the previous section. Karpeles described an instance from her fieldwork on folk songs in the southern Appalachians:

> The bearers of the tradition, who had put aside their songs because they felt them to be no longer in the fashion, have had their confidence restored by hearing them over the radio and on gramophone records, and by seeing them in print. This was exemplified by a singer in North Carolina who said: "When I forget Mother's songs, I know I have only to look at Cecil Sharp's book, and they will come back to me just exactly right." (1973, p. 101)

Historical recordings may also nourish the revival process. Recordings made by Hemetek over 30 years ago in Stinatz, Austria, have recently become important for villagers because most of the singers have died in the meantime; musicians are now turning to these recordings to find new ways of musical expression based on the tradition (U. Hemetek, personal interview, July 22, 2010). Norton recommends that as a part of the ongoing strategy to revitalize the endangered north Vietnamese genre *ca trù*, historical recordings be used to inform contemporary understanding, performance, and transmission (2009, June, p. 215).

Sound archives are integral to effective documentation, serving the functions of "collecting, storing, maintaining, cataloguing, documenting, publishing and making available recordings of music traditions as they are now for the benefit of musicians, scholars and other interested people in the future" (Stubington, 1987, p. 9). Umbrella networks have been created as hubs, such as Smithsonian Global Sounds (which also functions as a digital educational resource; Smithsonian Institution, 2013); the pan-European meta-archive DISMARC (*Discovering Music Archives*), encompassing over 30,000 audio recordings; and DELEMAN (*Digital Endangered Languages and Musics Archives Network*), which brings together over twenty prominent regional and international archives, including the *Archive of Maori and Pacific Music* (AMPM) housed at the University of Auckland, the *Pacific and Regional Archive for Digital Sources in Endangered Cultures* (PARADISEC), and the *Endangered Lunguages Archive* (ELAR) of the Hans Rausing Endangered Languages Program in the UK. Nettl gives an overview of the role of archives like these in musical preservation throughout the history of ethnomusicology (2005, pp. 161–171).

Ethnomusicologists continue working to counteract procedural flaws in documentation and archiving processes, recognizing that high-quality sustainable data and metadata are crucial for accessibility and dissemination. Most major projects in Western countries are now routinely accompanied by extensive guidelines for ensuring that processes of recording and collecting data and metadata meet international archival standards. Recent research has aided the move toward sustainable fieldwork data and their interface with archives and digital repositories, as well as concepts surrounding "best practice" (e.g. Barwick & Thieberger, 2006; Seeger & Chaudhuri, 2004). Nevertheless, from region to region and archive to archive, the processes of collecting, cataloging, classifying, indexing, storing, and preserving materials all remain variable in quality and nature, with national and international standards relating to access and use of recordings being particularly erratically implemented and monitored. This has understandably led to ethical concerns among some communities and scholars about misappropriation and misuse of materials (see Ellis, 1992, for one example).

Beyond the challenges of achieving "best practice" in documentation and archiving, the efficacy of efforts may be further jeopardized by factors outside the immediate control of researchers and communities. Technology changes at a rate so rapid as to make it difficult to keep pace. Recent computer software may be expensive; high-quality recording gear may require training to operate. Equipment required for playback of recordings quickly becomes obsolete, leading either to those recordings falling out of the public realm, or significant infrastructure requirements in terms of personnel, time, and funds to enable the transfer of copies to more recent formats. Storage discs, hard drives, reels, and tapes are subject to loss, damage, and deterioration, and like copying, the restoration of recordings is often a costly and time-consuming procedure. All these factors need to be taken into account in sustainability projects with documentation at their core.

Internationally, researchers and fieldworkers are increasingly recognizing the value and importance of ensuring that communities themselves have access to documentation—for example, by depositing recordings in local or locally accessible archives. Facilitating access in this way sometimes has the intended or incidental effects of renewing interest in a genre, strengthening pride in it, stimulating memories of it, or forming the basis for further cultural reclamation projects. These were all outcomes, for example, of *The Federal Cylinder Project*, which repatriated some early wax cylinder recordings of songs and narratives of American Indian communities (Gray, 1996).

An even more collaborative approach to documentation provides community members with training in the skills required to undertake the documentation of their own traditions. This approach builds capacity within the local community, minimizes outsider bias in documentation, and maximizes community ownership of the process and outcomes, among other benefits. Self-determination was one rationale behind the UNESCO project *Ethiopia: Traditional Music, Dance and Instruments*, which aimed to train a generation of local ethnomusicologists to document and archive Ethiopia's music genres, including by establishing ethnomusicology courses at the University of Addis Ababa (UNESCO/Norwegian Ministry of Foreign Affairs, 2006). Benefits of this type of collaborative approach notwithstanding, at times it proves challenging, not least due to the sometimes strikingly dissimilar aims in documenting of researchers and communities (e.g. Berez & Holton, 2006).

Online technologies are increasingly being used to store documentation and to disseminate the outcomes of documentation projects to the community and other interested parties. The *Plateau Cultural Heritage Protection Group* (in former incarnations, the *Tibetan Endangered Music Project* and *Plateau Music Project*), a grassroots cultural preservation program based in Xining City, China, is representative of some possible modes of dissemination and repatriation of the outcomes of music documentation (Tsering Bum & Roche, 2009). It makes available video clips on YouTube, prints and distributes written information in the local language to local communities, lodges recordings with international archives like PARADISEC, and has established links with two larger projects—*Digital Himalaya* (2013) and the *World Oral Literature Project* (2013b)—which are themselves developing digital collection, storage and distribution strategies for songs and other oral traditions from the Himalaya region and beyond.

Repatriation of old recordings raises issues relating to community ownership, protection of works, and protection of knowledge. When efforts to maintain or revitalize a music genre include the wide dissemination of recordings, concerns about copyright, economic rights, performers' rights, and intellectual property may become acute. There are often compelling arguments to make recordings available beyond academic circles and beyond the communities themselves. But if, as Romero believes, researchers should apply "imaginative strategies of commercialization and distribution of ethnographic records and film/videos" and draw on the mass media as the "principal means for reaching a wide audience" (1992, p. 206), the desire to promote information about situations of musical endangerment to as wide a public as possible needs to be balanced against ethical considerations, with the wishes of the community itself in the foreground.

This first category of practical approaches to sustaining music genres also encompasses the very identification of genres in need of support. As yet, there exists no widely-used, standardized, replicable tool that helps communities or researchers identify situations and degrees of musical endangerment (though Coulter, 2011, provides a useful example of how such a tool might look and work). Support mechanisms are therefore typically developed on a single-solution or reactive basis. Although the endangered status of some genres is obvious (as, arguably, in the case of many indigenous genres in Australia, Canada, the United States, and elsewhere), the endangerment of other seriously threatened genres may not be as apparent or may simply fail to attract research interest, increasing the risk that their communities will be deprived of access to support. Furthermore, a failure to systematically assess endangerment is likely to inhibit the development of effective support mechanisms, since assessing factors that are contributing to endangerment would help establish focus and priorities for action. Without systematic assessment, it is also difficult or impossible to accurately gauge the efficacy of any maintenance or revitalization initiatives that are implemented. This therefore represents a critical gap in both the theory and practice of ways to support endangered music genres.

1.3 RECOGNITION AND CELEBRATION

> …encouraging the celebration of endangered music genres at all levels from local to international, and recognizing, supporting, and encouraging musicians and music practices…

Of all initiatives celebrating music that may also strengthen musical vitality, festivals serve as perhaps the best example. Since at least the early 1900s, festivals have often played an important role in revival movements, and examples of festivals strengthening the vitality of musical traditions are scattered throughout the revival literature. By forming a new performance context for Indian *dhrupad* from the mid-1970s, for example, festivals were a central catalyst in the revitalization of that genre (Widdess, 1994). Livingston's description of why festivals and competitions are fundamental to revival movements may hold true for approaches toward music sustainability, too:

> These events are crucial to the revivalist community because revivalists meet each other face-to-face to share repertoire and playing techniques, to discuss the strengths and weaknesses of artists within the tradition, to actively learn and experience the revivalist ethos and aesthetic code at work, and to socialize among other "insiders." These events are fundamental to a revival's success for they supplement what can be learned from recordings and books with lived experiences and direct human contact. (1999, p. 73)

For indigenous peoples in particular, festivals represent strategic spaces to recognize, celebrate, and renew cultural traditions. Festivals have been lauded as "one of the few consistently positive spaces for Indigenous communities to forge and assert a more constructive view of themselves, both inter-generationally and as part of a drive for recognition and respect as distinct cultures in various local, national and international contexts" (Phipps, 2009, p. 30). By inspiring an indigenous community to identify more strongly with its musical heritage, or by confirming the value of the tradition in other ways (fiscally, for example), even non-substantive community events can benefit musical vitality and viability well beyond the duration of the event. On the other hand, it is also possible for the effect of these one-off events to last no longer than the events themselves. This depends a great deal on the level of community engagement, commitment, and ownership of the event.

With the rise of the mass media, festivals can be "truly global in scope; drawing self-consciously on the contemporary global communications networks of cultural diasporas, tourism and the media" (Phipps, 2009, p. 30). As in the case of Cape Breton fiddling in Canada in the 1970s, raising public interest in a "small" music genre may bring increased demand for it, and this in turn may pressure the media to allot it greater importance (Feintuch, 2006, p. 6). Another example of the role of the media in recognizing and celebrating musical heritage is the range of competitions celebrating traditional music skills and practices, such as these three in China: the *Television Contest of Erhu, Pipa, Dizi, and Guzheng*; the *National Folk Instrumental Music Television Contest*; and the *Chinese Folk Song Competition* held as part of the Nanning International Folk Song Festival. In many countries around the world, contests such as these often hold significant prestige, and achieving success in them can aid not only the career of a competing musician, but also potentially boost interest in the musical traditions they represent.

Festivals, competitions, and media promotion are not always wholly positive for the health of a genre or its associated musical practices. Essentially a facet of the global music industry, the phenomenon of the "festivalization of world music" (Bohlman, 2002, p. 137) has left residual effect on many genres, including their homogenization or standardization. In the case of *dhrupad*, "festivalization" has arguably encouraged the growth of the genre as a "parallel culture," rather than its integration into the mainstream: audiences are mainly local, and the festivals (and their embedded competitions) receive minimal press or national media coverage (Sanyal & Widdess, 2004, p. 281). Ellis voices further ethical concerns about the competitive nature of some festivals and their impact on communities (1992, p. 278). Overcoming these challenges may be difficult and will depend on the situation at hand, but as with most sustainability initiatives, it seems likely that odds of success will grow with a high level of community involvement in the festival process and product from the beginning.

The borders are sometimes vague between approaches to sustainability that recognize, support, and encourage music at a local level, and those that also work at a wider provincial, national, or international sphere. The Australian Aboriginal Garma Festival is one example, vigorously upholding local ownership while expanding to an event of national scope and, therefore, now representing "an intercultural gathering of national political, cultural and academic significance, and, simultaneously, a very local gathering of Yolngu clans on Yolngu land for Yolngu purposes" (Phipps, 2009, p. 38). Another instance is found in the revitalization of Vietnamese *ca trù*, where the establishment in the early 1990s of the local Hanoi Ca Trù Club and performing ensemble played a role in stimulating initiatives recognizing and celebrating the genre at national and international levels; the raised profile of *ca trù* has fed back to surge local interest and engagement in the genre.

UNESCO may be considered the primary driver of safeguarding approaches that recognize and promote endangered music and music practices at once locally and at a national or international level. From 2001, for example, the *Proclamation of Masterpieces of the Oral and Intangible Heritage of Humanity* paid homage to manifestations of cultural heritage in order to encourage local communities to protect them, and to raise awareness among local structures, national governments, and the wider public about intangible cultural heritage. While not without its problems (discussed later this section, and in Section 1.5), the *Masterpieces* program was successful in promoting awareness of the issues, creating a favorable environment for the drafting and ratification of the 2003 *Convention for the Safeguarding of Intangible Cultural Heritage*, and instigating a "surge in scholarly reflection" on intangible heritage programs (Seeger, 2009, pp. 114–115). This program was superseded in 2008 by the *Representative List of the Intangible Cultural Heritage of Humanity*. Another UNESCO list identifies *Intangible Cultural Heritage in Need of Urgent Safeguarding*; inscription on it typically escalates the local, national, and international profiles of the heritage in question, in addition to committing the relevant State Party to undertake certain safeguarding activities.

One particularly salient example of an initiative operating simultaneously at a local and a higher level is the *Living National Treasures* (sometimes *Living Human Treasures* or *Intangible National Treasures*) system that operates in several countries, originating in Japan in the 1950s. These schemes identify, support, and celebrate individuals who hold the highest skills in an aspect of the cultural heritage of a people. They aim to persuade artists to expand their artistic practice and pass their skills on to the younger generations, and to encourage younger people to "devote their lives to learning the skills and techniques of the identified cultural manifestations by holding out to them the possibility of future recognition and support, and national or international fame, if they are able to achieve the necessary level of excellence" (UNESCO Section of Intangible Heritage/Korean National Commission for UNESCO, 2002, p. 20).

Like festivals, competitions, and media promotion, these high-profile methods of recognizing and celebrating music and musicians have attracted criticism for their equivocal impact on the community (and cultural form) in question. Wang, for example, observes that the Taiwanese Ministry of Education Heritage Award for outstanding traditional musicians, implemented in 1985, "not only created a sense of competition among musicians and groups but also enhanced the reliance of musicians on scholars or other cultural bureaucrats as their mediators and patrons"; in 1994, the award was discontinued (2003, pp. 117–120). UNESCO's *Masterpieces* scheme has set a platform for some nation-states to manifest nationalist sentiment, by reifying the link between their nation-state and a cultural tradition, to the exclusion of cultural forms that are found across state borders (Seeger, 2009, pp. 121, 124–125). Titon argues that the same scheme suffered from a lack of satisfactory implementation mechanisms, and from a focus on the "masterpieces" themselves, over and above consideration of the persons who produce and sustain them, or their wider music-cultural ecosystems (2009b, p. 129). Thus, while "top-down" initiatives have proven an ability to promote prestige, recognize musical skill and knowledge, and celebrate and support musicians and music practices, they run the risk of being undermined by a complex set of issues, including a lack of grassroots understanding, resources, control, and ownership that typically characterizes approaches developed and implemented at the community level.

1.4 TRANSMISSION AND DISSEMINATION

> ...encouraging and supporting the transmission and dissemination of musical skills, knowledge, and practices...

The ways in which initiatives relating to transmission (from person to person) and dissemination (from place to place) can help maintain or revitalize a music genre are perhaps best explicated by reference to specific cases. One such initiative emanates from Thailand, where Thai classical music met with something of a revival due to the efforts of a local academic who introduced music schools into local shopping malls (QCRC, 2008a; see Example 1.2)🔊. Another is the music schools that were set up in African villages by the *Playing for Change Foundation*, a nongovernmental organization devoted to creating positive social change through music education. Supported by this foundation, the Kirina Music School in Mali opened in late 2010, with the aim of helping local people "preserve and share their musical traditions, which have been slowly disappearing due to lack of teaching resources" (Playing for Change, 2011, para. 3). Music education and the renewal of transmission processes also lie at the center of the *Revival of Afghan Music* project, launched in 2008 by the Afghanistan National Institute of Music. By training young musicians, who will (it is hoped) eventually go on to become teachers and music educators themselves, the project aims to help rebuild and revive Afghan musical traditions (Afghanistan National Institute of Music, 2013).

An interesting model of a transmission-based approach to music sustainability is the *Cambodian Living Arts* (CLA) community arts program, which since its founding in 1998 has supported over 500 students to develop the musical skills and knowledge that enable them both to earn a modest income and to help revitalize pre-Khmer Rouge music genres (Cambodian Living Arts, 2013). CLA provides master musicians with a wage, instruments, teaching space, and basic health care; students are provided lessons and instruments, and a limited number of scholarships are available. This transmission-based model holds loose parallels with certain music apprenticeship schemes in the United States, where arts agencies fund programs in which younger members of an arts community learn from respected elders (Titon, 2009a, p. 13).

In Southeast Asia, where Tan believes changing values and attitudes to tradition and modernity among young people are leading to the disappearance of traditional music (2008, p. 70), education may play an important role in music sustainability. Tan describes how a project in Malaysia, in which youths were given training in local music traditions which they then performed, stimulated interest in traditional music both among participants and among the wider community. With regard to the link to musical sustainability, she writes that such

> community-based music and heritage conservation programs...have empowered young people and the community to transcend ethnic barriers and take courage to speak for themselves. Empowerment ensures that musical traditions will be conserved in their traditional socio-cultural contexts of performance, rather than in the archives. (2008, p. 81)

Another example of a transmission-based revitalization initiative from this region emanates from Vietnam, where in 2002, the Ford Foundation funded a two-month program that enabled interested musicians from several northern provinces to learn the endangered genre *ca trù*. Following these classes, many participants began teaching the genre themselves, leading to the establishment of *ca trù* "clubs," which then became an infrastructure for teaching, learning, and performing (see Chapter 5).

The *Kantele Project* is another striking example of a music sustainability initiative centering on transmission processes. It was initiated in 1982 by the Folk Music Institute in Kaustinen in response to the low prestige and profile of the Finnish national instrument. By introducing the kantele into the music syllabus of all comprehensive schools, the project successfully raised the instrument's national public profile, and set a precedent for the introduction in 1983 of folk music into higher education. Ramnarine attributes the project's success to the endeavors of certain individuals, as well as "to the provision of instruments, teaching materials, and training for teachers—made available because of the value that the state continues to accord to folk music" (2003, p. 64).

In general, practical approaches to maintaining and revitalizing music genres that center on their transmission and dissemination are represented in the literature by specific instances such as those mentioned. In describing a scheme with transmission at its core, Graves (2005, pp. 137–139) is one of the few scholars to abstract the key elements in reviving the transmission of an endangered genre. The music in question is traditional English Northumberland *ceilidh* dance tunes. Their revitalization began a couple of decades ago, when a leading exponent of the tradition rightly recognized that the genre could be given a new lease by engaging local school students with it, and through them, the wider community. From those modest beginnings the organization FolkWorks was established, under whose auspices teaching resources were created and disseminated, master artists brought into schools to work with student ensembles, and summer music camps organized for teens and adults. Some of the young adults involved in these programs became interested in a career in folk performance, and eventually toured nationally. FolkWorks implemented a series of training workshops for schoolteachers, and in due course every school in Northumberland had a trained teacher able to offer basic instruction in the tradition. Graves generalizes the whole process in this way:

> The basic components form an elegant circle: exposure of students to traditional artistry in the classroom results in community performance opportunities; these inspire the most interested and talented students to pursue extracurricular

training; the best of these are given professional performance opportunities and are brought back for teacher training institutes; the teachers bring their new knowledge into their classrooms; and the cycle begins anew. (2005, p. 139)

This precedent has served as a model for a similar enterprise in Portland, Maine. One noteworthy feature of it is that, like the Kantele Project in Finland, it too illustrates the value of committed individuals in efforts toward musical vitality and viability.

From another angle, the field of Cultural Diversity in Music Education (CDIME) and the informal international network of this name may also hold theoretical insights into practical transmission-based approaches to sustainability. With a focus on pedagogy, it investigates the best ways to disseminate knowledge and practice about the world's music cultures in a range of formal and nonformal educational settings (Campbell et al., 2005). The very practice of cultural diversity in music education may aid the vitality of endangered music genres, which may feasibly find a new lease of life through transmission in different times and places. Children or youth learning in schools, for example, may "start playing with and exploring the possibilities, ... and expanding or in some way varying the tradition, ... and actually give credence to a more inventive nature of the genre" (P. Campbell, personal interview, March 4, 2010). Although research in the field of CDIME deals predominantly with transmission that occurs outside of the community whose music is being taught—sometimes with vastly different aims and in vastly different circumstances from transmission within its culture of origin—the field still holds some potential to inform the understanding (and practice) of the dynamics of music transmission across contexts and cultures.

Some of the approaches to maintaining and revitalizing music genres that encourage the transmission and dissemination of musical heritage and skills are spectacularly successful, like those described by Graves and Ramnarine. Others are far less so. Taiwanese state-funded *nanguan* training courses in elementary and junior high schools cultivated some grassroots appreciation and skills in the genre, but they also created tension among *nanguan* musicians over who would be involved in the program, how much they would be paid, and appropriate teaching methods (Wang, 2003, pp. 123–124). A number of scholars have also noted various risks in introducing a music genre into an institution (e.g. Cohen, 2009; Schippers, 2009). Campbell identifies some of these with regard to the introduction of Mexican mariachi into schools in the USA:

> Schools have systems, schools have bells, schools have timelines ... By way of oral lore, we find out that ... [teachers] go to workshops and they trade off a canon

of ten working songs and Mariachi becomes just that. So Mariachi becomes less rich .... It makes you wonder: was there more before it ended in the institution? (personal interview, March 4, 2010)

With this in mind, and despite some theoretical foundations from the field of CDIME, successful transmission-based sustainability initiatives represent promising but still under-researched prototypes for developing effective initiatives to support musical sustainability across other situations of endangerment.

1.5 POLICY AND ENTERPRISE

> ...protecting and promoting endangered music genres through legal measures, and through industry and cultural enterprise...

This section examines legal measures, policy instruments, and industry and enterprise initiatives that explicitly or implicitly serve to protect or promote music genres and music makers. Policies and regulations protecting and promoting music genres do not always relate directly to them; laws relating to media, education, and copyright, for example, can all affect musical vitality. These types of measures typically function chiefly at the national or transnational levels. National-level policies and regulations are of course largely dependent on the ideologies of those in power, and so vacillate from era to governmental era, and from country to country.

Blaukopf (1990, 1992) gives a number of examples of possible legal or contractual policy measures that may help protect "small" music genres—not least by raising funds for archiving, documentation, research, training professional musicians, or revitalization initiatives. Media consumption could be taxed, he suggests, by implementing license fees for television or radio ownership, for example. Phonographic companies and broadcasting bodies could be encouraged to make voluntary payments for their use of traditional music. Royalties could be payable upon use of folklore for economically gainful purposes, and those royalties in turn could be earmarked for cultural preservation or promotion purposes. Broadcasting policies could allocate a percentage of airtime to local music, thereby encouraging and celebrating local music and musicians, as well as providing a platform for its performance. Levies on blank cassettes could be used to compensate the authors of musical works for any lack of rightful remuneration due to piracy (nowadays, an internet-based equivalent could be implemented). Folklore could be copyrighted, meaning that the copyright is vested in the community.

In some countries, measures like these have been at least partly effective in protecting local music. One example is India, where All India Radio has played a significant role in preserving and promoting the Indian classical tradition. In other cases, policies do not exist, are inadequately reinforced, or are perversely implemented. Stobart's case study of music production and piracy in Bolivia explores the multifaceted nature of the challenges (2010).

At the international or transnational level, various declarations, conventions, and recommendations have formed tools of reference through which nation-states can take steps to protect their cultural heritage in spite of—or along with—mechanisms that promote it within a global market economy. These instruments form a foundation on which stakeholders, from local community members to national governments, may develop practical approaches to strengthen cultural (including musical) sustainability. The high profile of instruments like the *Universal Declaration on Cultural Diversity* (UNESCO, 2001), the *Convention for the Safeguarding of Intangible Cultural Heritage* (UNESCO, 2003a), the *Convention on the Protection and Promotion of the Diversity of Cultural Expressions* (UNESCO, 2005), and the *Declaration on the Rights of Indigenous Peoples* (United Nations High Commission for Human Rights, 2007) means that they hold considerable influence in supporting and promoting cultural heritage and diversity.

These instruments are supported by the efforts of nongovernmental bodies such as the US-based organization Future of Music, whose mission, through education, research, and advocacy, is "to ensure a diverse musical culture where artists flourish, are compensated fairly for their work, and where fans can find the music they want" (2013, para. 1). Other examples include Freemuse, which campaigns against unreasonable censorship and for the freedom of musical expression in all countries, and the World Intellectual Property Organization (WIPO), which aims to establish an appropriate relation between intellectual property rights and protecting traditional musical expressions. Responding to a call for guidance from indigenous organizations, archives, and cultural researchers, WIPO develops and maintains guidelines, codes of practice, protocols, and other resources for dealing with intellectual property issues that arise when archiving, documenting, recording, digitizing, and disseminating intangible cultural heritage. It also describes best practice and management of intellectual property in relation to festivals, which, as described earlier, hold some risk of adversely affecting local music genres.

The effect of national and international policy initiatives on local musics can be equivocal. While years of state intervention from 1980 brought Taiwanese *nanguan* increased visibility, it also arguably contributed to a compromise of the integrity of its musicians, as well as the "commodification, vulgarization, and theatricalization" of the music itself—and this quite aside from the overall failure of state intervention to solve problems of transmission (Wang, 2003, p. 152). The UNESCO strategy of proclaiming cultural "Masterpieces," too, has sometimes had unintended and damaging outcomes. The proclamation in 2001 of Bolivia's Oruro Carnival as a UNESCO *Masterpiece of the Oral and Intangible Heritage of Humanity*, for example, exacerbated conflict about the origins, ownership, and appropriation by Peruvians of Bolivian music and dance expressions (Stobart, 2010, p. 45). China's successful nomination of *khöömei* (throat singing) to UNESCO's *Representative List of the Intangible Cultural Heritage of Humanity* caused contention among some artists and officials in Mongolia, who argued that the tradition is Mongolian, not Chinese (Higgins, 2011).

Although the *Masterpieces* scheme did call international attention to the need to support intangible cultural heritage, the action plans resulting from the inscriptions to the *Masterpieces* list were sometimes so misconceived that, as Seeger noted, "if they had been applied it might have been worse than if they weren't"; often there were insufficient financial means to implement them in any case, resulting in local-level disillusionment about the scheme (A. Seeger, personal interview, March 22, 2011). In Croatia, certain proclaimed intangible masterpieces (not only musical ones) subsequently became "like a national park" where "you're not supposed to change anything" (S. Pettan, personal interview, July 30, 2010). Ramnarine sees the merit in recognizing and valuing music through such schemes, but warns:

> An ethnomusicologist can then fall into the traps of the local contestations, because by selecting one particular tradition that's recommended to a formal body such as UNESCO as an example of something which should be safeguarded, inevitably other traditions are not going to be presented.... And then there'd be all sorts of internal social political reasons why one tradition might be privileged over another—all kinds of relation dynamics that go on to determine what is going to represent the nation in a particular context in the safeguarding process. (Personal interview, March 16, 2011)

Titon describes two further equivocal cases: that of the Royal Ballet of Cambodia, where the UNESCO proclamation "entered local politics and worked against innovation, originality and development of new repertoire within the Ballet company" (2009b, p. 127); and that of Chinese *guqin*, in which case the proclamation ushered in a series of events which pushed aside the very tradition it wished to support, unwittingly helping to establish the music in a virtuosic, professional, presentational performance for the concert hall, which was contrary to the UNESCO proclamation's characterization of the music's heritage as an endangered, contemplative, amateur chamber music for the home. (p. 127)

While there continues to be extensive theorization, deconstruction, and critique of UNESCO's approach to cultural heritage and its safeguarding (e.g. the volume edited by Smith & Akagawa, 2009), ways to avoid (or even just accurately predict) the unanticipated ill effects of well-intended initiatives like the *Masterpieces* program have been the subject of only limited ethnomusicological investigation. To date, there is still no systematic evaluative process in place for the *Masterpieces* scheme, and any understanding of the effects of the program on the local communities involved remains anecdotal and piecemeal.

Endangered music genres are nowadays in a situation where they must contend with "the undisputable fact of a complete commodification and industrialization of musical production in areas hitherto untouched by capitalist transformation" (Erlmann, 1993, p. 4). In contrast with Malm's belief that it is almost impossible for national governments to influence the mass media through policies or recommendations (1992, p. 225), Romero considers the mass media "*the* realm, *par excellence*, in which well-intentioned cultural policies could produce a positive effect" on endangered musical traditions (1992, pp. 191–192). He believes, for example: "If in Peru the process of musical extinction is in some way being counteracted, it is because Indigenous and mestizo music is being featured on commercial discs" (p. 204).

This raises the issue of enterprise, whether in conjunction with policy or separate from it, and its role in strengthening the vitality of music genres. Cultural tourism, cultural entrepreneurship and businesses, cultural export strategies, and cultural enterprises as a part of economic development initiatives are just a few of the many possible links between enterprise and musical vitality and viability. Some types of enterprise seem to be an integral and fundamental characteristic of music revivals, pointing to their possible role in viability or vitality. According to Livingston, one feature most music revivals have in common is

> the emergence of a revival industry, by which I mean non-profit and/or commercial enterprise catering to the revivalist market consisting of concert and festival promotions, sales of recordings, newsletters, pedagogical publications, and instruments and supplies. Although many revivalists are embarrassed to admit

> this aspect of their movement given their general distrust of the commercial market and its massifying tendencies, it is an ethnographic fact. Indeed I would argue that it would be difficult for any revival to exist for more than a few years without entering into this phase. (1999, p. 79)

If Romero and Livingston are right, the role of enterprise may be an important consideration in furthering practical approaches to sustaining endangered music genres.

Vigilance should be exercised, though. As Graves warns (2005, p. 88), powerful links sometimes exist between the protection and the exploitation of cultural heritage. Among approaches aiming to raise the vitality of endangered music genres, perhaps nowhere is the threat of exploitation more real than in those mechanisms in which profitable enterprise and industry play a central role. In some ways, cultural homogenization is an advantage for multinational companies, for whom fewer consumer tastes means easier product and market development. Disturbingly, strategies "intended to buffer cultural heritage often result in consequences that are ruled by the model of the marketplace rather than the ecosphere" (Graves, 2005, pp. 88–89).

Recognizing this danger, some government and nongovernment policies and other mechanisms have been developed to support communities in protecting and promoting their cultural heritage in connection with enterprise. In 2006, the government of Newfoundland and Labrador made the development of cultural enterprise "while remaining sensitive to existing community practices" a key goal in its efforts to preserve intangible cultural heritage (Heritage Foundation of Newfoundland and Labrador, n.d., pp. 14–15). Another example is the *Stepping Stones for Tourism* program developed in collaboration with the Australian Government Department of Environment and Heritage, Aboriginal Tourism Australia, and Tourism NT (Stepwise Heritage and Tourism, 2008), which guides Australian Indigenous communities in developing and managing tourism that is sustainable for both themselves and their cultural heritage.

1.6 COORDINATION AND EVALUATION MECHANISMS

> ...monitoring, evaluating, coordinating and carrying forward the goals and objectives of sustaining endangered music genres...

Mechanisms that coordinate approaches and efforts in music sustainability may operate at a community, regional, national, or international level, and be carried out by a range of players, from the individual through to supranational bodies (see Table 1.1). Some community-level initiatives have been described earlier in this chapter, such as festivals and educational projects. A generalized example is when a local institution or school takes it upon itself to help maintain or revitalize a music genre, perhaps by running local festivals or performance events, purchasing musical instruments, or

Table 1.1 KEY PLAYERS IN SUPPORTING VIBRANT AND VIABLE MUSIC GENRES

Community-based institutions
Formal or informal, they may engage in some way with the cause of vibrant music genres, such as by driving grassroots-level cultural revitalization efforts or by advocating to government, media, or the public.

Training institutes/organizations
Their role in supporting musical viability may be explicit (as in the Revival of Afghan Music project at the Afghanistan National Institute of Music) or implicit (as in the promotion of cultural diversity in music education at the World Music and Dance Centre, Rotterdam).

Research institutes
These may drive research or documentation projects, run grant programs, engage in public advocacy, and provide publication and conference platforms. An example is the Australian Institute for Aboriginal and Torres Strait Islander Studies (accountable to, but independent from, government).

Non-government organizations
Their remit in whole or part may be to strengthen the vitality of cultural (or musical) heritage. These may operate on a local, regional, national, or international level. A prominent example of the latter is UNESCO (in particular, its Intangible Cultural Heritage division).

Foundations
These and other funding bodies may identify cultural support as a part or whole of their mission, such as the Christensen Fund. Lack of politically accountability means that foundations can be more flexible and take more risks when dispersing funds.

Profitable enterprises
It may be in their interest to protect or promote cultural expressions, such as those wishing to offset their impact on a minority or indigenous culture (e.g., mining companies), or those that profit from vital and viable cultures (e.g., cultural tourism businesses).

Local and national governments
These may play a role especially through their cultural and education policies and their attitudes to indigenous and minority peoples. Government bodies may also disperse funding for cultural projects.

Key individuals
These include community members, cultural activists, educators, researchers, business owners, philanthropists, and policy makers.

providing music tuition to individuals or groups. At a provincial, regional, or national level, coordinating strategies are well represented by the efforts of cultural institutions, such as the *China Intangible Cultural Heritage Protection Center*, an organization committed to promoting the cause of Chinese intangible heritage through research, education, promotion, and coordinating mechanisms, or the more local *Chengdu Intangible Cultural Heritage Protection Center* in Sichuan, China.

At an international level, UNESCO is the leading player in coordinating mechanisms. It represents a high-profile, well-established, and generally respected structure for promoting the diversity and vitality of cultures of the world, with proven ability to influence key decisions and actions in relation to sustainability and safeguarding. Its core aims in regard to intangible heritage are conducting advocacy, acting as a clearinghouse for the dissemination and sharing of knowledge and information, setting standards and forging international agreements, and helping member states implement national safeguarding measures, such as ongoing inventories of cultural heritage, appropriate policies, and competent legal, financial, and administrative measures (UNESCO, 2013). Despite its high profile, UNESCO's approaches to safeguarding have not escaped criticism. Some of the expressed concerns are raised later in this section.

Among UNESCO's mechanisms relating to safeguarding, one of the most significant is the 2003 *Convention for the Safeguarding of the Intangible Cultural Heritage*, the first UNESCO treaty specifically underscoring the importance of such heritage. Initiatives to facilitate the implementation of the Convention among States Parties continue to be developed. In 2009, for example, UNESCO released an online *Kit on Intangible Cultural Heritage*, "a basic reference and practical instrument for promoting and ensuring an effective understanding of intangible cultural heritage and the 2003 Convention by governments, communities, experts, concerned UN agencies, NGOs and interested individuals" (UNESCO, 2013, 'Publications and Documentation' section). The kit includes a set of downloadable fact sheets on safeguarding projects (Example 1.3 ◐). UNESCO also maintains an online *Register of Best Safeguarding Practices* showcasing projects, programs and activities that it believed best reflect the aims and principles of the 2003 Convention (UNESCO, 2013, "Lists and Register" section).

A multitude of international and transnational nongovernment organizations have been established to further UNESCO's goal to protect cultural heritage, founded on its principles or operating under its auspices. The *Asia/Pacific Cultural Centre for UNESCO* (ACCU), established in the 1970s, is one example. It organizes training courses for safeguarding intangible cultural heritage, hosts conferences around issues relating to the 2003 Convention, and for a time ran the *International Contest for Better Practices in Community Intangible Cultural Heritage Revitalization* (Asia-Pacific Cultural Centre for UNESCO, 2013). ACCU is largely subsidized by the Japanese government, and at times its continued existence has been at risk of discontinuation due to budget cuts.

The principles of UNESCO's declarations and conventions hold promise to form a conduit by which "small" music genres may be kept viable, especially if they are incorporated into evolving international agreements (like those on free trade or intellectual property). Yet UNESCO's safeguarding strategies do sometimes lead to unforeseen and unwanted consequences, as described earlier in this chapter in relation to the *Living National Treasures* and *Masterpieces* schemes. Titon puts this down to its very "remoteness" and a lack of "sufficient ongoing, on-the-ground connections (partnerships)" with cultural heritage workers and the culture-bearing communities themselves (2009b, p. 124); within the context of these schemes, the pivotal role of the community in safeguarding its own heritage has been problematized at some length (e.g. Blake, 2009, and others in that volume). Concern has been expressed too that experts in the relevant field do not have greater agency in moving forward UNESCO's goals:

> The 2003 UNESCO convention is now clearly dominated by politicians who quite often take a nationalist viewpoint. This is not always beneficial to safeguarding living culture in our world. Cultural policies are complicated and expertise is very much needed. (van Zanten, 2009, p. 42)

Various international bodies serve as networks for policy makers and other stakeholders to explore and exchange views and information on promoting cultural heritage and cultural diversity. The *International Network for Cultural Diversity* (INCD) (2003), dedicated to countering the homogenizing effects of globalization on cultural heritage, brings together culture-bearers, local communities, cultural institutions, researchers, and industry workers to promote cultural diversity and build international support for its cause. The *International Federation of Coalitions for Cultural Diversity* (2013), which facilitates cooperation and the development of common positions and actions between nations, played a role in developing the 2007 UNESCO *Convention on the Protection and Promotion of the Diversity of Cultural Expressions*. The *International Network on Cultural Policy* (Government of Canada, 2012) serves as an informal hub where national cultural ministers can discuss topical cultural policy issues and develop strategies to promote cultural diversity, and the *International Network of Lawyers for the Diversity of Cultural Expressions* (2011) is an independent association dedicated to providing legal counsel to civil society stakeholders and nation-states on issues relating to the implementation, evaluation, and interpretation of that same 2007 Convention.

Compared with these extensive international projects and networks that are coordinating and implementing the goals of safeguarding intangible cultural heritage, those specifically relating to music are relatively meager. Peak international music bodies such as the *International Music Council* (IMC) and the *International Council for Traditional Music* (ICTM; both with official relations with UNESCO), the *Society for Ethnomusicology* (SEM), and the *International Society for Music Education* (ISME) have some, but limited, engagement with the cause of musical diversity and music sustainability. While IMC-commissioned reports by Mundy (2001) and Letts (2006) offer useful suggestions for developing ways to support the diversity, vitality, and viability of music genres and music cultures, many remain unrealized.

The ideological support of these peak organizations for the issue of music sustainability is demonstrated by research partnerships (such as IMC's with the Australian-led project *Sustainable Futures for Music Cultures*), formal statements (such as the ICTM Australia-New Zealand Regional Committee's statement, endorsed in 2011, about the urgent situation of Australian Indigenous music and dance), and international conferences and events where sustainability is a theme (such as the 2010 symposium of ICTM's Applied Ethnomusicology Study Group). However, these organizations lack the administrative and financial resources that would enable them to play a more active part in coordinating approaches to sustainability. For this reason, most ways in which these peak bodies might help improve and standardize administrative, ethical, legal, financial, and practical matters relating to music sustainability—say by establishing guidelines and protocols for best practice, developing advocacy pitches, lobbying governments and other relevant bodies, evaluating practical efforts, centralizing information about potential funding sources, and creating networks for exchange of ideas and information—remain largely unrealized.

In particular, infrastructure in the form of hubs, gateways, and forums to pool and share resources about ways to support endangered music genres remains critically deficient. In the early 1990s, Blaukopf pleaded for the creation of a driving force behind the struggle for adequate legal policies, "a kind of lobby for traditional music.... if there is no such lobby, then certainly nothing useful will happen" (1990, p. 132). Around the same time, Malm argued that it was crucial

> to boost the informal international networks between music organizations and individual enthusiasts active at the national and local levels. These networks are today the most important agents for spreading music traditions that are not

> part of the commercial system. The enthusiasts and their networks are the only guarantee that at least some music traditions can live and develop according to conditions laid down by social, phsycological [sic] and physical needs and not only according to conditions laid down by the market. (1993, p. 351)

It seems that little progress has been made in the two decades since then. This was also the time that Romero proposed that "international cooperation should be one of the main strategies to be further explored by ethnomusicologists and cultural politicians in order to maximize their realm of action and effectiveness" (1992, p. 206).

Given the diversity of players in efforts to support music sustainability (as shown in Table 1.1), including educational institutions, nongovernment organizations, and governments, as well as recording companies, media organizations, and other agents whose primary concern is not musical viability per se, the establishment of national and international networks seems crucial in order to enable these players to pool resources and share knowledge, information, and experience. Networks (such as the one intended as an outcome of the *Sustainable Futures* project) could help further the conversation around best practice, facilitate the sharing of technical expertise relating to supporting sustainability, and help disseminate knowledge about methods and tools for supporting endangered music genres. They could serve to engage communities in making decisions about their music, and could help those in less developed regions to avoid the financial costs of reinventing approaches to sustainability that have already been tried and tested by wealthier countries. Importantly, they represent a way to develop clear advocacy arguments relating to the need for efforts to protect or promote musical diversity and the viability of "small" music genres; these are critical not only to raise public awareness of the issues, but also that of government and nongovernment organizations at the national and international levels.

1.7 CONCLUSIONS

This appraisal of music sustainability brings into relief some of the strengths, weaknesses, and gaps in current theory and practice. The key strengths may be summarized as follows:

- an understanding of, and some theoretical frameworks to describe, processes of transculturation, change, and revival of music genres, as well as theory on the relationship between globalization and culture,

including the equivocal effects of global markets on "small" music genres (Section 1.1);
- theoretical frameworks for understanding phenomena and processes of cultural, and specifically musical, diversity, and ways to protect them, as well as growing discourse on ecological models for cultural and musical sustainability (Section 1.1);
- extensive ethnomusicological experience and relatively well-funded initiatives of documentation and archiving, with procedural flaws being addressed through "best practice" (Section 1.2);
- keen awareness of ethical issues inherent in maintaining or revitalizing endangered music genres (particularly but not exclusively in relation to documenting and archiving), especially the importance of the principles of equality, collaboration, and reciprocity espoused by applied ethnomusicology (Section 1.2 and subsequently);
- specific instances of the ability of certain approaches supporting music at local, national, and international levels to increase the vitality and viability of music genres (e.g. festivals, transmission-based projects, and policy measures; Sections 1.3–1.5);
- extensive non–music-specific coordinating and evaluating mechanisms for safeguarding and sustainability, administered or driven by organizations like UNESCO, WIPO, and INCD (Section 1.6).

Another strength, which becomes apparent when viewing this chapter as a whole, is the ideological readiness of researchers, certain organizations, and other stakeholders to engage with research and applied efforts in music sustainability, as evidenced by a growing body of research and a range of practical initiatives in the area.

As is clear from the discussion in this chapter, some challenges to supporting music sustainability lie outside the immediate control of researchers or communities. Examples include the often limited availability of substantive funding and resources for practical initiatives; political or legislative forces that override efforts to sustain small music genres, such as unfavorable governmental attitudes to minority cultural expressions; and the equivocal impact on music genres of mass media, enterprise, and commercial ventures. While an understanding of these situations and processes is crucial to developing appropriate theory and practice of music sustainability, they are probably factors that maintenance or revitalization efforts will need to take into account, rather than focusing on overcoming them.

Several other shortcomings to current approaches supporting viable and vibrant music genres are eminently surmountable, however. The most critical gaps and weaknesses of current theory and practice relating to music sustainability may be summarized as follows:

- limited well-developed arguments advocating the need for efforts to maintain or revitalize small music genres (Sections 1.1 and 1.6);
- the lack of a systematic, standardized, replicable method to identify and assess situations of musical endangerment across a wide range of contexts (Section 1.2) (as opposed to the lack of a standardized way to *deal* with those situations, which is no doubt a necessity);
- limited knowledge-base on best ways to maintain and revitalize endangered music genres, despite the considerable success of specific approaches (for example, transmission-centered initiatives; Section 1.4);
- limited critical theoretical reflection on the possible effects of practical strategies intending to support music sustainability (e.g. policies, festivals, institutionalization, international instruments), despite recurring instances of equivocal and unexpected outcomes (Section 1.5); and
- limited music-specific measures that monitor, evaluate, coordinate, or carry forward the goals and objectives of sustaining and promoting endangered music genres (Section 1.6).

Before I investigate in Chapter 3 the extent to which the field of language maintenance might inform ways to repair these key shortcomings, language and music need to be assessed for similarities and differences in relation to factors that affect their sustainability. This is the aim of the next chapter.

CHAPTER 2

Language and Music Vitality
A Comparative Framework

Theories in language revitalization can bring new light to understanding music revitalization among indigenous minorities if we examine the differences and similarities while developing theories more appropriate to music revitalization. (Saurman, 2013, p.16)

This chapter aims to systematically identify the similarities and differences between language and music in relation to their vitality and viability.[1] Investigating the similarities lays the groundwork for identifying ways in which language maintenance might be accommodated within the theory and practice of music sustainability. By investigating the differences, we become aware of where caution might be exercised when transferring supporting approaches from language maintenance to music. The discussion is structured according to the *Five Domains of Musical Sustainability in Contemporary Contexts* presented by Schippers (2010, pp. 180–181), a framework that outlines broad issues affecting the viability of music genres (see Example 2.1🅞). Each section of this chapter is prefaced by the verbatim *précis* of the respective domain as it occurs in Schippers's framework.

---

1. A version of this chapter first appeared as the article: Grant, C. (2011). Key factors in the sustainability of language and music: A comparative study. *Musicology Australia* 33(1), 95–113. Reproduced by permission of the publisher (www.tandfonline.com).

2.1 SYSTEMS OF LEARNING MUSIC

> Systems of learning are central to the sustainability of most music cultures. This domain assesses balances between informal and formal training, notation-based and aural learning, holistic and analytical approaches, and emphasis on tangible and less tangible aspects of musicking. It explores contemporary developments in learning and teaching (from master-disciple relationships to systems based on technology/the world wide web), and how non-musical activities, philosophies and approaches intersect with learning and teaching. These issues play a key role from the level of community initiatives to the highest level of institutionalized professional training. (Schippers, 2010, p. 180)

For both languages and musical traditions, learning and teaching (implicit or explicit) are cornerstones of sustainability. Without them, intergenerational transmission does not take place, leading to the decline and eventual disappearance of the cultural heritage in question. Beyond this broadest similarity lies a range of more nuanced likenesses between language and music in relation to their transmission, as well as some significant disconnects.

Care is needed when drawing analogies between music transmission models and those for language transmission, especially in contexts of endangerment. The apparent similarity, for example, between the master-disciple system of learning music (perhaps best known in its centuries-old Indian manifestation *guru-śiṣya-paramparā*) and the master-apprentice model of language learning is misleading. For languages, the master-apprentice model (Hinton, 2002) is explicitly a safeguarding tool, implemented only where vitality is weak and viability in question, whereas for certain music genres it is the primary method of intergenerational transmission. This points to one divergence between language and music in relation to sustainability: in a characteristic vital and vibrant linguistic environment, in contrast with some musical ones, language transmission never takes place principally between two people alone.

According to one model from the area of Cultural Diversity in Music Education, the music learning process (within or outside of its culture of origin) may be viewed from the perspective of three continua: the analytic/holistic, the written/aural, and the tangible/intangible (Schippers, 2010, pp. 124–127). Each of these three factors pertains in the processes of language transmission, too. Like music, languages can be learned analytically (for example, with an explicit focus on grammar) or through more intuitive approaches, such as full immersion. Second, tangible aspects of the learning/teaching of music like technique and repertoire, and intangible ones like creativity and expression, also have their equivalences in language learning/teaching, which can focus on good pronunciation and syntactical accuracy (for example), or emphasize fluency and natural expression. Third, the explicit or implicit emphasis in language learning may either be on reading and writing (literacy) or on listening and speaking (as in most childhood language learning and in the pedagogical method known as the *communicative approach*).

With regard to this written/aural continuum, linguists generally agree that literacy is vital for successful language revitalization (Walsh, 2002, p. 17), not least because of its value in facilitating transmission: it vastly expands the range of learning resources that can be employed, it can act as a memory aide to expedite learning, and it enables transmission across otherwise prohibitive distances of time and space. For music, "literacy" (the ability to read notation) can likewise serve all these functions in the transmission processes. The concept of literacy in a language or music genre is of course meaningless without the existence of a means to write it down (orthography/notation). Researchers are well aware of the downsides of relying on written forms in transmission processes, one of which is the undesired standardization of traditions (as noted in Chapter 1.2). For sustainability of both languages and music, the distinction between descriptive and prescriptive orthographies (that is, for music, between transcription and notation) (Ellingson, 1992a, p. 157) helps distinguish between the roles of orthography in transmission and in documentation.

Although a written form is no guarantee of viability, a lack of orthography may in some instances hasten the decline of an endangered language or music genre (though it should also be noted that some genres, such as those with a basis in improvisation, cannot be notated because of their very nature). This is perhaps especially true since orally transmitted art forms and languages tend to be more variable in structure and content than those transmitted through written form. Tellingly, most endangered languages are orally transmitted ones (Grenoble & Whaley, 1998, p. 34). Despite the ambivalence of some linguists about the value of orthography for language viability, many researchers believe that writing systems are an advantage in the sustainability stakes, whether for music (notation is "an eminently useful tool for ensuring sustainability for complex musical structures;" Schippers, 2010, p. 67) or for languages:

> Communities with long-standing written traditions may be in a stronger position to hold on to a language despite reduced numbers of speakers, and certainly are in a stronger position for revitalizing a language which may in part need to be reconstructed on the basis of written records. (Grenoble & Whaley, 1998, p. 34)

Although the analytic/holistic, written/aural, and tangible/intangible continua themselves are relevant in the cases of both language and music, there may be wide divergences between language and music in how they are characteristically positioned along the continua within a learning context. Typically, for example, children learn their parents' language in the home, orally, holistically, largely through imitation, and without conscious intent. For this reason, much of the literature from language endangerment and maintenance places weight on intergenerational transmission between parents and children as the primary factor in viability (e.g. Fishman, 1991). Some music genres may be learned in a similar way (nursery songs, for example). But beyond the home, proficiency in music making may also be typically *primarily* learned in any number of other social contexts within a community: from a master or teacher, during social community gatherings, at rituals and ceremonies, or in an institutional environment. This greater variation in primary "domains" of music learning/teaching, and the corresponding difference in transmission approaches, holds important implications for developing appropriate mechanisms toward sustainability.

Another consideration in the sustainability of both language and music is the role of new media in learning and teaching; in recent years, these have featured increasingly in transmission processes. Audio and video technologies enable learning from a spatial or temporal distance; minidisc recorders and similar devices enable reinforcement of a lesson, and they can compensate for less time spent with a teacher (like "having the guru in one's pocket"; in Schippers, 2007, p. 127); CDs, DVDs, interactive multimedia resources, and the Internet act as learning stimuli or even surrogate teachers. Yet there are disadvantages to using technology as a tool in language and music transmission. Aside from the equipment being sometimes expensive, not always readily available, and requiring some training to use, technology may detract or distract from face-to-face methods of learning and teaching, which are arguably often the most effective (see Hinton, 2001). Also, for music, reliance on recordings (like the reliance on notation discussed above) does little to improve a learner's ability to improvise, a central skill in some musical traditions.

Like linguistic skills, musical ones may also be absorbed at a young age without formal tuition, through continual exposure. Tunstill (1987, p. 122) comments that "for the Pitjantjatjara, the acquisition of musical skills is as unproblematic as the acquisition of speech"; Dunbar-Hall recounts the following comment by a composer, performer, and teacher of Balinese gamelan, who describes his childhood experiences of music learning:

> [I learnt] just by listening, because in my village there is a gamelan ensemble and my father is the drummer. Everyday I follow[ed] my father to practice gamelan, and I try, but no teacher, I just try to learn and I just hear the technique, how the people play and I see and hear and I practice... I just watch and hear... if a grandfather is a musician, maybe anaknya ('his child') is a musician. (Dunbar-Hall & Adnyana, 2004, p. 148)

Particularly in such instances of "tacit knowledge," where musical skills and knowledge are acquired "by immersion in the everyday music and musical practices of one's social context" (Green, 2001, p. 22), the declining vitality of a genre within a society (for whatever reason) is likely to hold attendant repercussions for its transmission, and the risk is that this may mean a downward spiral for vitality. For languages, this is also true: whatever the initial impulse for a loss of speakers, the less a language is heard within a community, the less it is learned, and the less spoken.

Another factor in music and language viability is the issue of good teaching (however defined), whether implicit or explicit. Musical or linguistic competence does not necessarily translate into ability to teach well. The unlikelihood of recalling the process of learning a first language can make it difficult for native speakers to teach their language in a formal way without training. If music learning is explicit and continues beyond early childhood years, a music learner may be more likely to recall that learning process than the process of learning a mother tongue, yet still there is no guarantee that good teaching skills will result. For both language and music, the teaching skills of culture bearers may be a variable in the viability of a tradition. This is especially true when a language or music genre is endangered, since in that case explicit teaching may adopt a greater role in transmission processes. In fact, as languages become endangered, the processes of their transmission can begin to converge with those typical of some music genres (whether endangered or not): they become more formally and explicitly taught. Therefore, it is reasonable to suspect that the transmission processes of endangered languages and music genres hold greater synergies than in situations of linguistic vitality.

The five-domain framework that lends this chapter its structure does not explicitly attend to the various processes through which music comes into existence, yet compositional or creational mechanisms are certainly a factor in musical vitality. Not infrequently, music creation occurs simultaneously with its transmission (or indeed, the two are one and the same), meaning that this issue is well placed in this *Systems of Learning* domain. In the case of Tongan *lakalaka* (choreographed sung speeches), the atrophy of knowledge about compositional techniques contributed to an impoverished situation where existing repertory was reused rather than new repertory created (Kaeppler, 2004), although this situation has somewhat improved following UNESCO's proclamation in 2003 of *lakalaka* as a *Masterpiece of the Oral and Intangible Heritage of Humanity*. Composition as a deliberate and planned procedure is only one means by which new music comes into being; a process of improvisation is another, and yet another is supernatural beings or dreams investing individuals with songs (e.g. Marett, 2005). Language, by contrast, is generally not perceived to be "created" or "composed," and so these issues do not play a parallel role in linguistic sustainability.

Finally, this first domain of the five-domain framework acknowledges the role of nonmusical activities, philosophies, and approaches in systems of learning music. Here, the synergy with language learning is strong. Events such as ritual social gatherings at community houses, and the ideologies surrounding them, can provide children (and adults) with important opportunities to learn their (endangered) linguistic or musical heritage. Philosophies and approaches located externally to the culture can also directly affect systems of learning language and music and, therefore, sustainability. For some Australian Aboriginal communities, for example, hegemonic governmental attitude to bilingual education has at times presented a considerable danger to linguistic and wider cultural (including musical) viability.

2.2 MUSICIANS AND COMMUNITIES

This domain examines the role and position of musicians and the basis of the tradition within the community. It looks at the everyday realities in the existence of creative musicians, including the role of technology, media, and travel, and issues of remuneration through performances, teaching, portfolio careers, community support, tenured employment, freelancing, and non-musical activities. Cross-cultural influences and the role of the diaspora are also examined, as well as the interaction between musicians within the community. (Schippers, 2010, p. 180)

The positioning of a music genre within a society is a multifaceted phenomenon, and one that has, in many ways, defined ethnomusicological research for decades (witness, for example, Merriam's seminal work *The Anthropology of Music*, 1964). It embraces broad issues that include the social function of music within a community, its interconnection with nonmusical aspects of community life, and its economic basis in society. All of these issues interrelate with the sustainability of a genre.

In recent years, for example, music making for profit has in some cultures arguably overtaken music making for pleasure, and Mundy believes the "consumer boom in listening" has even effected a decline of actual music making in some communities (2001, p. 10), meaning fewer or less proficient musicians. Tongan *lakalaka* illustrates another kind of connection between the viability of a music genre and its positioning in society: when children were no longer taught relevant cultural traditions, aesthetics, or history as a core part of their school education, much of the in-depth cultural knowledge needed to compose poetry for it was lost (Kaeppler, 2004). A similar situation has arisen surrounding bardic singing in Aceh, Indonesia: the form requires strong Acehnese cultural and linguistic knowledge, but this is weakening as Indonesian (*Bahasa Indonesia*) takes hold (M. Kartomi, personal interview, October 21, 2010). These kinds of issues of social positioning hold less relevance to language sustainability, since language generally forms the basis for day-to-day communication in a society rather than serving discrete aesthetic, diversional, ritual, or other functions.

If the position of musician in a society is a specialist role, carries high status, or is viewed as requiring talent (Merriam, 1964), then these things may be powerful aids to the vitality or viability of a music genre (and conversely, a shift to low status may jeopardize viability). A case in point is the Western "pop idol" phenomenon, where musicians' prestige, talent, and status instigate disproportionately high media attention, public enthusiasm, and financial backing. By contrast, in a healthy linguistic environment, speakers hold no unique social function: within any one speech community (in contrast to the prestige of speaking one language or dialect over another, which certainly pertains), speaking that language is not perceived as special, or a talent or skill, and is considered neither of high or low prestige. Therefore, the various issues encompassed by this domain such as remuneration, interpersonal interaction, and the role of technology, media, and travel are unlikely to play as explicit a role for a speaker of a language as for a musician.

From an anthropological standpoint, Merriam proposes that even in those nonliterate cultures where music is an integral part of daily life, musicians hold a distinct specialist role within the community (1964, pp. 123–125). In view of this specialist role, musicians are often rewarded by society in some way that makes a real contribution to their living, whether through monetary remuneration, employment benefits, or gifts. Withdrawal of such recompense can play a role in the decline of a musical tradition, as demonstrated by the attrition in the mid-twentieth century of the Indian classical genre *dhrupad*, whose musicians faced financial hardship due to loss of royal patronage (Dutta, 1999). By contrast, remuneration for language speakers in a healthy linguistic context is atypical (though exceptions include language teachers, translators/interpreters, and artistic language users, like bards and poets). In this way, this domain embodies a key disconnect between music and language in relation to sustainability.

These and various other complexities of interpersonal relations may adversely affect the viability of both languages and music genres, especially when they are already endangered. Within certain indigenous cultures, for instance, internal laws governing cultural ownership enforce that only those who "own" song corpuses have the right to sing them (or to "give" them away); when those people are few, possibilities for transmission may be limited. In one instance, an Australian Indigenous elder decided to pass on secret and sacred men's business to a non-initiated female researcher, reckoning, "Well, it either dies with me, or I pass it on to [her]" (M. Walsh, personal interview, April 8, 2010). Taboos or restrictions sometimes exist about revealing one's knowledge of certain cultural practices to "insiders" (see for example Evans, 2001, p. 250, for language; Moyle, 1997, p. 78, for music) or "outsiders," like researchers. Internal "avoidance relationships" which proscribe interaction between certain kin are another variable in sustainability; Abley (2003) and Evans (2001) both cite poignant instances where such taboos have forbidden a fluent speaker to communicate in an endangered language with its other few remaining speakers. While they vary in type, then, issues of interpersonal relations are factors in the viability of both language and music.

Perhaps even more important in this regard than interpersonal relations, though, are intercultural ones. In an era when "cross-fertilisation no longer depends on the serendipity of travel or chance encounter[;] it can be at the touch of a button" (Mundy, 2001, p. 14), both musical and linguistic exchange is the rule rather than the exception. The myriad and complex possible results and responses to cross-cultural contact on music referred to in Chapter 1.1—revitalization, preservation, cross-fertilization, and impoverishment or abandonment of parts of the repertoire, among others—have direct parallels with the possible outcomes of languages in contact (Thomason, 2001). Kartomi even explicitly suggests that "the early stages of musical transculturation may resemble the initial stages of linguistic syncretism" (1981, p. 242), and Graves refers to a process of *creolization* when cultures come into contact, noting that the term is borrowed from linguistics (2005, p. 55).

A further possible outcome of contact between music cultures—Kartomi's "pluralistic coexistence of musics" (1981, p. 237)—incorporates notions of bi- or poly-musicality (Hood, 1960), which are paralleled in the language world by bilingualism and polylingualism. These phenomena imply that, for both languages and music,

> one might suggest that it is not a matter of either-or: *either* you keep your mother tongue and can function within your own community but remain isolated from the larger society whose majority language you do not speak, *or* you learn the majority language and get access to the larger society, but lose your mother tongue and what can be accessed through it. In other words, it is not a case of subtractive, but rather one of additive, language learning. (Maffi, 2003, p. 71)

Nettl, though, doubts the possibility of unbounded "additive" learning for music, assuming instead the notion of a maximum and roughly unchanging amount of "musical energy" within a culture:

> As Western music came into the lives of other of the world's peoples, they had to find ways of maintaining their older tradition with reduced energy, and this might mean a reduction in the number of people, or the amount of time, or the number of genres, styles, instruments henceforth devoted to it. (2005, p. 437)

This must also have its analogue in language: there is only so much linguistic communication that can be carried out in a community! According to Nettl, a complete embrace of a dominant music culture concurrently with the complete maintenance of its own music culture is absent as a response to (or result of) transculturation; this gives rise to his hypothesis that "addition to the musical culture of a society requires adjustments in the tradition already present" (1978, p. 129). For this reason, dominant languages and music genres often do encroach on minority ones, and recognition of this fact is a key instigator of purist attitudes within some music communities and speech communities. In turn, these attitudes affect sustainability in various ways (discussed in the next section).

In an individual, language loss or atrophy is always replaced by another language (barring aberrant circumstances like speech impairment), and at a community level, it always involves contact between at least two speech communities (Grenoble & Whaley, 1998, p. 27). This reality is alluded to by the term *language shift*, which underscores the move from one language to another. The term *music shift* has been adopted by at least one ethnomusicologist

(Coulter, 2007, 2011), but it is arguably less apposite than its linguistic counterpart: attrition of music-making skills or practice (whether in an individual or within a community) is not necessarily concomitant with that genre being replaced (or displaced) by another. As lifestyles changed, for example, entire corpuses of Maori paddling songs and food-bearing songs gradually died out, not because they were supplanted by other songs, but rather because they lost their function (McLean, 1996, p. 276).

The diaspora may play a decisive role in the future of endangered cultural expressions, both linguistic and musical. The portability of music means it can be (and often is) retained and practiced in diasporic spaces, and in this way, "small" music genres "can be kept alive by an international network of specialized performers spread out sometimes quite haphazardly around the world" (Malm, 1993, p. 350). In the dramatic case of the Polynesian atoll Takū, at imminent peril of being engulfed by rising seawaters, the autochthonous context is likely to disappear altogether, and the future of both language and music will be entirely in the hands of the diaspora (Moyle, 2007). In this era of globalization, where musical dissemination across the world is possible almost instantaneously, music has the ability to migrate even without human carriers.

Both musical and linguistic diasporic traditions often develop independently of their indigenous context—sometimes changing more rapidly as a result of the displacement and contact with other influences (e.g. Wang, 2003, p. 112), but sometimes more conservatively, due to preserved values and importance placed by the diaspora on continuing the true "tradition." Aubert cites two cases in point: French provincial songs of the seventeenth and eighteenth centuries survive in Quebec and Louisiana but not in France; and several genres among the Indian community of Trinidad, including seasonal chants linked to agricultural rituals, are now extinct in India but have been preserved intact in the Caribbean (2007, p. 74).

2.3 CONTEXTS AND CONSTRUCTS

> This domain assesses the social and cultural contexts of musical traditions. It examines the realities of and the attitudes to recontextualisation, cross-cultural influences, authenticity and context, and explicit and implicit approaches to cultural diversity resulting from travel, migration or media, as well as obstacles such as poverty, prejudice, racism, stigma, restrictive religious attitudes, and issues of appropriation. It also looks at

> the underlying values and attitudes (constructs) steering musical directions. These include musical tastes, aesthetics, cosmologies, socially and individually constructed identities, gender issues, as well as (perceived) prestige, which is often underestimated as a factor in musical survival. (Schippers, 2010, pp. 180–181)

Functions of speech and music differ, and therefore, so do their contexts. Typical language contexts include the home, the community, schools, workplaces, rituals and ceremonies, the media, government, law, and social services. Music is unlikely to be situated in some of these spaces; it is primarily found in community contexts (see Nettl, 2005, pp. 244–258, for an in-depth exploration of the uses and functions of music). By definition, music genres used in limited contexts have limited vitality, but not necessarily limited viability: Christmas carols are rarely heard for ten or eleven months of the year, but the genre seems unlikely to vanish any time soon. A language too can be viable even if it is not found across the full extent of possible contexts. Latin is a striking example: it is still the official language of the papal edicts and bulls, Catholic Roman rites, and an entire city-state, centuries after it was ever learned by children in the home as a mother tongue.

A notable point of disjuncture between contexts for language and music is that often the latter entails the concept of *performance* (in the sense of an individual musician or group's rendering or interpretation of a work, perhaps publicly, and perhaps in front of an audience), whereas communicative language contexts typically do not. Whether music is performed as part of a ritual, an informal community gathering, or a gala opera evening, a performance event is frequently a driving force behind music making, even if in many cases performance is "merely the residue of a process of far-reaching community involvement; preparations for the big ceremony can carry more content than their actualization as performance" (Graves, 2005, p. 63). This concept of performance also brings into relief a dichotomy between performer and audience, and in some ways and contexts, the role of the audience may be at least as important in issues of sustainability as that of the performer (see Domain 5: Media and the Music Industry).

New ways of life have resulted in disappearing sociocultural contexts for some genres of music, such as for the Maori paddling songs mentioned earlier, the songs sung by certain groups of women in India to lessen the drudgery of carrying water to wells ("now, there's a tap in the back yard"; Sethi, 2001, p. 85), and the Mongolian string fiddle genre *morin khurr*, whose decline resulted from the shift from nomadic life to urban settlement of Mongolian herding communities (UNESCO, 2012b). Other genres have successfully found new environments. Ramnarine describes various new urban performance contexts for Finnish folk music, including the striking and highly formalized situation of an examination within the Sibelius Academy's Department of Folk Music, a context that clearly departs radically from the traditional (2003, pp. 81–83).

In one way, then, a sustainable music genre is arguably one with the ability to reposition itself in new contexts and adapt to new social functions, and broadly speaking, the same can be said of languages. The vocabulary of the Aboriginal language Kaurna (probably last spoken on a daily basis in the 1860s) required some overhaul as it began to be taught within a school context in the late twentieth century. Learners and speakers developed new words (for example, for *computer, telephone,* and *to read*), devised a base-10 number system to enable counting into the millions, and coined expressions for sporting contexts and classroom use, such as "Empty the rubbish bin!" (Amery, 2002, p. 7). For both music genres and languages, then, it seems that not only are contexts themselves essential for viability, but so too is the ability to reposition, should those contexts shift radically or disappear altogether.

One issue addressed in this domain of the five-domain framework, but which in reality extends across and beyond all its domains, is community values and attitudes: toward the music genre itself, as well as toward learning and teaching methods, appropriate contexts, innovation and change in the tradition, and the use of media and technology, as well as more general community attitudes toward cultural diversity, gender roles, aesthetics, and a host of other nonmusical factors. For languages too, community constructs have considerable bearing on vitality and viability. For external influences to enter a linguistic or musical tradition, culture bearers must accept and adopt them; for a language or music genre to successfully adopt new functions, the community must be ideologically in favor of the change; for a language or music genre to successfully adapt to a changing sociocultural milieu, its carriers need to hold certain attitudes to "authenticity" and "tradition."

While all of the complex web of constructs that impact the vitality and viability of languages and music cannot be addressed at length here, two must be singled out as critical: first, a community's attitudes toward the tradition itself (that is, the prestige of a language or music genre in the eyes of its own community); and second, the community's attitudes and receptivity toward innovation and change. Regarding the latter, "mixed-up" language is sometimes rejected by community members of Australian Aboriginal groups, "who want either the old language or English and nothing else in between" (Thieberger, 2002, p. 324). Such an attitude could potentially break intergenerational transmission—and is one which linguist Walsh believes is, in the context of endangered languages, "completely potty" (personal interview, April 8, 2010). A musical analogue is quoted by Neuman, represented in this response of a highly respected master to an inquiry about the possible demise of the Indian instrument *surbahār*:

> You think that the ustads want to keep surbahars to themselves. It is wrong to think in that way. We do want to teach, but who is going to learn? It is such a big science, and if anybody asks for it and we give it then it would be like playing *vīnā* [the *bīn*] in front of a water-buffalo, so we only play for those who understand. (1980, p. 49)

A considerably more pragmatic attitude to change is that of one Finnish folk musician who, in response to an interview question about change in the tradition, replied simply: "Before it was like that and now it is like this" (Ramnarine, 2003, p. 213). Attitudes to broader cultural change also interplay with music and linguistic vitality and viability: the strength and uniqueness of the music culture of Takū are probably at least partially attributable to that community's ideological opposition to Christian missionary activity on the atoll—opposition that ended in practice, if not in principle, only in 1999 (Moyle, 2007, pp. 3–4). On the other hand, the local Balinese community, living in what is one of most heavy tourist areas in the world, has implemented various mechanisms that aim to balance tradition and innovation, mechanisms that strive to "protect their culture from the ravages of the international tourist trade while simultaneously taking full advantage of their economic opportunity" (Graves, 2005, p. 102).

One of the many instances of perceptions of prestige affecting musical viability is found in the Finnish *kantele*. Before the Finnish folk music revival of the late 1960s, the *kantele* was "seriously encumbered by prejudice, misplaced reverence and uncalled-for ridicule" (the words of Finnish musicologist Laitinen, reported in Ramnarine, 2003, p. 64)—and this despite its being widely perceived as the national instrument. Prestige is inextricably linked to aspects of other domains of the five domain framework, such as media attention and government policy. The improved status of the Welsh language during the 1970s and 1980s and the simultaneous retardation of its decline are both seen to be at least partly the result of the implementation of various policies, legislation, and media initiatives around that time. These initiatives include two Welsh Language Acts, the launch of a Welsh language television station, and the establishment of a Welsh Language Board (Welsh Assembly Government, 2003).

Closely related but not identical to the matter of prestige is this question: Do community members want their language or a particular music genre to survive, and if so, in what form? Ambivalence toward revitalization efforts is reflected in Stiles's experience of community language revitalization programs across four different cultures:

> All of the communities in these four programs experienced community objections to a program that taught the native tongue so seriously. Elders objected to the writing of the language (Cree and Hualapai); elders and parents feared teaching the children a language other than English because of past oppression for use of their native language (all programs); parents as non-speakers doubted the ability of their children to achieve fluency; and teachers were convinced the languages were unsuitable for academic endeavors. (Stiles, 1997, p. 257)

Paradoxically, there have also been instances where community members were in principle supportive of revitalization, but were unwilling to sacrifice effort or time to that end, rather employing what Walsh calls "avoidance strategies" (2002, p. 8).

Of course, a community consists of individuals who do not necessarily hold cohesive ideas about their language or music, or the maintenance thereof. In certain language revitalization efforts in North America, "there are individuals who are working their hearts out to try and relearn their languages et cetera; there are other people [within the same community] who couldn't care less; and there are others who actively discourage it because their particular view is . . . that it's a bad thing to keep that language going" (P. Austin, personal interview, June 16, 2010). These multifaceted constructs of culture bearers can be critical in the sustainability of both languages and music genres.

Although not made explicit by the five-domain framework, the constructs of significant outsiders—governments, policy makers, fieldworkers, researchers, and other power bearers—may also affect the sustainability of both languages and music genres, in at least three ways: by influencing the community's own attitudes toward their heritage; by making manifest these constructs and values in rules and regulations that affect the culture, whether favorably or unfavorably (see Domain 4: Infrastructure and Regulations); and by promoting to other outsiders their own values and attitudes in relation to the culture—for example, through academic, media, or advocacy platforms. Ursula Hemetek observes that not all researchers, for example, recognize the phenomenon of transculturation as worthy of study—there are those who "would not do any research on the diasporic or immigrant communities because this is not the 'real' music'" (personal interview, July 22, 2010).

A specific illustration the role of outsiders in musical vitality is found in the *dhrupad* revival, which was at least partly instigated when French scholar Alain Danielou "'revealed' this as the 'true' tradition of Indian music" and invited its musicians to perform abroad, thereby significantly raising the prestige of the genre (Schippers, 2009, p. 202). Another example comes from Konya, Turkey, where the US-based organization Cultures in Harmony recently negotiated the inclusion of women in the group of musicians accompanying the whirling dervish ceremony for the first time in its 700-year history (Cultures in Harmony, 2013; "Impact" section). Interventionist attitudes and practices like this may be beneficial to sustainability in some instances, but in others may have the opposite effect, or generate unexpected consequences. The literature on language maintenance is thick with instances of unforeseen results of intervention (e.g. NeSmith, 2009, for Hawaiian; Spolsky, 2005, for Hebrew).

This domain of Schippers's five-domain framework also encompasses the impact on sustainability of attitudinal obstacles such as cultural prejudice, racism, stigma, restrictive religious attitudes, and issues of appropriation. (It also refers to poverty, which I would argue is better placed within the next domain along with other non-attitudinal factors in sustainability, like war, civil unrest, and persecution.) Impinging on the totality of a culture, these attitudinal obstacles can affect the language as well as the music: Witness the fact that as late as the 1970s, the indigenous Sámi language was banned in some schools in Finland as the devil's language, and at least ten people are recorded as having been executed for singing the traditional Sámi joik (Ramnarine, 2003, p. 182). Despotic or totalitarian regimes may be particularly hostile toward musicians (more than language speakers), because of their explicit and unique role as carriers of culture, as in the heinous era of the Khmer Rouge in Cambodia in the 1970s, and the recent and ongoing years of Taliban repression and war in Afghanistan. The international organization Freemuse (Freedom of Musical Expression) works against conditions like these, advocating human rights for musicians and composers (2013). Certain other nongovernmental organizations advocate for freedom of cultural expression at large, sometimes with a significant focus on the rights of people to speak their heritage language (e.g. the US-based organization Cultural Survival).

Censorship of cultural expression is not always so insidious, or so obvious, as in cases of tyranny and despotism. For centuries, well-meaning evangelical missionary activities have explicitly and implicitly censored indigenous cultures the world over, separating children from their parents, disconnecting them from their culture, and denying them their heritage language and songs, thereby causing vast damage to cultural, linguistic, and musical viability (which is not to deny some positive outcomes of their activities). Censorship of quite another kind is the self-imposed censorship of a community on its own music making or language use. Whether conducive or obstructive to sustainability, this kind of censorship is almost always inextricably connected to ideologies (of kinship, gender, ownership, authenticity, transmission of tradition, and so on).

2.4 INFRASTRUCTURE AND REGULATIONS

> This domain primarily relates to the "hardware" of music: places to perform, compose, practice and learn, all of which are essential for music to survive, as well virtual spaces for creation, collaboration, learning, and dissemination. Other aspects included in this domain are the availability and/or manufacturing of instruments and other tangible resources. It also examines the extent to which regulations are conducive or obstructive to a blossoming musical heritage, including artists' rights, copyright laws, sound restrictions, laws limiting artistic expression, and challenging circumstances such as obstacles that can arise from totalitarian regimes, persecution, civil unrest, war or the displacement of music or people. (Schippers, 2010, p. 181)

Infrastructure requirements for making music and for speaking a language differ considerably, both in degree and nature. Unlike much music making, speaking a language generally does not call for specific locations, instruments, or other tangible resources to "create" or "perform" it. (Exceptions include some ceremonial or performative forms of language, which may be site-specific, and formal language learning contexts, which may employ a dedicated space). Also, primarily due to the interrelatedness of the World Wide Web and the commercialization of music (see Domain 5: Media and the Music Industry), virtual spaces are pivotal in sustainability of music genres, but not of languages (their potential or actual role in language transmission notwithstanding). At this level of infrastructure, then—tangible resources and places to create, perform, practice, and learn music—the parallels between language sustainability and music sustainability are limited.

A broader level of infrastructure, though, potentially affects both a community's language and its music inasmuch as it influences all aspects of life, including health, education opportunities, presence of technology and media, and perceptions of social and cultural identity. Infrastructure both relies on and is affected by economic circumstance, which is a key force in the sustainability of both languages (Grenoble & Whaley, 1998) and music genres (Letts, 2006). In fact, for music, economic circumstances are so crucial that they should arguably be added to the list of "challenging circumstances" identified in this domain as potentially obstructing music sustainability. This, however, brings to light another disjunction between language and music: The economic factors at play in musicians' (and audiences') lives, combined with the tangible resources often required to make music, mean that the impact of poverty on music sustainability is likely to be greater and more direct than on the sustainability of a language. Indeed, poverty may not in the least threaten the viability or vitality of a language (consider Bengali, spoken by well over 200 million speakers in Bangladesh and eastern India).

Like a lack of broad community infrastructure, other disadvantageous circumstances ("totalitarian regimes, persecution, civil unrest, war or the displacement of music or people" in Schippers' framework) may affect both language and music sustainability, simply inasmuch as these circumstances affect the totality of a culture. As mentioned earlier, the immediate peril of rising seawaters means that the Takū atoll (within Papua New Guinea political territory) is currently experiencing displacement of its people (Moyle, 2007), doubtless holding ramifications for both its linguistic and musical traditions, along with its cultural heritage at large. In Aceh, Sumatra, years of war (ending in 2005) significantly impeded the level of artistic energy in the population, which was "diverted to other things" (M. Kartomi, personal interview, October 21, 2010). The effect of challenging social circumstances on musical vitality and viability are not always adverse, however: the fact that no foreigners were allowed into certain communities in central Aceh for some decades during the war meant that these communities were better able to maintain their musical traditions, due to their isolation and a lack of foreign influence (M. Kartomi, personal interview, October 21, 2010).

This domain also deals with the role of regulations and policies in sustainability. At a local and regional level as well as at the level of nation-states, regulations often embody the attitudes to culture of governments, who are therefore key players in language and music sustainability. Artists' rights, intellectual property and copyright laws, and sound restrictions are all examples of regulations, normally government-imposed, affecting musicians and composers. Policies and laws impacting language use and language speakers differ in nature from these, but they are just as critical to sustainability: Among many others, they include laws relating to bilingual school education, to the use of minority languages in the workplace and the media, and to the provision of translation services in matters of social services. Government policies that significantly affect musical or linguistic sustainability (positively or negatively) do not necessarily directly refer to music or language or even culture but may instead relate primarily to education, immigration, ethnic discrimination, broadcasting, intellectual property, new media, e-commerce, and international free trade agreements, among other things (see Letts, 2006).

Over the past two or three decades, various international declarations have brought increased prominence to the importance of human, language, and cultural rights, and also to duties of governments and other bodies to honor them. Among them are the *Universal Declaration of Linguistic Rights* (Assembly of the World Conference on Linguistic Rights, 1996), the *Convention on the Protection and Promotion of the Diversity of Cultural Expressions* (UNESCO, 2005), and the *Declaration on the Rights of Indigenous Peoples* (United Nations High Commission for Human Rights, 2007). Although no declaration centers exclusively on music, the heightened awareness of cultural rights matters brought about by international tools like these have made significant inroads to protecting and promoting both linguistic and musical heritage.

2.5 MEDIA AND THE MUSIC INDUSTRY

> This domain addresses large-scale dissemination and commercial aspects of music. Most musicians and musical styles depend in one way or another on the music industry for their survival. Over the past 100 years, the distribution of music has increasingly involved recordings, radio, television and internet (e.g. Podcasts, YouTube, MySpace). At the same time, many acoustic and live forms of delivery have changed under the influence of internal and external factors, leading to a wealth of new performance formats. This domain examines the ever-changing modes of distributing, publicising, and supporting music, including the role of audiences (including consumers of recorded product), patrons, sponsors, funding bodies and governments who "buy" or "buy into" artistic product. (Schippers, 2010, p. 181)

The cuter the animal, it seems, the more likely it is to be earmarked for "rescuing"; advocates for any endangered species of insect would be hard pressed to gain the degree of publicity—or funding—that the panda has. Metaphorical license aside, it is interesting to draw the analogy with endangered music genres. The fate of unaccompanied Australian Aboriginal ceremonial songs performed by untrained voices and lasting half a minute may well fail to garner wide public attention, whereas the energy and rhythmic impulse of Cuban *son* holds high entertainment value by most standards. Entertainment value equates with commercial potential, which in turn helps the promotion and celebration of the music genre in question. An extension of the species metaphor to music genres and languages themselves is also telling. The enormity of the global music industry and the comparative paucity of commercial income generated by languages support the speculation that in the public perception, music is "cuter" than language, arguably giving it a significant advantage in the endangerment stakes.

This domain, then, represents perhaps the most significant disjunction between language and music in relation to issues of vitality and viability—namely, their contrasting potential as a commodity. Mundy even believes (perhaps naively) that "the best way to keep a small musical culture alive is to make it popular with a large enough number of people to make it a profitable profession for its exponents" (2001, p. 11). The commercial potential of music may hold particular promise for the sustainability of "small" music genres, as discussed in Chapter 1.1. The significant revival in the past four or five years of the lute-like Malian *ngoni*, for example, has been attributed to two recently released albums by artist Bassekou Kouyaté that enjoyed acclaim both within Mali and internationally (Durán, 2011, pp. 250–251).

Although size and dispersal of speaker population are variables in language viability too, those variables lack real potential to be mitigated by any such thing as a language "industry." Languages do not depend on global commerce *per se* for their vitality or viability, and it is hard to imagine a form of language that "does away with time and place," as Erlmann (questionably) believes world music does (1993, p. 12). It is true that a sustainable language needs to be a "profitable" enterprise for its speakers, but not necessarily fiscally: much more often it simply serves as the most efficient way to communicate—or it might "profit" speakers by expanding employment options, for example, or by acting as a marker of identity.

Mass media (those "that are designed to reach, and actually do reach 'mass audiences'—audiences larger than a live performance would reach"; Christensen, 1992, p. 121) are powerful mechanisms in the viability of small music genres, especially given their nexus with the music industry (as described in Chapter 1.1). Romero believes they are the most important forces of musical change, and critical to the sustainability of music genres (1992, pp. 191–192). Media attention and inattention, especially on television and radio, can be pivotal in the vitality and viability of endangered languages, too (as in the case of Welsh), even given the lack of a language "industry" as such.

As one example of a mass medium, the Internet provides insight into the powerful influence of media on cultural sustainability, both positive and negative. More than languages, the role of virtual spaces is pivotal to music sustainability, primarily due to their potential to reach mass audiences. Whether or not their use by individuals is fiscally stimulated, online tools like YouTube and iTunes have proven extremely effective ways to disseminate and distribute music, including small or endangered genres that may otherwise not have a voice in a regional or global environment. A delightful example of how technology and the Internet can work together to give voice to the music of minority cultures is found in one blogged video clip (Example 2.2⬤) showing a young Peruvian folk singer from Huayllar, Angaraes, in colourful traditional costume, dancing and singing a *huaylarsh* to the following words:

> How are you little friend, I want you to give me your email.
> Come on pretty faced friend, I want to get to know you better.
> See that I feel very in love, only through internet love.
> I think I am very much in love, give me your affection through internet.
> (Global Voices, 2009)

Alongside the questions this clip raises about shifting social functions of music, changing contexts, and tradition versus innovation, it also illustrates how technology and the internet can help promote the music of minorities. But woes of "Internet love" aside, the sometimes uneasy relationship between the World Wide Web and the dynamics of cultural sustainability mean that the Internet is not always the superlative tool for promoting endangered cultural expressions that it may at first appear to be. Among several other concerns is the fact that it creates an immediate power distance between culture bearer and consumer. As Bohlman observes, "pronouncements by media experts about the ubiquity of CDs, Internet, and the transnational recording industry notwithstanding, not everyone in the world has equal access to the technologies of world music, and most people in the world have no access" (2002, p. 133). Over a decade on, considerable inequities remain: Data from the UN specialized agency for information and communications technologies for 2013 indicates that 31 % of the population of the developing world uses the Internet, compared with 77 % of the developed world (International Telecommunications Union, 2013).

These access-related power inequities are of ethical concern in relation to endangered languages too, a fact expressed in UNESCO's *Recommendation on the Promotion and Use of Multilingualism and Universal Access to Cyberspace* (UNESCO, 2003c). Linguists have noted the two sides to the sustainability coin:

> The Internet paradoxically facilitates both language diversity and language domination.... Far from being a panacea for the very real threats to language diversity in the modern world, technology may well be playing an important role in diminishing real language diversity by supporting a more limited, essentially Eurocentric language pluralism. (Tonkin & Reagan, 2003, p. 7)

Parallel concerns arise in relation to other kinds of mass media, such as television and radio.

Just as mass media is not always wholly favorable to the sustainability of music genres, neither is the music industry itself. Aside from the considerable challenges to sustainability sometimes brought about by cross-cultural contact (which are multiplied infinitely by global music commerce), the music industry carries systemic anomalies that can fail musicians (as well as publishers, agents, recording companies, and composers). Piracy is a prime example: By depriving copyright holders of their profits, Mundy argues, it sometimes relegates music making to an unsustainable livelihood (2001, p. 13). Industry-related concerns like this do not affect languages or language speakers to anywhere near the same degree as they do musicians, though copyright, ownership, and intellectual property issues can and do arise with regard to appropriation of endangered languages by outsiders (Walsh, 2002, p. 7).

Dauenhauer and Dauenhauer write of a "legitimate fear" within one indigenous society of language-related materials being "appropriated, exploited, trivialized and desecrated by outsiders, and this fear has led many elders in the direction of secrecy" (1998, p. 91). Because of its wide commercial potential, music appropriation is an even greater danger than the appropriation or exploitation of language. Music sustainability may be implicated in various ways—for example, if the fear of exploitation leads culture bearers to be reluctant to engage with initiatives supporting viability (like documentation). The concern is not always located outside of the community, either: Viability is also jeopardized when communities themselves begin to "sell off" cultural heritage to outsiders, sometimes at the expense of maintaining it within the community and transmitting it to next generations.

This leads to the area of music tourism, a niche that has boomed in recent decades. Local music is promoted regionally, nationally, and internationally as a tourist drawing card, and music tours that offer "authentic" and sometimes participatory music experiences from Argentinean tango to West African drumming to Chinese opera are a growing phenomenon (Gibson & Connell, 2005). In an insightful overview of the paradoxes involved in re-presenting "traditional" music genres on the stage, Aubert offers the specific example of an ensemble from Kerala undergoing "a series of subtraction operations" in preparation for staged performances in Europe of tantric ritual music from Malabar, India: The ensemble trimmed the space and time requirements of the ritual, filtered out any aspects that would induce a feeling of voyeurism or discomfort in the audience (like trance and animal sacrifice), reduced the requirements and expectations of interaction with the audience, and generally de-ritualized the whole experience (2007, pp. 29–31). At some point the question must arise whether the staged version of the genre could even be called by the same name. While changes of this nature occur regularly in the "natural" development of music genres across the world, shows and performances like these that have been shaped for visitors or outsiders are not always gainful for sustainability. Tourism that instigates repackaged, devoid-of-context, exoticized culture can have "a high impact, socially and economically, on small-scale societies and communities. While the advantages may be short-term economic ones, the disadvantages are of a social nature and usually long term" (Langton, 1994, p. 20).

These important considerations for the sustainability of music genres are negligible in the case of languages, which are unlikely to be tailored to outsiders' tastes for economic reasons. Yet there are certain ways in which tourism can benefit both endangered languages and endangered music genres. A little ironically, it seems that endangerment is one attribute of a language that can excite tourism, bringing it recognition and national celebration (as in the case of the Norman language, celebrated in La Fête Nouormande; Johnson, 2005, pp. 74–75). Musical vitality too can be strengthened through tourism, as the festival phenomenon has proven: the establishment in 1968 of the *Kaustinen Festival of Folk Music* helped raise the profile of Finnish music after a time of neglect (Ramnarine, 2003), and as already mentioned, festivals were a central catalyst in the revival of Indian *dhrupad* from the mid-1970s (Widdess, 1994).

2.6 CONCLUSIONS

The foregoing discussion points to both considerable similarities and considerable differences between languages and music genres in relation to factors that impact upon their vitality and viability. Table 2.1, in effect a précis of this chapter, synthesizes these synergies and disconnects into a comparative framework (also downloadable as Example 2.3 ⓞ). Like the chapter itself, the framework is structured according to the *Five Domains*

Table 2.1 COMPARATIVE FRAMEWORK: KEY SYNERGIES AND DISCONNECTS BETWEEN MUSIC AND LANGUAGE IN RELATION TO THEIR SUSTAINABILITY

Domain 1. Systems of learning music. *Level of synergy: very high*
SYNERGIES: Like music, the sustainability of languages is dependent on systems of learning and teaching, as well as related issues such as teacher training. As for music, approaches to language learning can be situated along various continua, such as the written-aural and the analytic-holistic. New technologies and developments in teaching and learning languages are often linked with sustainability, in that they relate to effective transmission. Nonlinguistic factors intersect with learning and teaching languages, as nonmusical ones do for music.
DISCONNECTS: Typical contexts for language learning differ from those for learning music, though as a language becomes endangered its transmission process may more closely resemble that of some music genres. Everyday communicative language is generally not perceived to be "created" or "composed" in the same way as music is.

Domain 2. Musicians and communities. *Level of synergy: moderate*
SYNERGIES: Interpersonal and intercultural contact and the dynamics of a community moving from using one language to another are critical factors in language sustainability, as they are for music. The diaspora also potentially plays a role in language sustainability, as it may (perhaps even more so) for music.
DISCONNECTS: The different social role of language and language speakers compared with music and musicians means that many issues in this domain (including social positioning, remuneration, and career paths) disconnect with language sustainability issues.

Domain 3. Contexts and constructs. *Level of synergy: very high*
SYNERGIES: For language as for music, sociocultural functions and contexts and the capacity to adapt to changes in them are critical for sustainability. Attitudes to tradition/innovation, recontextualization, cross-cultural contact, and context affect language and music sustainability, as do constructs surrounding specific languages and music genres, such as prestige. Also playing a part in language and music sustainability are the broader attitudes of a community, such as those relating to cultural diversity, identity, and gender roles (which for example may be the root of obstacles like stigma and prejudice). The constructs of significant outsiders impact in important ways on both language and music sustainability.
DISCONNECTS: Typical everyday language contexts are broader than those of music, and do not generally entail the notion of performance.

Table 2.1 (CONTINUED)

Domain 4. Infrastructure and regulations. *Level of synergy: high*
SYNERGIES: As for music, political and economic circumstances (censorship, prejudice, persecution, war, poverty, population displacement), as well as levels of community infrastructure, can greatly affect language viability. Policies and regulations imposed from either within or outside of the community can have enormous bearing on language and music sustainability alike.
DISCONNECTS: Speakers of a language generally require fewer tangible resources than musicians to perform or create their language, being unreliant for example on instruments or specific performances sites. Virtual (internet-based) infrastructure is less critical to the sustainability of languages than to that of music genres.

Domain 5. Media and the music industry. *Level of synergy: low/very low*
SYNERGIES: The sustainability of languages (particularly when endangered) and of music genres are both closely connected with attitudes of the media (especially television and radio). Both are sometimes also linked to the impact of tourists and others who in some way buy into language use or music making.
DISCONNECTS: Language and music have vastly contrasting potential as a commodity. As a rule, languages do not depend on an industry *per se* for their vitality or viability, and for this reason, industry-related issues in music sustainability, such as dissemination and distribution, as well as challenges such as piracy, intellectual property issues, appropriation and exploitation, technological access, and the sometimes equivocal effect of tourism on cultural sustainability, are lesser concerns in language sustainability, though they can play a role.

of Musical Sustainability in Contemporary Contexts (Schippers, 2010, pp. 180–181). It indicates an approximate level of synergy of each domain with issues of language sustainability (very high/high/moderate/low/very low). Admittedly this is a crude system, not least because certain aspects of a domain may hold high synergy while others of the same domain may significantly disconnect. I hope it proves useful, however, in representing the broader key findings of the chapter.

Based on the discussion in this chapter, core synergies between language and music in relation to their sustainability include the dynamics of their transmission (Domain 1), the interplay between the vitality of a language or music genre and the social and cultural constructs and attitudes that surround it (Domain 3), and the impact of economic and political circumstances (including policies and regulations) (Domain 4). This raises a number of questions: Are there language-based transmission initiatives, like the successful Maori *kōhanga reo* ("language nests"; King 2001), that might hold resonance with potential (or actual) music-specific initiatives toward sustainability (Domain 1)? How might tried and tested ways of raising the prestige of an endangered language within a community help inform similar situations for music (Domain 3)? To what extent could language-related precedents indicate possible effects of policies and regulations on the vitality of music within a culture or community (Domain 4)?

The dissimilarities between language and music discussed in this chapter suggest where language maintenance strategies are less likely to be amenable to adaptation for music. Initiatives that aim to expand the domains of use of an endangered language—from the school to the community to the workplace, or to legal and government spheres, for example—may be only indirectly relevant for music genres, if at all (Domain 3). Conversely, there are likely to be effective ways to support music sustainability that will lack precedent in language maintenance: most obviously, those engaging industry and commerce as a promotional mechanism (Domain 5).

It might be observed that not all domains of the *Comparative Framework* are likely to affect the sustainability of music (or language) equally. This is true both for specific cases of musical endangerment as well as at a general level, though there appears to be little consensus in the literature regarding which aspects are the most critical overall. Ellis, for example, believes that "the most serious impediment to the preservation of traditional music in some living form...is likely to be the dominant society's belief that music is a useless form of communication" (1992, p. 275)—a factor of Domain 3: Contexts and Constructs. Romero, on the other hand, argues that the mass media (Domain 5: Media and the Music Industry) is "usually considered the main force of musical change" (1992, p. 200), and for this reason it can act as "the ultimate factor in cultural disintegration" (p. 195). Further research investigating the relative importance to sustainability of each domain would progress understanding of the dynamics of music sustainability, but that may only become possible as ethnomusicology attains a better grasp of those dynamics in a range of specific contexts.

In addition to being affected by the issues relating to the five domains, sustainability of both languages and music genres is also linked to issues relating specifically to maintenance and revitalization, such as the extent, quality, and overall efficacy of current or past efforts to support viability, and the degree and quality of existing documentation and archiving. Another key issue is the sometimes profound effect of maintenance efforts themselves on communities and their cultural expressions (referred to several times in Chapter 1 with regard to music). Beyond their intended outcomes, maintenance efforts can influence sustainability in a variety of ways, for example via the prestige that is sometimes created around a music genre or language as a direct result of the interests and efforts of outsiders to protect or promote it.

I have already argued that an understanding of the synergies and disconnects between language and music in relation to their sustainability is needed to gauge how and to what extent language maintenance strategies may inform ways to support the viability of music genres. In this way, the *Comparative Framework* represents necessary groundwork for the following chapter, which explores how recourse to the field of language maintenance may help address the weaknesses and limitations of current theory and practice of music sustainability (as identified in Chapter 1). By affording the extensive experience and discourse of this field a place within investigations into issues of musical vitality and viability, Chapter 3 embraces the central purpose of this book.

CHAPTER 3
Learning From Language Maintenance

> I think it obvious *that* ethnomusicology can learn from linguistics, just as it can learn from musicology, anthropology, aesthetics, philosophy, human biology, and physics. The real question is *what* ethnomusicology can learn from linguistics. (Feld, 1974, p. 212; italics mine)

In this chapter, I investigate how, and to what extent, the field of language maintenance might help repair weaknesses and gaps in current approaches to music sustainability. I will take as a point of departure the five key gaps identified in Chapter 1:

1. the need for a systematic, standardized, and replicable method to identify and measure music endangerment;
2. the need to further develop advocacy efforts to maintain and revitalize endangered music genres;
3. the need to improve the knowledge base on optimal ways to maintain and revitalize endangered music genres;
4. the need for critical theoretical reflection on the possible effects of practical strategies intending to support music sustainability, especially given recurring instances of equivocal or unexpected outcomes; and
5. the need to develop music-specific structures that monitor, evaluate, coordinate, or carry forward the goals and objectives of music sustainability.

Taking into account the synergies and disconnects between languages and music genres in relation to sustainability (as identified in the *Comparative*

Framework of the previous chapter), I now consider each of these five points in turn, examining how theory and experience from the field of language maintenance may be able to inform each.

3.1 DEAD OR ALIVE? IDENTIFYING AND ASSESSING MUSIC ENDANGERMENT

While research (especially in the field of intangible cultural heritage) has helped identify the manifold *causes* of musical endangerment, it remains unclear what actually constitutes endangerment—how it might be recognized, defined, or measured. Here the field of language maintenance proves informative in two ways. First, it points to some of the complexities of identifying and assessing degrees of endangerment; and second, it presents a variety of tools used by linguists to assess language endangerment, some of which may serve as prototypes for developing similar tools for music.

Defining what constitutes language endangerment has proven a difficult and contentious task. Consider one of the seemingly simplest gauges for the vitality of a language: the number of speakers it has. Should only fluent speakers be counted (or for music genres, only accomplished musicians)? What counts as a fluent speaker (accomplished musician)? What does *speaker* (*performer/musician*) even mean (cf. Blacking's exploration, 1973, of how the concept of *musician* differs greatly from culture to culture)? Should those terms refer to competence or deed (consider a master musician who no longer performs or a speaker who no longer uses her mother tongue)? Where to draw the line between a language and its dialects (between one music genre and another)? These questions aside, the figure for the number of speakers that linguists have chosen as indicating vitality diverges wildly: Garza-Cuarón and Lastra (1991) declare the vitality threshold to be 500 speakers (for Mexican languages), while Krauss (1992) cites 100,000 as a "safe" number in general, with less than 10,000 speakers indicating endangerment. Other researchers regard as imperiled some languages with a substantial speaker population, such as Catalan, with over 11 million speakers (cf. Walsh, 2005, p. 294). These considerations from language maintenance (described by Tonkin, 2003, and others) suggest to ethnomusicologists that measuring vitality will be no easy task. Perhaps more helpfully, they also indicate some specific challenges ethnomusicologists are likely to encounter, and in some cases point to possible solutions.

For languages, no single factor sufficiently indicates vitality. Although critical speaker mass (however defined) may in some circumstances serve as a convenient proxy, it cannot be used as the sole determining factor in the strength of a language. Many Australian Indigenous languages may never have had more than a relatively small speaker population (under 1,000) but remained stable for millennia until a few generations, even decades, ago. Likewise, the number of musicians of a genre (however defined) is an inadequate measure of musical vitality: A genre may find itself in peril even if there are many musicians (consider the potential immediate impact of unfavorable new political circumstances, such as repressive regimes). On the other end of the spectrum, low musician numbers can be a woolly concept too; de Ferranti explains (in a footnote, mind you) that the title of his book *The Last Biwa Singer* "is not intended literally, but as a characterization," since this form of Japanese narrative singing continues in two "modern biwa" traditions (2009, p. 13).

In developing ways to identify and assess endangerment, linguists have taken a holistic approach: Language vitality assessment tools almost always try to account for the multitude of linguistic and nonlinguistic factors at play. Intergenerational transmission is often considered to be the most critical factor, but many other variables are also taken into account, including the official status of the language; community literacy; and the geographical concentration of the speaker population, its location relative to a dominant culture, its economic base, and the language's prestige relative to surrounding languages. As the *Comparative Framework* of the previous chapter shows, many of these factors also affect the vitality and viability of music genres, warranting similarly holistic approaches to identifying and assessing musical vitality.

In spite of the complexities, a number of typologies and classifications of language endangerment exist, including by Schmidt (for use with Australian Aboriginal languages; 1990), Dixon (1991), Fishman (1991), Kinkade (for indigenous Canadian contexts; 1991), Edwards (1992), Wurm (1998), McConvell and Thieberger (2001), UNESCO (2003b), and Lewis and Simons (2010). The most common kind of typology positions any given language into one of about five or six categories, ranging from *safe* (or *viable* or *strong*) to *extinct* (see Figure 3.1 for one example). *Endangered* languages are those falling in between, often subdivided into categories like *moderately endangered*, *severely endangered*, and *moribund*. These classes are typically distinguished from each other by variables such as the strength (or weakness) of social contexts and functions, proportion of the population speaking the language, degree of threat from more dominant languages, and/or strength of intergenerational transmission. It is not difficult to conceive of classification systems whereby music genres are positioned along similar graded scales. (Nor is it difficult to imagine the academic consternation any such system or set of descriptors would generate! Concerns about

Safe (5): The language is spoken by *all generations*. There is no sign of linguistic threat from any other language, and the intergenerational transmission of the languages seems uninterrupted.

Stable yet threatened (5-): The language is spoken in most contexts by all generations with unbroken intergenerational transmission, yet multilingualism in the native language and one or more dominant languages has usurped certain important communication contexts. Note that multilingualism alone is not necessarily a threat to languages.

Unsafe (4): Most but not all children or families of a particular community speak their language as their first language, but it may be restricted to specific social domains (such as at home where children interact with their parents and grandparents).

Definitively endangered (3): The language is no longer being learned as the mother tongue by children in the home. The youngest speakers are thus of the parental generation. At this stage, parents may still speak their language to their children, but their children do not typically respond in the language.

Severely endangered (2): The language is *spoken* only by *grandparents and older generations*; while the parent generation may still *understand* the language, they typically do not speak it to their children.

Critically endangered (1): The youngest speakers are in the *great-grandparental generation*, and the language is not used for everyday interactions. These older people often *remember* only part of the language but *do not use* it, since there may not be anyone to speak with.

Extinct (0): There is no one who can speak or remember the language.

Figure 3.1 Graded typology of language viability. (Text: UNESCO Ad Hoc Expert Group on Endangered Languages, 2003, pp. 9–10)

these kinds of typologies are raised later in this section and at length in the following chapter.)

One of the most significant international tools to assess language vitality and viability is UNESCO's *Language Vitality and Endangerment* (2003b; Example 3.1 ⓞ). It identifies nine factors in language vitality, and provides a quantitative way to measure each (such as the graded numeric scale in Figure 3.1, the first of the factors of this framework, which relates to intergenerational transmission). For any language, the measurements of these nine factors, taken as a set, indicate its vitality. The framework has found widespread use, including in the preparation of UNESCO's *Atlas of the World's Languages in Danger* (Moseley, 2009); Grenoble and Whaley note that the framework "ha[s] been endorsed by a relatively large group of linguists from around the world" (2006, p. 4). Again it is possible to conceive of a comparable methodology for assessing music endangerment, whereby a number of factors are identified as contributors to vitality; where each of those factors can be quantified and qualified; and where their summative assessment indicates the level of vitality of any given music genre. (It is this very kind of methodology I attempt to develop in the next chapter.)

Like many other graded-scale typologies of language endangerment, UNESCO's *Language Vitality and Endangerment* takes inspiration from Fishman's seminal *Graded Intergenerational Disruption Scale*, or GIDS (Fishman, 1991, 2001), which assesses the degree of disruption to the intergenerational transmission of a language. GIDS identifies eight stages of endangerment, and suggests interventions to reverse language shift at each stage. At the most critical stage of endangerment, for example, Fishman recommends reassembling the vestiges of the language from elderly speakers and teaching them to demographically unconcentrated adults. For lower levels of endangerment, he suggests trying to expand the functions of the language in workplaces, higher education, government, and the mass media. Of any typology of language endangerment, GIDS has probably provoked the most discourse within the linguistic literature (e.g. Dauenhauer & Dauenhauer, 1998; Reyhner, Cantoni, St. Clair, & Parsons Yazzie, 1999; Walsh, 2002). A number of modifications and adaptations have been proposed, both generally (e.g. Hinton, 2003; Lewis & Simons, 2010; McKay, 1996) and in specific contexts (such as for Australian Indigenous languages, in Lo Bianco & Rhydwen, 2001).

At least one ethnomusicologist has recognized the potential for GIDS to be adapted for music: as part of his doctoral research, Coulter modified the tool in order to assess the vitality and viability of the music genres of the indigenous Alamblak people in Papua New Guinea's lowland Sepik region. His adaptation resulted in a five-stage *Graded Music Shift Scale* (GMSS) (2007). Inspired by Lewis and Simons's Expanded GIDS (2010), Coulter subsequently modified and expanded his GMSS to eight levels (2011). While problematic in certain details (such as the implied correspondence between *language shift* and *music shift*, critiqued in the *Comparative Framework*; cf. Chapter 2.2), Coulter's two incarnations of GMSS represent useful attempts to adapt a language vitality framework for music.

Other kinds of tools for assessing language vitality often seem to trade the simplicity of graded classifications for more complicated but fine-grained assessments. Edwards's typology presents a nuanced matrix of 33 macro- and micro-variables that affect the vitality of minority languages, including geographical, historical, political, sociological, educational, economic, and linguistic factors (1992, pp. 49–50). His framework is taken up and modified by Grenoble and Whaley (1998), who argue the case for a hierarchy among the variables. Adopting another approach altogether, McConvell and Thieberger (2001, p. 56) tentatively propose a quantitative language endangerment index for use within an Australian context, calculated as the ratio of the percentage of speakers in the 0–19 age group to that of the 20–39 age group; if the index is less than or equal to 1, the language may be called endangered. Maybe due to their pedantry, or the specificity of the information required to undertake the assessment, these tools have stimulated less interest or use among linguists (and communities) than the various graded classification systems—a consideration for those wishing to develop well-utilized tools assessing music vitality and endangerment.

Just like the complex task they aim to undertake, these various tools to measure language vitality are by no means unproblematic. In some ways, any one tool is bound to cater only inadequately to the multitude of dynamic, complex sociolinguistic situations found across the globe. Some linguists have expressed "considerable reluctance" at having to "force languages into the procrustean bed fashioned in the GIDS workshop" (Walsh, 2009, p. 134) or into the molds of other frameworks. Peter Austin believes that in carrying out assessments, linguists have sometimes "paid too little attention to individual differences, differences between the performance, the behavior, the characteristics, the usages of individuals," tending instead to "want to lump people into groups of classes so that they can process the quantitative data" (personal interview, June 16, 2010). He argues for "a much more subtle, qualitative analysis of the particularities of individual contexts and situations, and individuals—individual speakers, individual performers" (personal interview, June 16, 2010). Appraisals of the usability, accuracy, and generalizability of UNESCO's *Language Vitality and Endangerment* in particular have led to a number of criticisms and suggestions for improvement. Especially notable is the study by Lewis (2006), which, among other aims, sets out to pinpoint the theoretical flaws of the framework by subjecting 100 languages to analysis in terms of its nine factors. In 2011, UNESCO itself released a background paper critiquing the framework and its reception by experts, as well as reviewing how it had been applied since its development eight years earlier (UNESCO Culture Sector, 2011).

Despite the criticisms, these various assessment tools have been crucial in advancing theory and practice of language maintenance and revitalization. Their use goes well beyond merely diagnosing situations of language endangerment: they have also helped clarify the factors contributing to endangerment in specific contexts; helped indicate the urgency for maintenance or revitalization strategies; helped guide and focus priorities for those strategies; and helped direct funding and resources to languages in most need (for example, in the context of Australia's National Indigenous Languages Survey, for which UNESCO's framework was employed; Australian Institute of Aboriginal and Torres Strait Islander Studies, 2005). Assessment frameworks may also be used diachronically to assess changes in the vitality of languages over time (for example, by comparing the data presented in the sixteen editions of *Ethnologue* since 1951). This capacity to assess change in vitality over time is important. It assists researchers and communities to better forecast the likely short- or medium-term trajectory of a given language, and perhaps even more crucially, it represents a way to systematically evaluate the efficacy of any maintenance strategies that are implemented. This possibility for evaluation vastly increases the likelihood that maintenance strategies will be systematically improved over time.

All these usages of language vitality assessment tools have potential parallels for music. Such a tool could help identify genres in danger—a necessary capability to determine the extent of global musical endangerment. It could also help us understand factors contributing to the endangerment of those genres, develop and evaluate appropriate response strategies, and monitor and better predict changes in their vitality. The task of trying to develop a framework suited to evaluating any music genre is formidable, just as it is for languages. Yet despite the challenges and likely imperfections of any such framework, precedent from language maintenance presents a strong case for developing such a tool.

3.2 DEVELOPING ADVOCACY FOR MUSIC SUSTAINABILITY

Arguments promoting the importance of music both generally and within communities (and to a somewhat lesser extent, arguments promoting the importance of a diversity of musics) are relatively well represented in the academic literature. Indeed, five of them serve as a rationale for this book, as presented in the Introduction. Sometimes these kinds of arguments emerge in the public sphere too—to help promote multicultural festivals, for example, or to validate culturally diverse school music programs. They typically incite little or no opposition; in most Western societies at least, advocacy *against* vibrant and diverse musical communities is anomalous.

The type of advocacy I refer to in this section is both more contentious and complex: It relates to the need for intercession in the endangerment of music genres. Advocacy for this cause comprises two main components: (a) promoting awareness of the fact that certain music genres are in danger (or may become so, without action); and (b) justifying the need for concerted action (arguably the more difficult of the two). I discuss each of these components in turn, relating them to relevant language advocacy arguments.

Promoting Awareness

A number of linguists (including Austin, 2008, and Crystal, 2000) believe that communicating with the public about the vitality and viability of languages is a fundamental part of language maintenance efforts. Public awareness about language endangerment and its repercussions increases the likelihood that key stakeholders in language viability—endangered-language speakers themselves, as well as policy makers, funding bodies, journalists, and the media—will be more receptive and sympathetic to the cause. In turn, this may facilitate program implementation, policy changes, or securing funding. For similar reasons, promoting awareness of *music* endangerment is likely to be an important part of music sustainability strategies (and may even form a strategy in its own right): the groundswell of public understanding created by advocacy efforts has the potential to influence political and social action, resulting in change favorable to musical vitality and viability. Without convincing and thoughtful justification, efforts to maintain and revitalize music genres run the risk of being charged with some of the same offenses as the now-discredited "salvage ethnomusicology" (including romanticism, paternalism, and hegemony).

In the context of raising awareness of language endangerment, some of the most valuable data are the various striking statistics that indicate the extent of the problem: the total number of languages spoken across the world (7,105 according to the 17th edition of Ethnologue; Lewis, Simons, & Fennig, 2013) and the proportion of these at risk of extinction (about half by the year 2100; Krauss, 1992, p. 6); their population distribution (96% of the world's population speaks 4% of its languages, so 96% of the world's linguistic diversity is maintained by only 4% of its population; Austin, 2008, p. 81); the rate of decline in linguistic diversity (20% over the period 1970–2005; Harmon & Loh, 2010), and the rate of language "death" (about one every fortnight; Crystal, 2000, p. 19). Admittedly, the numbers often vary significantly from source to source—*Ethnologue* defines language death differently from Crystal, for example, thereby placing the rate of death at "only" six per year since 1950 (Lewis, Simons, & Fennig, 2013). Nevertheless, data like these have proven immensely valuable in driving home to policy makers, funding bodies, and the general public the need for urgent action to support endangered languages. They are frequently cited in media reportage, public seminars and events, and materials and publications for nonspecialist and nonacademic audiences. In this way, they have been instrumental in securing support and funding for endangered languages.

By contrast, extensive data like these do not yet exist for music endangerment. Even figures on the number of music genres in the world are hard to come by in the literature—although the immense difficulty of arriving at even an approximate number is clear. There exists no authoritative map plotting the distribution of the world's music genres, such as is presented for languages in *Ethnologue*, nor any wide-scale data on their vitality, such as in UNESCO's *Atlas of the World's Languages in Danger*. Nor is there any way to measure global changes or trends in musical diversity or vitality, such as the quantitative *Index of Linguistic Diversity* developed by Terralingua. Compared with linguists, then, ethnomusicologists currently have a far smaller stockpile of information to draw from when promoting awareness of endangerment. Further research on the extent of global musical endangerment is therefore urgently needed; anecdotal accounts or incidental studies are unlikely to build a sufficiently strong case for action. Precedent from language maintenance (as in *Ethnologue* and the *Atlas*) suggests that such a vast task may be achieved through the collaboration of a number of experienced researchers with strong community and academic networks within their region of expertise. Preliminary studies may focus on particular regions or particular types of communities (e.g. indigenous ones).

For languages, a number of specific projects have proven relatively successful in raising public awareness of endangerment. One is UNESCO's annual *International Mother Language Day* on February 21st, which aims (among other things) to promote linguistic diversity. While an *International Music Day* exists (proclaimed by the International Music Council), its purpose is to promote music in all sections of society, rather than to advocate for issues of music endangerment and sustainability, or global musical diversity. Another salient example of a language-related public advocacy project is the annual *Endangered Languages Week* run by the *Hans Rausing Endangered Languages Project* at the School of Oriental and African Studies in London; academic papers run alongside talks, displays, discussions, debates, films, and workshops for the general public, most of them free of charge. Given that music arguably has a greater ability to capture the public imagination than languages (*Comparative Framework* 2.5), comparable initiatives like an annual "*Endangered Music Cultures Week*" or "*International Day of Local Musics*" could be highly successful in promoting awareness of music endangerment.

Advocating Action

Linguists are continually called upon to state and defend their role in issues of language viability. Nonspecialists (like funding agencies and journalists) have sometimes responded dubiously to the call of linguists to protect linguistic diversity, with cynical reactions like: "Naturally you linguists want to keep all those languages around, as a kind of artificial zoo at public expense, just so you can study them" (in Krauss, 1998, p. 109). One response from linguists—and ethnomusicologists too—to these kinds of concerns about a researcher profiting (career-wise or otherwise) from working with more marginalized communities is to espouse and ensure reciprocity and partnership in all aspects of the research (Galla, 2008).

Another reaction linguists sometimes encounter in response to their work is: "Surely one language is better, more harmonious?" (cf. Davis, 2003). Given that most people enjoy and recognize the value of a diversity of musics, ethnomusicologists are less likely to encounter this sentiment in their work (though a hierarchy of music cultures exists in the minds of many, often with Western classical music at the top). Probably more likely is general indifference within majority groups that music genres of certain communities are atrophying. One possible way to counteract this indifference is to promulgate the various arguments that articulate the personal and social value of music genres, several of which I presented in the Introduction as the rationales for this book.

Perhaps more challenging and complex than these kinds of publicly voiced concerns about language or music sustainability efforts are those raised by people with an expert understanding of the issues: researchers and activists themselves, and the communities with whom they work. In the case of languages, philosophical and practical concerns about maintenance and revitalization have sparked vehement debate among scholars, fieldworkers, culture bearers, and other stakeholders. Four key issues recur in the language maintenance literature, each with relevance to music sustainability (explored in some depth in Grant, 2012a). First, some linguists deem efforts to sustain languages or music genres to be interfering with their natural processes of growth, change, and decline—and therefore neither wise nor ethical (a little redolent of *Jurassic Park*). Second are concerns about the purism embodied by the very notion of sustaining an endangered tradition: What is it that should be sustained? How can natural processes of change be reconciled with the ideology of sustainability? Third, activism in the fate of a language or music genre carries the risk of researcher interventionism in a community; while issues of researcher–community power balances have long been discussed in ethnomusicology, that discipline has not always considered the unique issues generated by contexts of musical endangerment. Finally, endangered-language activists have faced repeated accusations that maintenance strategies simply don't work, or that they too frequently entail unanticipated or equivocal outcomes. The discourse in the language maintenance literature surrounding each of these concerns represents an invaluable resource for ethnomusicologists, who might draw on the various linguistic rejoinders to these arguments to construct firmer theoretical, philosophical, and ethical bases on which to ground their own work on music sustainability.

Thus, if advocating to the public about activism in music sustainability is important, advocating within the discipline of ethnomusicology is at least as much so. While the vast majority of sociolinguists are aware of the situation and extent of language endangerment—after all, an entire subfield of their discipline has developed around it—the same cannot yet be said of ethnomusicologists, whose training often comprises ethnographic work within one or two communities, and from whom the bigger picture can sometimes disappear from view. Many linguists believe that awareness and action within their discipline is crucial (particularly, but not only, for the documentation of endangered languages). Dixon accuses linguists of "errors of attitude" (1997, p. 137) with regard to their apparent apathy to the global predicament of languages, reasoning the following:

> If every linguistics student (and faculty member) in the world today worked on just one language that is in need of study, the prospects for full documentation of endangered languages (before they fade away) would be rosy. I doubt if one linguist in twenty is doing this. (p. 137)

If these beliefs are indicative, ethnomusicologists' awareness of the need for music sustainability efforts, and their engaged commitment to that end, will be imperative to the success of those efforts. Some advances in this regard are promising, such as the Australia-New Zealand ICTM Regional Committee's formal statement in 2011 highlighting the need for urgent support of the many highly endangered Indigenous Australian music and dance traditions. However, widespread commitment within the discipline is unlikely to gain traction until such time as ethnomusicologists better understand the extent and nature of music endangerment, hence the necessity of conducting further research in the area. Greater recognition within academia of the value and importance of community engagement and service will also help matters along; this issue has been a significant bugbear for university-employed linguists, whose time spent engaging with communities (for example, in providing expert advice on revitalization activities) has typically gone largely unrecognized and unrewarded by their institutions.

In addition to advocacy directed toward experts and toward the general public, linguists have noted the importance of a third kind: that which targets endangered-language communities themselves. This "internal advocacy" has mostly centered on raising community awareness about the options for influencing the trajectory of the language. It differs significantly in nature and approach from advocating to outsiders, and I address it in the next section as a maintenance strategy in its own right.

3.3 DEVELOPING MAINTENANCE AND REVITALIZATION STRATEGIES

In Chapter 1.4, transmission-based approaches to boosting the vitality and viability of music genres were identified as promising but under-researched pathways to supporting music sustainability. Certain successful transmission-based approaches to language maintenance potentially represent models that could be adapted for use with music. One example is language nests, cultural and language immersion centers for young children, operating in New Zealand (Spolsky, 2003) and Hawai'i (NeSmith, 2009) since the early 1980s, and which continue to be adapted for use in other contexts (including recently in Mexico; Bojórquez, 2010, pp. 111–112). Another are the master–apprentice programs developed in California in the early 1990s, which pair an older native speaker of an endangered language with a younger learner and focus on oral transmission in a nonformal learning situation (Hinton, 1997; these language programs differ fundamentally from the master–apprentice methods of transmission common to some music genres, as discussed in Chapter 2.1). Other types of endangered-language immersion programs with slightly different approaches have also proven at least partially successful (see Hale, 2001). Careful reference to the *Comparative Framework*, in conjunction with an assessment of the kinds of music genres that may be appropriately transmitted in these ways, would clarify the extent to which transmission-based language maintenance initiatives may serve as prototypes for transmission-based initiatives that support music sustainability.

Transmission-based approaches to supporting music sustainability are only one kind of approach; Chapter 1 also described initiatives that focus on *documentation and preservation; recognition and celebration; policy and enterprise; and coordinating and evaluating mechanisms*. Across all of these areas, language maintenance provides a raft of possible models for developing music-specific sustainability strategies. Yet for music, as for languages, the success of a strategy in one context is no reliable indicator that it will work in others. There can be no one-size-fits-all remedy for endangerment, no one recipe. Each situation is unique, and each strategy must take into account the degree and causes of endangerment, socioeconomic and political circumstances, the attitudes and aspirations of the community concerned, and the human, financial, and material resources at hand.

For this reason, rather than exploring how particular language maintenance strategies (like language nests or apprentice programs) might be adapted for use with endangered music genres, in this section I instead draw on language maintenance theory in order to propose and describe a broader set of circumstances in which *any* chosen strategy is likely to be successful. In this way, the theory I present remains relevant (I hope) to the diverse global situations of music endangerment. Such theory is arguably needed to develop consistently effective approaches to supporting endangered music genres that are tailored to, and appropriate for, local conditions. I therefore leave aside an investigation of ways to adapt, for music, specific language maintenance strategies, and instead I highly recommend this as a topic for further academic study.

Research into specific language maintenance initiatives can generate understanding of the factors influencing their success, and this understanding may, in turn, be able to inform theory on music sustainability. Take the Hebrew language revival, for example—arguably one of the most successful. Linguists have identified a number of factors favorable to that revitalization effort, including the fact that Hebrew was already extensively documented (cf. the Hebrew bible); that the language was considered prestigious (positive construct); that anyone had the right to speak it (lack of ownership); that loanwords and foreign words were borrowed freely without adverse connotations (lack of a purist ideology); and that it could be revived anywhere, not only in its place of origin (lack of place restriction) (Zuckermann & Walsh, 2011). Given the similarities between music and language viability with regard to issues of documentation (cf. *Comparative Framework*, Chapter 2.1), prestige (2.3), ownership (2.2), authenticity and purism (2.3), and the role of the diaspora (2.2), the case of Hebrew holds promise to yield useful theoretical insights for music sustainability. Analyses of other language revitalizations hold potential to yield further insights.

For ethnomusicologists, one potentially valuable resource from language maintenance is linguists' analyses of the optimal conditions in which an endangered language is most likely to gain ground (or in which maintenance strategies are most likely to succeed). A number of linguists have attempted to theorize those factors that "turn up so frequently that they could be recognized as postulates for a theory of language revitalization" (Crystal, 2000, p. 130). By way of example, Box 3.1 presents three such lists, each framed slightly differently, by Yamamoto (1998), Crystal (2000), and Walsh (2010).

Box 3.1 DESIRABLE CONDITIONS FOR LANGUAGE MAINTENANCE: THREE THEORIES

Nine factors that "help maintain and promote the small languages" (Yamamoto, 1998, p. 114):

1. the existence of a dominant culture in favor of linguistic diversity;
2. a strong sense of ethnic identity within the endangered community;
3. the promotion of educational programs about the endangered language and culture;
4. the creation of bilingual/bicultural school programs;
5. the training of native speakers as teachers;
6. the involvement of the speech community as a whole;
7. the creation of language materials that are easy to use;
8. the development of written literature, both traditional and new;
9. the creation and strengthening of the environments in which the language must be used.

Six conditions under which "an endangered language will progress" (Crystal, 2000, pp. 130–143):

1. its speakers increase their prestige within the dominant community;
2. its speakers increase their wealth relative to the dominant community;
3. its speakers increase their legitimate power in the eyes of the dominant community;
4. its speakers have a strong presence in the educational system;
5. its speakers can write their language down;
6. its speakers can make use of electronic technology.

A "wish-list" for language revitalization programs (Walsh, 2010, pp. 26–32):

1. cultural awareness, and acknowledgement of the language-culture connection, within the community;
2. community cohesion;

3. community control of the revitalization process;
4. acknowledgement that language is only one part of the revitalization process and that other cultural activities need to be integrated into that process too;
5. a sizeable knowledge base and access to information on the language;
6. access to linguistic expertise;
7. recognition of the fallacy of the claim that learning the language will be easier for a person of the same ethnic background, and that teachers must also be of that ethnic group ("overcoming the genetic fallacy");
8. foregrounding oracy over the "easier" option, literacy;
9. appropriate use of technology;
10. trained teachers of the language;
11. sustained commitment from Elders;
12. a regional support network;
13. willingness to draw on existing resources from elsewhere and adapt them to the local situation;
14. funding (useful, but not an essential ingredient for success);
15. ability to address problems but not be overwhelmed by them.

The *Comparative Framework* helps identify which of those factors that linguists commonly believe affect the success of language maintenance strategies are also likely to affect the efficacy of strategies supporting music sustainability. Areas of overlap include the role of training and teacher training in transmission (*Comparative Framework*, Chapter 2.1), prestige (2.3), community commitment to sustainability strategies (2.3), and broader socioeconomic circumstances (2.4). The framework also indicates some of the probable differences in these conditions, relating to the role of orthography in sustainability (2.1), the social functions of language and music within a community (2.2), the infrastructural requirements for music making versus language speaking (2.4), and the role of media and the (music) industry in sustainability (2.5).

Ethnomusicologists have not yet made a sustained effort to consolidate an experience-base from which to empirically compile a list of favorable conditions for music sustainability, like those proposed for languages. Through careful recourse to the *Comparative Framework*, however, linguistic understandings of desirable conditions for language maintenance strategies signal several probable desirable conditions for music sustainability strategies. Below, I propose a tentative list of six of the most likely desirable conditions for music, positioning them against precedent (or lack thereof) from the field of language maintenance. Over time, further research and empirical evidence will lead to refinements to this list. As other conditions prove advantageous, they may be added, too.

The Support of the Community as a Whole

For both music and language, the role of the community in sustainability strategies is critical and multifaceted. The attitude of a language's own speaker community toward it may be the most crucial factor in the success of language maintenance efforts (UNESCO, 2012a, "What can be done to save a language from disappearing?" section), and the *Comparative Framework* identified the attitude of the community (narrowly defined as the community of practice, rather than the wider society in which a music genre is located) as being critical to the sustainability of music genres too (Chapter 2.3). Even if a community's attitude to a language or music genre is favorable, this does not necessarily always convert into sustained, active commitment to maintaining or revitalizing it; "unspoken but deep doubts, fears and anxieties about traditional language and culture may actually mean that people are not willing to become personally involved" (Grenoble & Whaley, 2006, p. 48). Commitment to the cause, then, in addition to a favorable community attitude to the tradition in question, is a highly desirable precondition for the success of music sustainability strategies, as it is for language strategies.

The field of language maintenance confirms that it is essential for community members to have (and to *feel* they have) control over maintenance projects and processes. Aside from the ethical imperative, training community members themselves to implement maintenance projects or engaging them in other ways throughout the process has improved outcomes, as well as saving time and generating a sense of community ownership (Berez & Holton, 2006, pp. 73–74). One important role of the outsider may be to alert communities to the possibilities for maintenance. Michael Walsh describes how, in his work with certain Australian Aboriginal communities, the community attitude toward the future of their language changed "in about ten minutes" from pessimism to "boundless optimism" when alerted to the various possibilities for revitalization (personal interview, April 8, 2010). This is likely to hold true for music sustainability initiatives, too: for their success, the community has to care, "or at least be talked to enough so that they understand. They may have given up; they may say, 'I don't care any more,' but you may find that underneath that statement of not caring there's actually something else going on" (A. Seeger, personal interview, March 22, 2011). For both music and languages, community agreement about how to approach maintenance is also important; in Walsh's experience, "if the community cannot reach consensus most of the time then the success of the language revitalization programme will be put in jeopardy" (2010, p. 28).

The Ideological Willingness of the Community to Explore New Pathways for the Genre

It is eminently likely that a community ideology of purism or insistence on authenticity sometimes adversely affect the viability of endangered music genres (Grant, 2012a). The converse is certainly the case: An open approach to exploring new possibilities has boosted the vitality of a number of genres, as demonstrated in the cases of Finnish "new" folk music (Ramnarine, 2003, p. 70), the "reinvention" of Mexican mariachi (Sheehy, 2006, pp. 79–89), and the revival, modernization, and social recontextualization of Hungarian folk music (Frigyesi, 1996, p. 54), among many other examples. Like music genres, languages too need to be permitted to adapt to new contexts to survive (*Comparative Framework* 2.3). One striking example is the Australian Aboriginal language Kaurna, where a flexible community attitude has allowed the language to adapt in accordance with the demands of new contexts and functions (Amery, 2002, p. 7).

Many linguists therefore agree that a purist community ideology often (but not always) adversely affects the sustainability of an endangered language, by denying it the processes of innovation and change that normally feature in living, vital languages. For successful maintenance strategies, then, it is arguably preferable that communities adopt an approach which recognizes that endangered cultural expressions are situated within inevitably changing environments, and which gives them the resilience to cope with shifting contexts by embracing, rather than resisting, change. Whether of music or language, community approaches to sustainability might not only aim to preserve the past, but to allow adaptation to the changing environment in ways consistent with the naturally dynamic expression of cultural traditions over time. The issue of a community's willingness to traverse new pathways will be explored at more length in Chapter 5 specifically in relation to Vietnamese *ca trù*, where authenticity and upholding the true tradition are key points of debate and dispute.

Recognition in the Wider Social Context of the Value of Musical/Cultural Expressions

Although the lists of desirable preconditions for language maintenance in Box 3.1 only refer indirectly, if at all, to the favorable wider social positioning of languages, this factor is demonstrably critical to the success of language maintenance strategies. The impact of socioeconomic and political circumstances on the viability of both languages and music genres was confirmed in the *Comparative Framework* (2.3), with favorable circumstances likely to vastly increase the chances of success of maintenance strategies. Consider the unfeasibility of implementing maintenance strategies in repressive political circumstances or situations of extreme poverty, versus situations where a rich diversity of vibrant cultural expressions is extensively supported through policy, regulations, funding, and research.

It is feasible that the wider context may not be given greater due in the lists by Yamamoto, Crystal, and Walsh because it is one of the most difficult to influence—in some cases, impossible. This is one reason why Walsh (2010) believes that Crystal's six conditions overreach the requirements for language revitalization, at least in the Aboriginal Australian context: he argues that some of them are simply not realistic (for example, that Aboriginal-language speakers will increase their wealth relative to the dominant community, or their prestige within it, at least in the near future). Despite the difficulty of influencing this condition, I nevertheless include it here as a probable important factor in the success of music sustainability strategies.

Adequate Resources for Learning, Teaching, Rehearsing, and Performing

Not represented in the language-related lists presented earlier, this fourth favorable condition for music sustainability strategies develops from a finding of the *Comparative Framework* (2.4), that tangible resources and infrastructure play a more critical role in the vitality of music genres than of languages. Particularly on the topic of resources for creating, rehearsing, and performing, the language maintenance literature is not overly informative, since language production in its normal communicative function does not typically entail these notions (*Comparative Framework* 2.3).

More helpful is the substantial research and experience from language maintenance that relates to the role and use of learning and teaching resources in endangerment contexts. Since endangered languages often rely on explicit learning and teaching for their transmission (*Comparative Framework* 2.1), endangered-language communities and linguists have invested much time and effort into developing resources and materials specifically for use in these situations of endangerment (e.g. Hinton & Hale, 2001). Learning and teaching materials like these may not exist at all for music genres that are traditionally orally transmitted. In cases of endangerment, the vitality of those genres may be boosted if community members have ready access to a range of high-quality learning materials. Learning and teaching resources for endangered languages may be useful in stimulating ideas for music-related learning materials for use specifically in contexts of endangerment (cf. *Comparative Framework* 2.1). Investigation of this possibility is recommended as a topic for further inquiry.

The Means for the Community to Access and Utilize Electronic Technology

Like the previous condition, this one emanates from the *Comparative Framework* (2.5) rather than from language maintenance theory itself: specifically, from its finding that media (including, particularly, electronic technology) play a far more critical role in the sustainability of music genres than of languages. While some aspects of the role of technology in music sustainability will therefore need to be researched independently from language maintenance precedent, theory and practice relating to the use of technology in language maintenance may still be relevant to music in a number of ways. Language maintenance may indicate ways to expand and improve the use of electronic technology in archiving and documentation practices, provide precedents for establishing technology-related policy that supports endangered cultural expressions (cf. for example, UNESCO's recommendation on multilingualism in cyberspace, 2003c) and, more generally, point to some of the challenges and risks involved in using technology in situations of cultural endangerment or in maintenance and revitalization efforts.

Perhaps most importantly, through the models of specific successful projects, language maintenance demonstrates possible ways to employ technology in music sustainability strategies. There are hundreds of examples. Three notable ones are *FirstVoices*, a suite of online tools and services designed to support Canadian Aboriginal communities to archive, learn, teach, and revitalize their languages (First People's Cultural Foundation,

2011); *Ninti Ngapartji*, the Pitjantjatjara language and learning website (Ngapartji Ngapartji, 2013); and the computer-assisted Hawaiian-language learning project *Leoki* (see Warschauer et al., 1997). Successful initiatives like these not only demonstrate the value of electronic technology in situations of the endangerment of cultural expressions, but also indicate concrete ways in which it may be employed. In conjunction with the *Comparative Framework*, this is another recommended field for further investigation.

A Knowledge Base and Access to Documentation on the Genre

Walsh's wish list of desirable conditions for language maintenance includes "a sizeable knowledge base and access to information on the language" (2010, p. 26), since attempts to revitalize may clearly be impeded by a lack of information about a language. For music too, the extent of available information may determine the success of maintenance strategies, and so a sizeable knowledge base and access to documentation on the genre is a desirable precondition for music sustainability strategies also. In underscoring the importance of a knowledge base in strategies to counter endangerment, linguists have theorized about the role of written documentation in maintenance efforts (Crystal and Yamamoto both table the importance of the written language in maintenance strategies; cf. Box 3.1). Language maintenance also points to the unique functions and uses of a knowledge base in endangerment contexts, which may differ somewhat from those in contexts of cultural vitality. Consider, for example, the ethical imperative that fieldwork materials elicited from communities be made available quickly (Nathan, 2006, p. 62).

For both endangered languages and endangered music genres, documentation and revitalization are intimately connected and may be seen as two sides of a coin rather than separate or mutually exclusive activities (Grant, 2010). Documentation has proven essential in sustaining and revitalizing certain traditions that may otherwise have been lost. Ethnomusicologists are already very familiar with the relationships between documentation and music revivals (cf. Chapter 1.1), and in several recorded instances, the repatriation of archival recordings has renewed a community's interest and practice of a tradition (Chapter 1.2). It is possible that documentation and archiving may play an even more important role for music revitalization than for languages, since it is arguably easier to recover a musical tradition from documentation (and to stimulate its growth in a new form) than it is to re-situate a documented language within a society.

3.4 REFLECTING ON AIMS AND OUTCOMES OF STRATEGIES

While a recurrent theme in the literature is the often unanticipated outcomes of practical strategies intending to support music sustainability (Chapter 1 describes a number of examples, particularly in relation to festivals and top–down interventions), ethnomusicological inquiry offers little by way of critical theoretical reflection on appropriate responses to this situation.[1] Should communities and researchers try a different approach? Redefine the aims of sustainability projects? Accept some randomness of outcomes? Abandon them altogether? Discourse within the field of language maintenance raises all these questions; it also offers a number of answers that may hold relevance for efforts in music sustainability.

On balance, attitudes about the efficacy of language maintenance strategies to restore languages to full use tend toward despondence. Pronouncements of endangered languages as a "hopeless cause" (Newman, 1998, 2003) reverberate through the literature. With regard to Irish, a language often paraded as a failed maintenance attempt, McCloskey writes: "The smell of failure has hung around the 'revival' movement like a corrosive fog for decades" (2001, p. 43). The raft of recurrent problems with Australian Aboriginal language maintenance programs has led to the abandonment of several of them; problems include obstructive government policy, a lack of skills and resources, community criticism, inadequate or mismanaged funding, lack of long-term planning, "tokenism" in the content and organization of programs, and a lack of communication between communities involved in maintenance activities (Amery, 2002; Schmidt, 1990, pp. 82–101). The top–down Eurocentric nature of some language maintenance programs is no help. Contending that "an honest evaluation of most language revitalization efforts to date will show that they have failed" (Grenoble & Whaley, 2006, p. ix), some linguists arrive at the conclusion: "What, then, is the solution for dying and endangered languages? I'm sad to admit that I'm not sure that there is one" (Carnie, 1996, p. 112).

Evidently, ensuring the viability of a music genre is no easy task either—though it may be argued that the odds of successfully sustaining a music genre are higher than for a language, because of music's greater ability to recontextualize (*Comparative Framework*, Chapter 2.2) and its significantly greater commercial potential (2.5). It is certainly possible to halt or even reverse the decline of a music genre. In the early twentieth century the

---

1. This section draws on my 2012 article "Rethinking safeguarding: Objections and responses to protecting and promoting endangered musical heritage" in *Ethnomusicology Forum* 21(1), 39–59.

popularity of Korean *p'ansori* ("epic storytelling through song") began to dwindle, but post-1964, when it was declared Korea's Important Intangible Cultural Property No. 5, "its fortunes were reversed, and its audience grew once more" (Howard, 2006, p. xii). In Thailand, the academic Sugree Charoensook of Mahidol University, Bangkok, set up music schools for Thai (and Western) classical music in shopping malls. Wong observes that the Thai classical music tradition was considered in danger of dying out, but its fortune "was turned right around by [Charoensook] recognizing the fact that there was a new population ready to engage with it in a very different way" (QCRC, 2008a; Example 1.2 🔊). The case of Vietnamese *ca trù* is a third example, explored at length in Chapter 5.

The track record for languages is not all bad either. Perhaps foremost among the success stories is Hebrew, for some the only unmitigated example of revitalization. In certain domains, the Welsh language has gained strength, partly due to bilingual education programs and increased political and cultural awareness of the language. Language loss has also been arrested in the case of Maori in New Zealand, though full intergenerational transmission is yet to be restored. Speaker numbers of the indigenous Hawaiian language have grown since the 1970s, when various revitalization strategies were implemented, including language immersion schools. Abley (2003), Austin (2006), Fishman (1991), and Thieberger (2002) explore other examples.

Despite these successes, purposeful language maintenance strategies cannot always claim full credit for revitalization. With regard to the revival in recent years of the Manx culture and language, certain political, economic, and social forces having nothing to do with planned revitalization initiatives may have been just as crucial in changing the fortunes of the culture (Wilson, 2008). Even the revival of the Hebrew language happened with little deliberate planning, and some scholars believe it would not have been nearly as successful without a remarkable confluence of sociopolitical factors that would be impossible to deliberately recreate in the case of other endangered languages (Nahir, 1998).

Music genres too display a sometimes surprising ability to revitalize themselves: after over a decade of near inutile official recognition and financial support for the Korean folk genre *p'ungmul* ("a familiar, yet declining age-old rural practice"), four South Korean percussionists, later named SamulNori, accomplished its revitalization "almost literally overnight" (Hesselink, 2004, pp. 405, 408). Two neo-African popular music genres, Creole *kawina* and Ndjuka Maroon *aleke*, underwent an unplanned "sudden revitalization" in Suriname in the late 1980s to early 1990s (Bilby, 1999, p. 267). The revitalization of rural folk songs in Serbian towns in the 1990s has been described as "a spontaneous, intuitive response" to newer genres and to the suppression of traditional music (Jovanović, 2005, p. 39). In these (and similar) cases, the role of the mass media and the world music market is often of considerable importance.

Not infrequently, the results of language maintenance strategies have been unanticipated. In the case of the Hawaiian language, the limited interaction between native speakers and the increasing number of second-language speakers, coupled with the fact that most educators of the language were not native speakers, played a role in the unexpected development of a new language that has been labeled "neo-Hawaiian" (NeSmith, 2009, p. 3). The revitalization of Hebrew has resulted in not only quite a different language, but also an unanticipated cost in terms of loss of other languages (Spolsky, 2005, p. 2163). A number of music sustainability strategies have also resulted in unexpected outcomes; several of these were tabled in Chapter 1.

On the other hand, the unanticipated results of maintenance strategies can be positive as well as negative. Although a description and revitalization project with the endangered Yan-nhaŋu language of Eastern Arnhem Land failed to produce any more speakers, the researchers argue that the benefits of the project have been plenty, including a raised profile of the language within the community, substantial documentation, improved confidence in asserting links between language and traditional sites and practices, and increased academic research and publications resulting in heightened awareness of the existence of the Yan-nhaŋu people as a distinct group (Bowern & James, 2010, p. 367). Zuckermann and Walsh add that even wider benefits may result from efforts that support the viability of languages:

> A small investment in language revitalization could yield very significant dividends. Language revival can result in the saving of vast amounts of money and resources going into housing, social services and health intervention to little effect. A small investment into language revitalization can make an enormous difference to society. Public health can benefit from language intervention. (2011, p. 123)

These observations are arguably potentially true for music too, which also has close links to individual and community identity and social cohesion. The utilitarian spin-off effects of strategies supporting music sustainability within a community may therefore be considerable.

For these reasons, in the case of both languages and music genres, even token revitalization may be a wholly acceptable outcome of sustainability strategies. For some languages (like Australian Aboriginal Kaurna, where written records have been the only knowledge base for reconstructing the language), a formulaic approach was adopted: an inventory of phrases, expressions, and functional language has been reinstalled into the community in appropriate contexts, such as in welcome-to-country speeches, opening speeches for town events or art galleries, and at funerals (Amery, 2002). Some linguists object to equating this with a living language: "If the only words of Wiyot that you use are *yes* and *no*, and only in a particular semiceremonial context, this is no longer a language, any more than musicians are speaking Italian when they say *andante* and *fortissimo*" (Dalby, 2003, pp. 250–251). Others linguists argue that when formulaic usage benefits the community, it constitutes success:

> You put that much investment into language revitalization and the dividends will be ten, fifty, a hundred-fold. Because what happens is you get Indigenous people whose lives are literally turned around, where instead of being totally dysfunctional, they feel good about themselves, they've regained their identity. So to shock people, I say, "Look, I don't care whether they only know ten words and they 'mispronounce' the whole lot of them." If the effect has been to take a dysfunctional person... [and] move from that to a person who's living a good family life and likes himself and stuff, well I don't care what it looks like, how authentic it is, or anything else–that's the way to go. (M. Walsh, personal interview, April 8, 2010)

In brief, music sustainability strategies may or may not end up restoring endangered music genres to their "original" contexts, regaining lost repertoire, or fully reviving skills and technical expertise in musicians. They may or may not stimulate new directions for a genre, such as new repertoire, styles, contexts, functions, and techniques. It should be remembered that fully reactivating the former vitality of a music genre may in fact be at variance with the community's priorities, which may lie rather within areas such as sociocultural identity, intrinsic worth and self-esteem, or links with heritage. This is perhaps especially true of disenfranchised communities, where cultural expressions are often the lynchpin of individual and community identity. Hence Walsh's striking statement: "Even 'failure' in language revitalisation is worthwhile!" (2002, p. 22).

Experience from language maintenance therefore indicates that music sustainability efforts should not be judged solely on the criterion of increasing the long-term viability of a genre, but also on wider economic, social, and political outcomes. Linguist Julia Sallabank suggests that ethnomusicologists and linguists alike should engage in "prior ideological clarification" (after Dauenhauer & Dauenhauer, 1998) of the goals of their strategies: "Are you trying to get everybody speaking again, or everybody singing? Or will you be satisfied with a few symbolic bits? Or somewhere in between? What is this language or music going to look like in the future?" (personal interview, June 17, 2010).

Already, certain music sustainability strategies embrace broader objectives that benefit the individuals and community under study. Ahmad Sarmast, the director of the *Revival of Afghan Music* project, hopes that his program's initiative will not only help revive traditional Afghan musical instruments and forms but also destroyed lives; half of all places at the project's Afghanistan National Institute of Music are reserved for disadvantaged and underprivileged children. For Vietnamese *ca trù*, the ultimate purpose of implementing sustainability strategies may also be something more, or other, than ensuring the viability of the genre for its own sake: Its reclamation may, for example, play a role in establishing "a future in which pre-revolutionary traditions and sentiments have a respected place in a rapidly changing, 'modern', Vietnam" (Norton, 2005, p. 50). These sentiments embody a broad and open-minded perspective on aims and outcomes for music sustainability strategies.

3.5 DEVELOPING COORDINATING MECHANISMS

Tackling the problem of endangered music genres in a coordinated way promises to optimize the outcomes of efforts toward sustainability. During a conference assessing the 1989 *Recommendation on the Safeguarding of Traditional Culture and Folklore* (held at the Smithsonian Institution, Washington, in June 1999), one delegate observed:

> I see here a lot of foot soldiers, most of us winning a battle here or losing one there—yet painfully conscious that we are actually losing the war. What concerns me is that even as we win or lose our little battles, we are nowhere near evolving a game plan for the war. Is there a general in our army? An SOS number to call? (Sethi, 2001, p. 86)

Language maintenance can help develop a game plan for music sustainbility, by offering a range of conceptual prototypes for mechanisms to help monitor, evaluate and co-ordinate efforts. Some of these mechanisms already exist in some form or other; they include umbrella organizations, centralized funding agencies, registers of best practice, research databases, and resource hubs where stakeholders exchange ideas and pool resources. Some language-related coordinating measures may also provide preexisting infrastructure on which music-specific coordinating mechanisms may be built. Both these possibilities—conceptual prototypes and preexisting infrastructure—are explored in this section.

For both linguists and endangered-language communities, the means to share and disseminate knowledge and expertise about successful language maintenance efforts has proven highly useful. Online open-access "registers of good practice," for instance, stimulate ideas about possible ways to approach sustainability, provide exemplars of projects, indicate common pitfalls, and offer hands-on solutions. One such register has been developed by E-MELD (Electronic Metastructure for Endangered Languages Data), a project that aims to formulate and promote good practices in digitizing data on endangered languages, to demonstrate those practices through an online "showroom," and to communicate with the research community about standards and recommendations (2006). The development of a comparable repository of music-specific "good practices" could benefit from reference to these language-specific precedents—as well as those for cultural heritage at large, such as UNESCO's *Register of Best Safeguarding Practices* referred to in an earlier chapter.

Sharing ideas and experiences relating to music sustainability may be as simple as establishing an online vehicle for the purpose. The Endangered Languages and Cultures blog is one example, a moderated online platform for advancing scholarly inquiry into the endangerment and maintenance of languages and cultures (PARADISEC, 2013). A select group of regular bloggers (mostly linguists) and their invited guests contribute to a broad-ranging dialogue on documentation, fieldwork, technology, education, projects, resources, and other issues relating to endangered languages and cultures. Presently, few posts deal specifically with issues of music endangerment or sustainability, despite the fact that the topic fits directly within the scope of the blog. The blog's infrastructure could be immediately better utilized by those working with endangered music genres; an added benefit of capitalizing on this preexisting resource is the potential it creates for a cross-disciplinary language–music discourse on sustainability issues.

Another important aspect of coordinating approaches to music sustainability is finding ways to disseminate, assess, compare, and review relevant research. One of the first tasks to this end will be to gather information on past and current studies of endangered music genres, and where possible, to make those studies easily accessible in a centralized location for scholarly inspection, reflection, and critique. One precedent from linguistics is the online database of language endangerment levels compiled by researchers at the World Oral Literature Project (2013a). The data are assembled from *Ethnologue*, UNESCO's *Atlas of the World's Languages in Danger*, and from the work of an individual researcher (conservation biologist William Sutherland). The database also cross-references to collections, recordings, and documentation of oral literature across the world, and for each language, to other referenced and frequently updated online sources. In this way, the database represents a tool that centralizes research on language endangerment. As these data grow for music, an equivalent music-specific tool will be increasingly called for.

A centralized resource network could serve as a means to share tools like this, as well as other resources, ideas, research outcomes, project outcomes, and practical experiences surrounding issues of music endangerment and sustainability. Establishing a network that operates at the international level would ensure the widest scope for both access and input to the network. Several language precedents exist for international resource networks on endangerment and sustainability, including the Consortium for Training in Language Documentation and Conservation founded in 2012, which aims to foster networking and collaboration across the world among those involved in issues of training, and the longer-established Resource Network for Linguistic Diversity (RNLD), which aims to advance the sustainability of indigenous languages. RNLD, founded in Australia in 2004, is a particularly successful international resource network. An active e-list is a vehicle for energetic discourse between network members. The network's website itself is a centralized source of information about grants, projects, media reportage, conferences and events, training opportunities, relevant blogs and lists, links and online resources, policy matters, and opportunities for activism and advocacy relating to language endangerment and maintenance. The following list of possible objectives for a comparable "Resource Network for Music Sustainability" takes inspiration from the missions of RNLD and the Consortium, as presented on their respective websites:

- to construct a clearinghouse of resources and materials relating to music endangerment and sustainability, accessible to researchers, communities, and other stakeholders across the world;
- to provide an international forum for sharing approaches and methods in initiatives that support music sustainability, including advice on technology;
- to facilitate and foster discussion about the objectives and outcomes of projects currently being developed and implemented;
- to identify and share successful practices;
- to encourage partnerships and collaborations between researchers, governments, nongovernment organizations, businesses, and communities of varied backgrounds and expertise;

- to promote relevant activities and projects and to organize informal gatherings for community activists, researchers, and others interested in music sustainability; and
- to take into account a wide variety of perspectives and approaches by bringing together stakeholders from communities, institutes, universities, cultural centers, government, and elsewhere.

Some, but not all, of these objectives are intended as outcomes of the *Sustainable Futures for Music Cultures* project in Australia (QCRC, 2013), which will draw to completion soon after this book goes to print.

In addition to a resource network for sharing resources, experiences and knowledge about music sustainability, there is also a need for an international organization supporting endangered music genres at a more general and public level—one that operates outside of the interests of any particular group and that is accessible to all. Drawing on the discussions in earlier chapters, Box 3.2 formulates a manifesto for such an organization—an imaginary "Foundation for Music Sustainability"—modeled on the manifestos of two prominent international organizations that support endangered languages, Terralingua (2013) and Foundation for Endangered Languages (2013).

Box 3.2 EXEMPLAR STATEMENT OF PURPOSE, BASED ON MODELS FROM LANGUAGE MAINTENANCE, FOR AN ORGANIZATION SUPPORTING MUSIC SUSTAINABILITY

FOUNDATION FOR MUSIC SUSTAINABILITY:
STATEMENT OF PURPOSE

Foundation for Music Sustainability is an autonomous international non-profit organization committed to supporting the vitality and viability of music genres.

A. *Foundation for Music Sustainability* recognizes
  1. that music in all its diversity is a fundamental part of the world's intangible cultural heritage;
  2. that many music genres around the world, especially those of indigenous and minority peoples, are under threat (a concern reflected in the 2003 UNESCO Convention for the Safeguarding of Intangible Cultural Heritage); and

3. that the decline or loss of music genres within a community potentially holds wider repercussions both within and beyond that community—for example, in terms of individual and community identity and social cohesion.

B. *Foundation for Music Sustainability* declares
1. that music constitutes an important and unique expression of culture within human societies, and that expressing culture is a basic human right;
2. that communities should have the right of self-determination with regard to their music and its future; and
3. that such decisions should be freely made with due regard for economic, social, cultural, community, and humanitarian considerations.

C. Therefore, *Foundation for Music Sustainability* undertakes
1. to raise awareness of endangered music genres through all available means, both within and outside the communities where those genres are located;
2. to support the transmission and performance of endangered music genres where appropriate, prioritizing the right of communities to self-determination;
3. to increase participation and promote autonomy of communities themselves in all aspects of music sustainability efforts, through training, mentoring, resource sharing, networking, and advocacy;
4. to forge partnerships in and across communities, between culture bearers, fieldworkers, researchers, nongovernmental organizations, and other stakeholders, in relation to issues of music sustainability;
5. to establish ethical and other principles to guide fieldworkers, researchers, and communities in their activities supporting music sustainability;
6. to monitor policies and practices affecting music making and musicians, and to seek to influence the appropriate authorities where necessary;
7. to support research and documentation of endangered music genres, by providing or indicating avenues for training, financial assistance, or disseminating outcomes;
8. to assemble and make available information that facilitates supporting the sustainability of music genres;

> 9. to raise greater public awareness of the importance of music sustainability and the need for strategies that support it; and
> 10. to disseminate information on all the above activities as widely as possible, at all levels from the local to the international.

Such an organization could help effect a coordinated approach to supporting music sustainability that engages not only with specific communities, but also with governments, nongovernment organizations, funding bodies, and the wider public, to advocate for the importance of vibrant and viable music cultures and to develop strategies to further that goal. A resource network, discussed above, may form one part of this organization.

For languages, efforts to carry forward the goals and objectives of maintenance efforts are largely reliant on grants; funding bodies, therefore, play a key role in those efforts. Significant funding bodies include the Foundation for Endangered Languages (based in the UK), the Endangered Languages Fund (USA), and the *Dokumentation der Bedrohte Sprachen* ["Documentation of endangered languages"] project of the Volkswagen Stiftung (Germany). A particularly notable funding source is the *Hans Rausing Endangered Languages Project* at the School of Oriental and African Studies in London, which provides substantial annual research grants for the documentation of endangered languages across the world. The project also comprises an archiving initiative and an academic training program (including postgraduate courses in endangered-language description, documentation, and field linguists). Although a comparable initiative is probably beyond the immediate sights of music sustainability—it was a £20 million donation from a charitable fund that led, in 2002, to the establishment of the *Hans Rausing* project—current ways of funding language maintenance projects indicate possible approaches to manage funding of music sustainability projects in the future. In 2009, the Musical Futures Foundation was set up with the intention to raise and distribute seed money to fund community-driven sustainability initiatives; as this book goes to print, the Foundation is not yet operational (QCRC, 2013, "Contact us: Musical Futures Foundation" section).

3.6 CONCLUSIONS

The discussion in this chapter points to five main ways in which language maintenance may help repair key gaps in current theory and practice of music sustainability. First, a range of tools from language maintenance may represent models for identifying and measuring music vitality, including UNESCO's Language Vitality Framework (Section 3.1). The development of a similar tool would permit the systematic identification and assessment of situations of musical endangerment across the range of global contexts.

Second, advocacy efforts relating to music sustainability may usefully draw on advocacy approaches and arguments for language maintenance (3.2). I suggested that one key requirement for effective public advocacy will be a firm understanding of the extent of music endangerment globally, and that further ethnomusicological investigation in this area is therefore warranted. Precedent from language maintenance suggests how this research might be carried out (namely, through the collaborative efforts of experienced ethnomusicologists across the world with strong regional expertise and networks). Another requirement for effective public advocacy is awareness among ethnomusicologists of the central issues in music endangerment. For this reason, as knowledge about the extent of music endangerment grows, so too should the need for consolidated response be promoted within the discipline—for example through training and educational opportunities, conferences and workshops, and published research.

Third, I argued that understanding preconditions for the success of language maintenance strategies is likely to advance our knowledge of the best ways to support endangered music genres, and I suggested that music-related strategies should be continually reviewed to refine our understanding of desirable preconditions for their success (3.3).

Fourth, in exploring how linguists approach the dilemmas of inefficacy or unexpected outcomes of language maintenance strategies, I suggested that their perspectives may guide ethnomusicologists in defining realistic aims and outcomes of music sustainability strategies (3.4). The objectives and success of music sustainability strategies might be defined not, or not only, in terms of securing the viability of the genre in question but also in wider social, political, and economic terms.

Finally, I described a number of coordinating mechanisms for language maintenance and how they may represent potentially valuable prototypes and infrastructure for music-specific coordinating mechanisms (3.5). Two specific examples served to illustrate this, relating to a music-specific resource network on sustainability and to a nonprofit international organization to support the goals and objectives of music sustainability efforts. Overall, then, to some degree, language maintenance holds the potential to inform all five issues in music sustainability under consideration in this chapter.

This brings to a close the first part of this book, which has identified key areas in music sustainability that require developing and some ways in which recourse to language maintenance may help do so. In the second part, I develop a tool that permits systematic identification and assessment of situations of musical endangerment. For reasons presented earlier this chapter, I believe this currently represents the most pressing undertaking in matters of music sustainability. Chapter 4 develops and presents the tool, and Chapter 5 applies it to gauge the vitality of a specific music genre.

CHAPTER 4

How to Identify and Assess Endangerment

The Music Vitality and Endangerment Framework

In 2002–2003, UNESCO invited an international group of expert linguists to develop a framework for determining the vitality of a language, in order to assist in developing policy, identifying needs, and implementing appropriate maintenance measures. This UNESCO Ad Hoc Expert Group on Endangered Languages subsequently elaborated the landmark concept paper *Language Vitality and Endangerment* (2003; Example 3.1 🔾). *Language Vitality and Endangerment* presents nine factors contributing to the degree of vitality of any language. Each factor is measured qualitatively (against the best-fitting description) and qualitatively (against a numeric scale of 1–6, or in real numbers). In this way, the Expert Group proposes, these nine factors taken collectively can indicate the level of vitality of any language:

1. Intergenerational language transmission
2. Absolute number of speakers (measured in real numbers)
3. Proportion of speakers within the total population
4. Trends in existing language domains
5. Response to new domains and media
6. Materials for language education and literacy
7. Governmental and institutional language attitudes and policies, including official status and use
8. Community members' attitudes toward their own language
9. Amount and quality of documentation.

It is this seminal tool that I take in this chapter as the basis for developing a comparable tool for identifying and assessing music endangerment, the Music Vitality and Endangerment Framework (MVEF). In Chapter 1, I argued that the lack of a systematic way to identify and assess endangerment across the range of global contexts is a major gap in current approaches to music sustainability. Such a tool is important for at least three reasons: (1) to enable diagnosis of situations of music endangerment and determine the urgency to implement initiatives toward sustainability; (2) to ensure the right remedial action is taken, as assessing the factors causing endangerment will help establish focus and priorities for action; and (3) to enable methodical evaluation of the efficacy of any efforts to maintain or revitalize the music genre.

My decision to adopt the UNESCO *Language Vitality and Endangerment* framework as a foundation for the MVEF has several grounds: its development and endorsement by a group of esteemed experts in the field; its use in national and international spheres; and its association with, and use by, the high-profile international organization UNESCO. A model for music vitality closely aligning with UNESCO's ideology may find easier movement in the international arena than one based on a lower-profile model.

4.1 MODIFYING THE LANGUAGE FRAMEWORK

Before constructing a framework to assess music vitality and endangerment based on UNESCO's model, I wish to make several general points about necessary modifications to the language framework. The need for these modifications arises in part from the differences between language and music in relation to their vitality as identified in the *Comparative Framework* of Chapter 2, and in part from certain inadequacies of the language framework (some of them acknowledged by UNESCO itself in a background paper reviewing and soliciting feedback on the use of the framework; UNESCO Culture Sector, 2011). The modifications include changes in terminology, an increased weight placed on assessing change, the introduction of a way to assess so-called *emergent* music genres, and some other minor adaptations.

Terminology

The process of adapting the *Language Vitality and Endangerment* framework for music demands a careful consideration of terminology. Most fundamentally, the term *music genre* needs defining (the *Language Vitality and Endangerment* framework does not offer a definition of *language* at all). Consistent with the rest of this book, in the MVEF I use the term *music genre* to describe a discrete musical tradition or form, while *music culture* refers to a society's total involvement with music.

To describe groups of people who share a language and sociolinguistic practices, the language vitality framework refers to *speech communities*. *Music communities*, though, is both a more oblique and problematic term: is such a community comprised only of musicians? Of audiences too? How does it relate to the idea of *musicking*—of music as a social experience? How does it position cultures or groups of people that engage with several music genres (which is in fact the norm)? In developing the MVEF, I use the term *community*, which has the advantage of imprecision: As defined in the Preface to this book, it may refer to a group of people who share their musical heritage by virtue of their common geographical, cultural, or ethnic background, but it may also denote a "community of practice" (Wood & Judikis, 2002, p. 12), that is, in this case, a group of people bound together first and foremost by their musical practice and interests. This wider definition is necessary to encompass the range of groups who are the primary custodians or carriers of music genres, whether endangered or vital.

Following the launch of the 2009 edition of UNESCO's *Atlas of the World's Languages in Danger* (Moseley, 2009), its editor-in-chief reportedly received vitriolic correspondence from individuals who took offense at their heritage language being referred to as *extinct* (as I learnt at a symposium that year). In addition to being potentially affronting to those individuals and communities who still identify with their heritage language, the term *extinct* arguably disallows the possibility of reclamation, reconstruction, or revival, which can be achieved—with sufficient documentation and community motivation—even in the case of a language with no remaining speakers. For these reasons, some linguists argue that *dormant* or *sleeping* may more appropriately describe languages whose last speaker has died, especially where a community still identifies with the language; the editors of a recent volume on Australia's Indigenous languages were "rather insistent" that their contributing authors avoided terms like *moribund, dead*, and *extinct* (Hobson, Lowe, Poetsch, & Walsh, 2010, p. xxvii). Taking into account these concerns, but believing that *dormant* and *sleeping* may be too euphemistic to describe some nonvital, nondocumented music genres (or for that matter, languages) without an identifying community, in the MVEF I have chosen to adopt the more neutral term *inactive* to refer to nonvital music genres.

Assessing Change

If a language scores highly or relatively highly on many of the nine factors of the *Language Vitality and Endangerment* framework, but most factors show a downward trend in recent years, this in itself can be an important gauge of endangerment. This is one major drawback of the language framework: the tension between its static nature and the natural dynamism of language use. For some factors of UNESCO's framework, like "number of speakers," a measure that places primary importance on the rate and direction of change would arguably better indicate vitality or endangerment. Considerations about the importance of change in assessing the vitality of music genres have led to my significantly modifying certain factors of the original language framework.

Four factors of the MVEF, then, place primary emphasis on diachronic assessment: the change in the number of proficient musicians (Factor 2); the change in number of people engaged with the genre (Factor 3); change in the genre itself and associated music practices (Factor 4); and change in its functions and performance contexts (Factor 5). Evaluated synchronically (that is, by the number of proficient musicians, the number of people engaged in the genre, the genre itself, and its performance functions and contexts), none of these factors represents a very legitimate gauge of vitality, and they all become particularly problematic when comparing two or more genres. A better indicator of vitality is the way they change over time.

By contrast, the other eight factors of the MVEF adopt a synchronic approach, although the change over time in these factors may also be relevant to vitality. A shift in community attitudes, for example, may reflect something about the vitality of a genre, as may any change in infrastructure or resources required for musical practices. But for each of these factors, it is arguably the current situation that is even more crucial. The extent and quality of the *existing* documentation is more relevant to vitality and endangerment than a comparison of past documentation with present; *current* community attitudes and government policies even hold more sway than their shift; availability of performance resources *now* impacts more on vitality than how this has changed over time; and so on.

Assessing Emergent Genres

The majority of frameworks developed to assess language vitality, including Fishman's GIDS (*Graded Intergenerational Disruption Scale*) and UNESCO's *Language Vitality and Endangerment*, were developed to help assess the language situation of a community before any maintenance efforts began to take effect. Now that situations are more common where a language has already undergone some degree of revitalization, new circumstances are manifesting that are not adequately catered to by these schemata. Children who have learned a revived language in school, for example, may begin to teach it to their parents, a situation that invalidates the premise that older generations teach younger ones. These so-called *emergent* languages therefore challenge the assumption that situations of endangerment must deteriorate inexorably; empirical evidence now indicates that the process of language loss "does not inevitably have to progress unidirectionally toward extinction" (Krauss, 2007, p. 9). Krauss revises his earlier estimates of the extent of language moribundity and extinction to account for this fact, and Lewis and Simons's (2010) modification and augmentation of Fishman's GIDS is also partly in order to cater for emergent situations.

Although efforts to revitalize endangered music genres have not yet gained the same degree of momentum as efforts relating to endangered languages, there nevertheless also exist *emergent* music genres: genres that have undergone some degree of revitalization, whether due to "spontaneous" revivals or engineered sustainability initiatives. Many of the music genres that have been inscribed on UNESCO's *List of Intangible Cultural Heritage in Need of Urgent Safeguarding*, for example, may be classified as emergent: not by virtue of the recognition of their precarious viability, but for the international prominence and recognition gained by inscription, the resulting funding and resources, and the positive community attitudes toward the genre demonstrated by its (required) support of the nomination. As efforts to support endangered music genres build momentum, more emergent situations will no doubt arise.

For these reasons, any framework to assess music vitality should also be developed from the perspective of revitalization as well as endangerment, to ensure it is equipped to deal with the sometimes atypical circumstances presented by emergent genres. Given the emphasis in the MVEF on change over time, which can thereby signal the increasing vitality of emergent genres, the only other significant modification needed to make the MVEF appropriate for emergent situations is to Factor 1: Intergenerational transmission (see Section 4.2).

Other Modifications

The first six factors of UNESCO language framework are identified as "major evaluative factors of vitality"; the remaining three deal with community attitudes, government and institutional attitudes, and issues of documentation. Yet as I describe in Chapter 3, attitudes and constructs are often crucial, even determining, in the vitality of music genres. For this reason, the factors relating to attitudes are still grouped together in the MVEF, but they are not relegated to a secondary role in vitality: The division between "major evaluative factors" and other factors is removed in the MVEF.

One drawback of the UNESCO language framework is that some of the graded scales for assessing each of the nine factors fuse more than one assessment criterion within a single grade description, thereby increasing the possibility that any particular description only will partly "fit" with a given circumstance (a shortcoming noted by Lewis, 2006, and UNESCO Culture Sector, 2011). In developing an equivalent framework for music I have attempted to tease out disparate components of the scales, in most cases by simplifying the grade descriptions. The fact remains that for certain music genres, the graded descriptions may remain incongruous. If none of the descriptions for a particular factor adequately describe a genre, those descriptions should be adapted as necessary to fit the particular situation at hand, and the specific purpose of the assessment itself. The grade descriptions provided in this chapter may therefore be viewed as examples only. Approaching them in this way will help avoid strained or artificial classification, though significant adaptations to the descriptions may affect comparability between genres. In certain cases, the grade descriptions might be better dispensed with altogether, and only a numerical grade selected as an indicator of vitality (0 [nonvital] to 5 [vital]). In the rare case that a factor itself is inapplicable to the music genre in question, or if it is not a valid indicator of its vitality, it may be omitted altogether. In short, the MVEF should not be adhered to dogmatically but rather remain subservient to human judgment.

Neither should the MVEF be regarded as a closed framework. With ongoing changes and developments in the intersections between music genres and societies, it is possible—probable, even—that key factors in music vitality and viability will shift over time. A retrospective stance illustrates the point: If a music vitality framework like the MVEF had been developed a hundred years ago, mass media and industry may not have featured in the framework at all. In an imaginative analogy, Michael Walsh described how nineteenth-century natural scientists, recognizing that platypuses and echidnas fitted no existing classification of animal,

> created the category *monotremes* .... they recognized that they had an animal that didn't fit the existing classification. And I'm saying there are languages that don't fit the existing GIDS or UNESCO classifications. So don't think of that as

a problem for the language, any more than: blame the echidnas because they're just a bloody nuisance to the theory. You have to absorb these language situations into an enriched theory that actually describes the situation [at hand]. (personal interview, April 8, 2010)

Thus, although the twelve MVEF factors may represent a useful system for thinking about the viability of music genres in the current milieu, the framework should be revisited on an ongoing basis and revised as necessary.

4.2 BUILDING A NEW FRAMEWORK FOR MUSIC

Drawing on the synergies and disconnects between language and music in relation to their sustainability as identified in the *Comparative Framework* (Chapter 2), the rest of this chapter uses UNESCO's structure as a foundation on which to build a tool to assess musical vitality and endangerment, the MVEF (*Music Vitality and Endangerment Framework*). As in the language framework, intergenerational transmission is Factor 1, since it can be used in isolation as an indicative measure of musical vitality or endangerment. All diachronic factors come next (Factors 2–5), followed by one factor assessing response to media and industry (Factor 6), and two assessing resources for music practices (Factors 7–8). The next three factors relate to attitudes (Factors 9–11), and the final factor assesses documentation (Factor 12).

Factor 1: Intergenerational Transmission

The *Comparative Framework* identified intergenerational transmission as a key indicator of both musical and linguistic vitality. Yet not all music genres are typically learned by children, or even by all members of a community, and music is not typically present in the variety of domains in which languages are found within a community (such as in the workplace or in commerce). The scale for this factor of UNESCO's framework therefore requires considerable adaptation to make it useful for music. For example, given that some music genres might be atypical or even taboo for children to learn, I have changed the language framework's references to *children, parent generation*, and *grandparent generation* to *youngest appropriate generation, middle generations*, and *older generations*. Also, the notion of "use" in the language vitality framework (as in "the language is used by all ages") has been replaced with "performance"—in the broadest sense of music

Table 4.1a GRADE DESCRIPTIONS TO ASSESS
FACTOR 1: INTERGENERATIONAL TRANSMISSION FOR
NON-EMERGENT MUSIC GENRES

Degree of endangerment	Grade	Intergenerational transmission
safe	5	The music genre is performed by all appropriate ages and is transmitted intergenerationally.
unsafe	4	The music genre is performed by all appropriate ages, but transmission to the youngest appropriate generation is weakening.
definitively endangered	3	The music genre is performed mostly by the middle generations and up.
severely endangered	2	The music genre is performed mostly by the older generations.
critically endangered	1	The music genre is performed only by the very elderly, and then only partially and infrequently.
inactive	0	There exists no performer of the music genre.

making of the genre in question—without necessarily implying something formal or public.

In most situations, the youngest generation that retains proficiency (in an unbroken chain of intergenerational transmission) can be taken to indicate strength of intergenerational transmission, as displayed in Table 4.1a.

However, in emergent situations where a music genre is undergoing revitalization, intergenerational transmission may have been broken. For languages, Lewis and Simons (2010) suggest that in emergent situations the measurement of vitality should be the oldest generation, in an unbroken intergenerational chain, that is once again proficient; vitality is achieved when all generations are again speaking the language and passing it from older to younger generations. For music genres (and arguably for languages too), however, intergenerational transmission in emergent situations may take various forms: All generations may make efforts to learn the genre; the middle generation may learn the genre first (perhaps from recordings and other documentation) and then pass it to the younger generation, while the older generation remains inactive; the oldest generation may teach the youngest, skipping the middle generation altogether; or in some cases, the youngest generation may begin to teach middle or older generations. This somewhat complicates the development of grade assessments for this factor, but Table 4.1b offers relatively general descriptions that might be used in emergent situations (and, as always, adapted to suit the situation

Table 4.1b GRADE DESCRIPTIONS TO ASSESS FACTOR 1: INTERGENERATIONAL TRANSMISSION FOR EMERGENT MUSIC GENRES

Grade	Intergenerational transmission
5	The music genre is performed by all appropriate ages and is transmitted intergenerationally in an unbroken chain from older to younger generations.
4	The music genre is performed by all appropriate ages, though is not (yet) transmitted intergenerationally in an unbroken chain from older to younger generations.
3	The music genre is being reestablished among more than one appropriate generation.
2	The music genre is being reestablished among only one generation.
1	The music genre is being reestablished among only one generation, and then only partially and infrequently.

at hand). Note that a "Grade 0" would be meaningless here, since by definition this assessment is to be applied to genres that are being revitalized.

Factor 2: Change in the Number of Proficient Musicians

In addition to the challenges of identifying and interpreting the number of musicians of a genre (described in Chapter 3.1), an adaptation for music of the language vitality factor "absolute numbers of speakers" needs the very different roles of "musician" and "speaker" in a group to be taken into account (see *Comparative Framework*). For some music genres, for example, it may be typical for there to be only a handful of hereditary master musicians within the community, whereas for other genres (especially song), almost everyone in the community may participate. This means that considerable caution would need to be exercised in using absolute numbers as an indicator of musical vitality, and numbers would be an inappropriate indicator altogether of the comparative vitality of more than one music genre. This is not to say that absolute numbers are entirely discountable; "any community needs a critical mass of participants to maintain itself" (Graves, 2005, p. 34). Just as for speakers of a language, a small number of musicians means that a music genre is much more vulnerable to attrition, as when musicians age and pass away.

With regard to the UNESCO framework, Lewis considers the measurement of this factor—a raw number—to be an anomaly and suggests that the number "needs to be set in some sort of interpretive framework so that its contribution to the overall evaluation becomes more evident" (2006, p. 25). Especially given the added complexities of interpreting numerical indicators of musical vitality, this factor of the MVEF assesses the *change* in numbers of musicians over time. Such a diachronic assessment is arguably a more accurate indicator of the vitality or endangerment status of a genre, and it also enables meaningful comparison between genres. The period of 5–10 years has been chosen as the time frame to assess trends, although a series of assessments for longer (or shorter) periods of time will yield even more accurate data on trends in musical vitality. For some genres, a different time frame may be chosen, according to the situation at hand and the purpose of the assessment.

In offering no definition of *speaker*, the *Language Vitality and Endangerment* leaves open the distinction between proficient, semi-proficient, and basic language skills, and between native and nonnative speakers, potentially leading to substantial discrepancies in data. This factor of the MVEF suggests that only proficient musicians be taken into account; other musicians are accounted for in the next factor, which deals with the number of people engaged with the genre altogether. This raises the issue of the widely divergent notions of "proficiency" across genres and cultures. A folk singer with low technical ability, for example, may be considered proficient on the basis of a thorough knowledge of repertoire, while for other genres, especially "classical," high technical skill may be the precondition for being considered accomplished. The meaning of "proficiency" should therefore be gauged from the perspective of the genre and of the community itself.

Table 4.2 suggests grade descriptions for assessing this factor. Those genres with no proficient musicians may be allocated a "Grade 0," even in cases where this represents little or no change in the number of musicians over the time frame being assessed.

Table 4.2 GRADE DESCRIPTIONS TO ASSESS FACTOR 2: CHANGE IN NUMBER OF PROFICIENT MUSICIANS IN THE PAST FIVE TO TEN YEARS

Grade	Change in number of proficient musicians in the past 5 to 10 years
5	Significant increase in proficient musicians
4	Moderate increase in proficient musicians
3	Little or no change in numbers of proficient musicians
2	Moderate decrease in proficient musicians
1	Significant decrease in proficient musicians
0	No proficient musicians

Factor 3: Change in the Number of People Engaged with the Genre

One factor the language framework assesses is the proportion of speakers within the total population of a group, however defined. Yet just as "absolute number of speakers" is not an appropriate indicator of the vitality of a music genre, assessing the "proportion of musicians in relation to the total population of a group" is also problematic. In the most vital possible language environment, the proportion of speakers in relation to the total population will be 100%. For certain vital genres of music, the proportion of musicians in a community might only be maximally one in 50, or even one in 500; this reflects the different social roles of the musician and the language speaker, as described in the *Comparative Framework*. For other genres, such as certain song corpuses of indigenous groups that call for full community participation, the figure may be closer to 100%. Even the "proportion of people engaged with a music genre" is not ideal: there exist genres in which very few people within a given population engage, yet these genres are still in a relatively strong position (Western classical opera in Europe being an interesting case in point).

A better indicator is the *change* in the number of people engaged with a music genre in relation to the total population of a group: that is, the change in number of those who partake in the music genre in any number of ways, whether through community music making, learning, teaching, listening to recordings, attending performances, or "consuming" the music in other modes appropriate to the community and the genre in question. One illustration of this is the recent concern (among some) about a weakening vitality of Western classical music (perhaps in contrast with opera, mentioned earlier): it is the *decrease* in the number of people *engaged* with that tradition (indicated by audience size, for example)—not the small proportion of musicians within the population, nor even a decrease in the number or proportion of its musicians per se—that has fueled the concern.

Table 4.3 provides grade descriptions for this factor. As in Factor 2, 5–10 years has been selected as the time frame for assessment. Again, those genres with no musicians of any level may be allocated a "Grade 0," even in cases where this represents little or no change in the number of people engaged with the genre.

Factor 4: Change in the Music and Music Practices

How quickly a music genre changes and the form that change adopts can be critical indicators of the vitality of a music genre. The *Language Vitality*

Table 4.3 GRADE DESCRIPTIONS TO ASSESS FACTOR 3: CHANGE IN NUMBER OF PEOPLE ENGAGED WITH THE GENRE IN THE PAST FIVE TO TEN YEARS

Grade	Change in number of people engaged with the genre in the past 5 to 10 years
5	Significant increase in people engaged with the genre
4	Moderate increase in people engaged with the genre
3	Little or no change in people engaged with the genre
2	Moderate decrease in people engaged with the genre
1	Significant decrease in people engaged with the genre
0	No people engaged with the genre

and Endangerment framework does not offer a way to assess the rate and direction of change in a language, although arguably this is an important indicator of language vitality too.

It is not possible to make a blanket statement about whether change is beneficial or detrimental to the vitality of music genres—to say, that is, that fast change means a vital genre whereas slow change indicates lower vitality, or vice versa. This is wholly genre-dependent; the rate of change in a music genre must always be considered in relation to the inherent values of the tradition. The musicians of Balinese *gamelan kebyar* believe that to keep that tradition static amounts to stagnation; old pieces are continually reformed and reconstructed and new ones constantly created. Change represents high vitality. Conversely, the sacred music of Balinese *gamelan gong gede* is considered best preserved unchanged: high importance is placed on retaining the "purity" of the tradition (Hood, 2010). In genres with this kind of aesthetic, fast change may be representative of low vitality, as attempts are made to palliate the genre.

To gauge the degree to which change reflects increasing or decreasing vitality, the rate of change also needs to be positioned against its direction. For genres where "positive" change takes the form of new repertoire (for example), the community may consider other types of change—the introduction of technology or new media in performance, say, or a relaxing of traditional gender roles—to be inherently harmful. Other communities may embrace technological innovations, leading to an invigoration of the genre. In any two situations, then, the change itself may be identical, but its implications for vitality may be opposite. Assessment of this factor must therefore be thoroughly grounded in an understanding of the constructs surrounding the genre being assessed. Table 4.4 suggests grade descriptions for assessing this factor.

Table 4.4 GRADE DESCRIPTIONS TO ASSESS FACTOR 4: PACE AND DIRECTION OF CHANGE IN THE MUSIC AND MUSIC PRACTICES IN THE PAST FIVE TO TEN YEARS

Grade	Pace and direction of change in the music and music practices in the last 5 to 10 years
5	Pace and direction of change in the music and associated music practices reflect significantly increased strength of the genre
4	Pace and direction of change reflect moderately increased strength
3	Pace and direction of change reflect little or no change in strength
2	Pace and direction of change reflect moderately decreased strength
1	Pace and direction of change reflect significantly decreased strength
0	Pace and direction of change reflect no or almost no strength

Factor 5: Change in Performance Contexts and Functions

In the language vitality framework, "Factor 5: Response to new domains and media" relates to the capability of a language to expand into new educational (school), workplace, and community contexts, as well as broadcast media and online environments. For certain music genres though, expansion into new contexts may be neither a desired nor appropriate shift. Some genres (like ritual music, for example) may be intimately bound with one specific context and function. The grade descriptions for this factor therefore emphasize the *nature* of change in performance context(s) rather than their *quantity*, as in the language framework.

For music genres, shifts in context often closely reflect or instigate shifts in social function, and so both are given weight in this factor of MVEF. (The issue of function is nowhere explicitly addressed in the *Language Vitality and Endangerment* framework, since the primary function of all languages is the same—that is, communicative.) It should be noted that the presence of two or more music cultures in one community is not necessarily a threat to either the context or function of the music genres. In fact, a multiplicity of music *cultures* (as well as genres) within a community might nowadays be considered the norm, just as many languages may co-reside within a single community. A music genre need not be the main genre within a community for it to be vital, and musicians and other community members do not have to be "monomusical" (see *Comparative Framework*).

Although the period of 5–10 years may again prove a useful guide for assessing this factor, a diachronic assessment of performance contexts and functions is most important for the intermediate stages of change or stasis

Table 4.5 GRADE DESCRIPTIONS TO ASSESS FACTOR 5: CHANGE IN PERFORMANCE CONTEXT(S) AND FUNCTION(S) IN THE PAST FIVE TO TEN YEARS

Degree of endangerment	Grade	Change in performance context(s) and function(s) in the last 5 to 10 years
integral contexts and functions	5	The music genre continues to be performed in one or more regular, well-established contexts and holds integral function(s) within the community.
expanding contexts or functions	4	The music genre has expanded to new context(s) and function(s), and is performed regularly or semi-regularly.
static contexts or functions	3	Context(s) and function(s) for the music genre have remained largely static, even in relation to changing environments. The genre is performed regularly or semi-regularly.
formulaic contexts and functions	2	The music genre is performed only in irregular formulaic contexts and functions.
highly limited formulaic contexts and functions	1	The music genre is performed only on exceptional occasions in formulaic contexts and functions.
inactive	0	The music genre is not performed in any context for any function.

(Grades 3 and 4 of the scale above). When a music genre enters the critical state of being performed only in formulaic, nontypical contexts and functions (Grades 1 and 2), synchronic assessment begins to be of more relevance for evaluating vitality. These considerations are built into the grade descriptions for this scale (see Table 4.5).

Factor 6: Response to Mass Media and the Music Industry

Response to media and industry is a significantly greater indicator of vitality for music genres than for languages (*Comparative Framework*), warranting the greater emphasis placed on it in the MVEF through the inclusion of this factor. In almost all cases, the mass media (including radio, television, and the Internet) and the music industry have the potential to substantially affect the vitality of a music genre. The way a genre responds to these entities—and vice versa—is a key factor in assessing endangerment.

For those genres where engagement with the media and industry is considered gainful for vitality, *robust* (Grade 5) may mean the music genre is a vibrant part of the local, national and even international media and music industry (though the internet has eroded clear distinctions between

Table 4.6 GRADE DESCRIPTIONS TO ASSESS FACTOR 6: RESPONSE TO MASS MEDIA AND THE MUSIC INDUSTRY

Degree of endangerment	Grade	Response to mass media and the music industry
robust	5	The genre displays significant strength in its engagement with and response to mass media and the music industry.
strong	4	The genre displays strength in its engagement with and response to mass media and the music industry.
coping	3	The genre displays an ability to cope in its engagement with and response to mass media and the music industry.
weak	2	The genre displays weakness in its engagement with and response to mass media and the music industry.
very weak	1	The genre displays significant weakness in its engagement with and response to mass media and the music industry.
unable to cope	0	The genre displays an inability to cope in its engagement with and response to mass media and the music industry.

these levels). For other genres, such as certain kinds of ritual music, *robust* will mean resilience against, or even resistance to, encroachment of mass media and the music industry. At the other end of the scale, an inability to cope (Grade 0) may be represented in some cases by a lack of engagement with the media or the music industry altogether, or by mass media and the music industry heavily encroaching on the genre. As with other factors of the MVEF, then, the grade descriptions for this factor in Table 4.6 need to acknowledge the different values across genres in relation to their response to, and engagement with, mass media and the music industry.

Factor 7: Infrastructure and Resources for Music Practices

More than languages, music genres often demand infrastructure and resources for their creation, transmission, rehearsal, and performance, such as musical instruments, musical paraphernalia, technological equipment, and dedicated spaces for creating or performing. In many cases, the unavailability or inaccessibility of these resources will jeopardize the vitality of the genre in question. This factor of the MVEF addresses this consideration, and also responds to one of the key differences between languages and music in relation to vitality: the concept of creating or composing music.

This factor of the MVEF encompasses the impact on vitality of the quality and availability of learning and teaching resources for various ages and

Table 4.7 GRADE DESCRIPTIONS TO ASSESS FACTOR 7: ACCESSIBILITY OF INFRASTRUCTURE AND RESOURCES FOR MUSIC PRACTICES

Grade	Accessibility of infrastructure and resources for music practices
5	All infrastructure and resources required for creating, performing, rehearsing, and transmitting the music genre are easily available and accessible.
4	All infrastructure and resources required for creating, performing, rehearsing, and transmitting the music genre are accessible, but not necessarily easily.
3	Most but not all required infrastructure/resources are accessible.
2	Some but not all required infrastructure/resources are accessible.
1	Some required infrastructure/resources are only accessed with great difficulty.
0	Some required infrastructure/resources are completely inaccessible.

musical abilities, including song books, scores, pedagogical games, recordings, digital audio/video recorders, online learning technologies, and multimedia resources. The existence, type, extent, quality, and accessibility of these resources will all affect transmission processes, and therefore the vitality of the genre. Table 4.7 provides grade descriptions for assessing this factor.

Factor 8: Knowledge and Skills for Music Practices

Just as tangible resources and infrastructure are necessary for the vitality of many music genres, intangible resources are also often needed for creation, transmission, and performance. Examples include the sociocultural and musical knowledge and skill needed for the creation of new repertoire, the linguistic knowledge and ability needed for the creation of new song texts, and knowledge of systems and methods of transmission and pedagogy (as opposed to transmission itself, which is addressed under Factor 1). Where community members lack easy access to these intangible resources, the vitality of the genre may be threatened (see *Comparative Framework*).

One clear example of the way systems of knowledge can affect the vitality of a genre comes from Bali, where at the beginning of the twentieth century, *gamelan gong gede* were eclipsed by the increasingly popular *gamelan kebyar*—except in the highlands, where a deeply ingrained social system of ritual domains called *banua* govern the musical associations who own and maintain these antique orchestras. Here orchestras are preserved largely because membership into these *banua* ritual domains is contingent upon reciprocal services between its members. Unlike lowland gamelan groups who own and operate their gamelan independently, highland groups stay loyal to their *banua* ritual networks. As a result, few groups have abandoned

Table 4.8 GRADE DESCRIPTIONS TO ASSESS FACTOR 8: ACCESSIBILITY OF KNOWLEDGE AND SKILLS FOR MUSIC PRACTICES

Grade	Accessibility of knowledge and skills for music practices
5	The community holds all knowledge and skills required for creating, performing, and transmitting the music genre, and these are easily available and accessible.
4	The community holds all required knowledge and skills, but these may not be easily available or accessible.
3	The community holds most but not all required knowledge and skills.
2	The community holds only some of the required knowledge and skills.
1	The community holds only a little of the required knowledge and skills.
0	Required knowledge and skills are almost or completely absent in the community.

their *gong gede*, resulting in the survival of this unique orchestra type (Hood, 2010, p. 92).

Table 4.8 suggests grade descriptions for assessing this Factor 8.

Factor 9: Governmental and Institutional Policies Affecting Music Practices

Although—unlike languages—most music genres do not usually have an official status within a nation-state, governments and government bodies generally have explicit policies and/or implicit attitudes toward cultural heritage and the arts. Even if these do not refer directly to music and musical practices, they often deeply affect them (*Comparative Framework*, 2.4).

Because a government often has no specific music policy, in the grade descriptions for this factor (Table 4.9), I refer to "cultural expressions" rather than specifically to music. The terms on the left to describe each grade have been retained from the language framework, but they adopt slightly different meanings with their new definitions (e.g. "differentiated support" refers here to attitudes and policies that distinguish between the unique needs of cultures or genres, and is therefore more favorable than "blanket support").

Factor 10: Community Members' Attitudes Toward the Genre

Much of the literature about endangered languages emphasizes that community members' attitudes toward their language, including their commitment to revitalization efforts, are a key factor in vitality. A number of

Table 4.9 GRADE DESCRIPTIONS TO ASSESS FACTOR 9: OFFICIAL ATTITUDES TOWARD THE MUSIC GENRE

Degree of support	Grade	Official attitudes toward the music genre
differentiated support	5	The music genre is supported through specific cultural policies developed and implemented in consultation with culture bearers.
blanket support	4	The genre is supported through overarching policies supporting cultural expressions, without differentiation and without consultation with culture bearers.
passive assimilation	3	No explicit policy exists for supporting (or hindering) diverse cultural expressions, such as the music genre.
active assimilation	2	Implicitly or explicitly, the government encourages the abandonment of small or nonmainstream cultural expressions, for example by providing education only in the language and culture of the majority group.
forced assimilation	1	Government policy explicitly declares the majority group to represent the only recognized culture. Small or nonmainstream cultural expressions are neither recognized nor supported.
prohibition	0	Performance of the music genre is prohibited. It may be tolerated in private social contexts.

variables often combine to form community attitudes toward language, including economic factors, the perceived prestige of the language, and literacy levels within the community (Grenoble & Whaley, 1998).

The strong parallels between constructs and attitudes toward languages and those toward music genres, and the effect of both on the vitality of the heritage in question, was established through the *Comparative Framework*. Just as with languages, members of a community are not usually neutral toward their musical expressions. They may take pride in a particular music genre, or they might be ashamed of it or view it as old-fashioned, with repercussions for its vitality. If community members view the music genre as representative of their cultural identity, but that identity is seen as a hindrance to economic mobility and integration into the majority society, they may harbor negative attitudes toward the genre. In some communities, there may be individuals or subgroups whose attitudes and opinions about the music genre are more highly esteemed or influential, such as elders within indigenous communities. In assessing this factor (using the grade descriptions in Table 4.10), it is the balance of community support that needs to be gauged.

Table 4.10 GRADE DESCRIPTIONS TO ASSESS FACTOR
10: COMMUNITY MEMBERS' ATTITUDES TOWARD THE MUSIC GENRE

Grade	Community members' attitudes toward the music genre
5	Community support for the maintenance of the music genre is very strong.
4	Community support for the maintenance of the music genre is strong.
3	Community support for the maintenance of the music genre is moderate.
2	Community support for the maintenance of the music genre is weak.
1	Community support for the maintenance of the music genre is minimal.
0	No community members support the maintenance of the genre.

Factor 11: Relevant Outsiders' Attitudes Toward the Genre

In addition to governmental and community attitudes, the attitudes of other relevant outsiders can also have a substantial impact on the vitality of a genre. Researchers, academics, fieldworkers, activists, commercial enterprises, funding bodies, and nongovernmental organizations can all directly affect the vitality of a music genre—for example, through their research, projects, lobbying and activism, and revitalization efforts. The impact may also be indirect, such as when the very interest of an esteemed outsider shifts the attitudes of the community itself. A lack of interest in a music genre from those outsiders deemed relevant (e.g. commercial enterprises) may be detrimental to the vitality of the genre.

It cannot be assumed that outsider interest always signals support for the sustainability of a genre. This is especially true of interest from profitable enterprises that place financial gain over and above the wishes of the community, but even academic interest may be insidious. In the early 1990s, for example, one veteran Chinese folk performance scholar claimed, "My basic aim in investigating folk beliefs is to eliminate their influence" (Jiang Bin, cited in McLaren, 2010, p. 32).

Table 4.11 provides grade descriptions for assessing this factor.

Factor 12: Amount and Quality of Documentation

UNESCO's language vitality framework argues that in order to assess the urgency for documenting a language, the extent and quality of existing documentation needs to be known. Information about existing documentation, it suggests, helps speakers design efforts toward documentation and maintenance, as well as enables linguists to formulate suitable projects

Table 4.11 GRADE DESCRIPTIONS TO ASSESS FACTOR 11: RELEVANT OUTSIDERS' ATTITUDES TOWARD THE MUSIC GENRE

Grade	Relevant outsiders' attitudes toward the music genre
5	Support of the music genre by relevant outsiders is very strong.
4	Support of the music genre by relevant outsiders is strong.
3	Support of the music genre by relevant outsiders is moderate.
2	Support of the music genre by relevant outsiders is weak.
1	Support of the music genre by relevant outsiders is minimal.
0	Support of the music genre by relevant outsiders is absent altogether or attitudes to the genre are adverse.

Table 4.12 GRADE DESCRIPTIONS TO ASSESS FACTOR 12: DOCUMENTATION OF THE MUSIC GENRE

Nature of documentation	Grade	Documentation of the music genre
superlative	5	Abundant high-quality documentation exists in a range of formats, including audiovisual.
good	4	Adequate high-quality documentation exists.
fair	3	Adequate documentation exists in varying quality.
fragmentary	2	Limited documentation exists in varying quality.
inadequate	1	Documentation is very limited or is of unusable quality.
undocumented	0	Documentation is nonexistent.

on the language in collaboration with the community. The language framework combines several components within each grade description for this factor, assessing within a single grade the existence (and quality) of grammars, dictionaries, texts, literature, everyday media, and audio and video recordings.

Following Lewis's recommendation to simplify and "unpack" these descriptions (2006, p. 27), I keep the grade descriptions general for this factor in the MVEF (see Table 4.12). For most music genres, extensive well-annotated, high-quality audio and video recordings will represent the most important type of documentation. The amount and quality of recordings will often (but not always) be indicative of the amount and quality of other types of documentation, such as transcriptions/scores, books, and other written materials. In addition to comprehensiveness, accessibility, and availability of metadata, appropriate archiving of documentation may also be considered an aspect of its quality.

The *Language Vitality and Endangerment* framework emphasizes the importance of an orthography for the vitality of a language (see Factor 6: Materials for language education and literacy). The lack of an orthography inhibits the range of domains in which a language can be employed, therefore limiting its vitality with possible repercussions for viability, but the lack of a way to write down a music genre does not necessarily limit its vitality in the same way. A notation system for a music genre is therefore not as significant a factor in vitality as an orthography is for a language, and the MVEF places no special emphasis on it. Nevertheless, a notation system does represent an additional and sometimes more durable form of documentation than recordings and may therefore be taken into account in assessing matters of documentation.

4.3 CONCLUSIONS

In sum, the following twelve factors affect the vitality of a music genre (downloadable, with the grade descriptions, as Example 4.1 🅞):

Factor 1. Intergenerational transmission
Factor 2. Change in the number of proficient musicians
Factor 3. Change in the number of people engaged with the genre
Factor 4. Change in the music and music practices
Factor 5. Change in performance contexts and functions
Factor 6. Response to mass media and the music industry
Factor 7. Infrastructure and resources for music practices
Factor 8. Knowledge and skills for music practices
Factor 9. Governmental policies affecting music practices
Factor 10. Community members' attitudes toward the genre
Factor 11. Relevant outsiders' attitudes toward the genre
Factor 12. Amount and quality of documentation

Along with their grade descriptions, these twelve factors form the Music Vitality and Endangerment Framework (MVEF). Just as with the language framework, the vitality of music genres cannot be gauged simply by adding the numbers from the grades in the framework, and it is recommended that such addition not be done. Also, I reiterate that these twelve factors, and the descriptions and scales for each, are only offered as guidelines, and should be adapted as befits the situation and purpose of the assessment. Under no circumstances should the MVEF be uncritically applied (which some linguists believe sometimes has been the case, regretfully, with UNESCO's language framework).

In addition to helping gauge the vitality of a music genre, the MVEF can also indicate the areas where a genre is most in need of support. An MVEF evaluation may be carried out by a community to gauge its own musical vitality and determine an appropriate course of action, if required, or it may be used by external bodies such as governments, nongovernment organizations, research institutions, cultural advocacy bodies, and funding agencies as a means to help inform policy decisions, to make sure resources and funds are directed where they are most viable, and to steer research and documentation efforts in collaboration with the community. These possibilities, and some of the challenges inherent in them, are discussed further in Chapter 6.

In addition to these uses of the framework, each of its twelve factors also may serve as an important tool for comparison between music genres. Comparing the vitality of genres (either within or across communities) has several functions, perhaps the most important being to help ascertain the relative severity of endangerment. In conjunction with a careful consideration of community attitudes, as well as any other factors critical to revitalization prospects of music genres, a comparative tool may help ensure that sustainability projects are implemented where they are most viable and that funding is appropriately channeled. Comparison of vitality could also serve to alert agencies to the state of musical diversity at the regional, transregional, and global levels, which in turn may inform development of national and international policy promoting that diversity.

In his assessment of 100 languages of the world using UNESCO's language vitality framework, Lewis found that, to some extent, that framework "ask[s] some new questions and the existing data repositories don't have the data, or have not organized their data in such a way that they can readily answer those questions" (2006, p. 23). With current knowledge, such a survey for music based on existing data would probably be altogether unfeasible, since extensive information on the world's music genres relating specifically to the factors of the MVEF is even less readily available. In some ways, this is not a bad situation. If a tool such as the MVEF could be used starting from the incipient stages of international research into music endangerment and vitality, complete and consistent data may be gathered from the beginning, facilitating the coordination, reporting, collation, and tracking of information.

In the next chapter I turn to a specific music genre, the emergent north-Vietnamese tradition of *ca trú*, to demonstrate how the MVEF might work in practice.

CHAPTER 5

Measuring Up

Putting the Framework to Work

This chapter demonstrates how the *Music Vitality and Endangerment Framework* (MVEF) presented in the previous chapter may be applied to assess musical vitality and viability. After providing a short historical background to *ca trù*, I give my reasons for choosing it for this assessment, and I comment briefly on some considerations in carrying out the task. The core of the chapter comprises an assessment of the vitality of *ca trù* according to the twelve factors of the MVEF.

5.1 A SHORT HISTORY OF CA TRÙ

Ca trù is a chamber music genre of the majority Việt (Kinh) people in northern Vietnam. Nowadays, it typically involves three musicians—a female singer, who also players a small bamboo slab (*phách*), a male player of the three-stringed lute (*đàn đáy*), and a beater of the "praise drum" (*trống chầu*; traditionally a knowledgeable member of the audience). Before the 1980s, the most common name for the genre was *hát ả đào*; various other names exist, including *hát cô đầu, hát nhà tơ, hát nhà trò,* and *hát ca công*.

Ca trù was an established genre by the 15th century. Its performance contexts and functions shifted over time; each had its own repertoire of songs and, sometimes, also dances. Historically, specific functions for *ca trù* included *hát thờ*, to worship the village guardian spirit, and to praise *ca trù*'s ancestors; *hát thi*, competitive singing within *ca trù* communities to recognize and honor the skill of their musicians; and *hát chơi*, for the entertainment of the upper and middle classes in society, including literati, mandarins, and noblemen. By the early 20th century, the three main contexts for *ca trù* were aristocratic homes for ceremonies and celebrations (where the genre was referred to as *hát cửa quyền*), at village communal houses and temples for worship or ceremony (*hát cửa đình*), and in private homes for entertainment (*hát chơi*) (Nguyễn P. T., 1991a, p. 12).

In the early 20th century, French colonization of Vietnam brought increasing Westernization, and an urban economy prospered. Many rurally based *ca trù* singers moved to the cities, especially to Hanoi, and here *hát chơi* performance opportunities flourished with the growth in "singing houses"—private homes, most often, made available in the evening for this purpose. By the 1940s, however, these singing houses had become associated with opium smoking and prostitution, not involving *ca trù* singers themselves but young women known as *cô-đầu rượu*, who served in the establishments. The reputation of *ca trù* soon shifted from an elite refined art to "an amusement pleasure of vulgar people and boors" (Lê, 2008, p. 282), and the growing moral questionability surrounding the genre was one reason for a government crackdown on its venues, leaving the musicians nowhere to perform. New public opinion of *ca trù* as a form of debauchery meant that musicians became ashamed to be associated with it. Decades of war from 1945 on meant the destruction or closure of other performance venues for *ca trù*, especially the communal *đình* (temple-houses) (Vietnamese Institute for Musicology, 2008b).

Social and economic upheaval after the 1945 August Revolution and the Communist victory in the 1945–1954 Franco-Vietnamese war also played a role in the demise of the genre (Jähnichen, 2008, p. 161). The Cultural and Ideological Revolution in Vietnam (1954–1986, thus encompassing and extending beyond the era of Mao's Cultural Revolution in China in the 1960s and 1970s) saw the rise of *cải biên nhạc tộc dân* ("neotraditional" music), which represented a government-approved way of managing the country's cultural image and giving voice to the revolutionary ideology. Many traditional genres were suppressed or banned during this era, including *châu văn* (trance music), *nhạc lễ* (ritual music), and *ca trù*, all of which were seen to incorporate superstitious or backward practices (Arana, 1999, p. 120).

For all these reasons, *ca trù* was rarely performed from the 1950s to the late 1980s, and much musical knowledge was lost during this time. The genre essentially had "no prestige, no money, no infrastructure, no training, no audience" (Schippers, 2009, p. 201). Musicians with thorough knowledge of the art no longer practiced it, leading Vietnamese musicologist Phạm Duy to believe by the mid-1970s that *ca trù* was almost extinct

(1975, p. 100). Even though a recording made in 1976 of singer Quách Thị Hồ by expatriate musicologist Trần Văn Khê gained international recognition after Trần introduced the recordings to UNESCO's International Music Council, Trần himself conceded in 1982 that the genre was one "whose beginnings lay in the 15th century, its golden age in the 19th, at the start of the 20th century took its first backward step, and is presently experiencing its end" (cited in Jähnichen, 1997, p. 9).

In 1986, incited by an economic crisis and a deteriorating standard of living, the Vietnamese Communist Party launched *đổi mới*, its renovation or reform policy that signaled the shift from a state-subsidized economy to a free-market one, which increased acceptance of international influences and trade. In 1987, the Political Bureau's Resolution Number 5 recognized freedom of artistic expression, at least for all artistic works that were "not anti-socialist, anti-Party and anti-government" (Lê, 1998, p. 113). In this way, *đổi mới* and the end of the Cultural and Ideological Revolution opened the way for the reappearance and revival of prerevolutionary music genres, including *ca trù*. This situation led within a few years to the development of projects like the UNESCO-approved *Vietnamese Court Music Revitalization Plan* funded by Toyota Foundation, which aimed to revive former central-Vietnamese genres through documentation, education programs, and research (Osamu, 2001).

So it was that by the early 1990s *ca trù* musicians who had not practiced their art for decades found themselves in an environment where it was possible to do so. In 1991, the first official state-supported *ca trù* club was established, the Hanoi Ca Trù Club, which served for a time as one of the few places where musicians and listeners could meet and enjoy the genre. Several more voluntary, nonprofit clubs were established in following years, in both urban and rural areas. Performances and training opportunities for musicians grew. Research interest also developed, and several local conferences on *ca trù* took place. In 2000, the First Open Ca Trù Hanoi Festival was held, providing an opportunity for *ca trù* artists from Hanoi and further afield to meet for the first time (Lê, 2008, pp. 289–294).

In the 2000s, the spate of *ca trù* revitalization initiatives continued to grow, from clubs, festivals, classes, and promotional activities to conferences, workshops, and research and documentation projects. In modern-day Vietnam, tradition is "no longer antithetical to the modern or in need of reform"; instead, it is "being used to bolster national identity, which many cultural nationalists consider to be threatened by the forces of globalisation" (Norton, 2009, p. 21). Since the 1990s, *ca trù* has also increasingly represented a way of renegotiating Vietnam's cultural history

(Wettermark, 2010a) and remembering its idealized past (Norton, 2005). The government now recognizes the value of traditional music genres— economic as well as ideological. Testament to this fact is that in 2009, backed by the Vietnamese Ministry of Culture, Sports, and Tourism, *ca trù* was officially inscribed on the list of *UNESCO Masterpieces of Oral and Intangible Cultural Heritage in Urgent Need of Safeguarding*.

Nevertheless, opinions remain mixed about the future of *ca trù*. Some sources suggest hopefully that the genre has merely been "sleeping peacefully" for the last sixty years (Vietnamese Institute for Musicology, 2008a); others deem that *ca trù* "is now disappearing" (Trần & Nguyen, 2007–2010) or is even already "buried in the dust of time" (Nguyễn T. T., 2008).

5.2 CARRYING OUT THE VITALITY ASSESSMENT

Any of hundreds of music genres could be used to illustrate the practical application of the MVEF, but the checkered history of *ca trù* indicates that the genre might form an interesting case study in viability. The availability of sufficient recent source material relating to vitality and viability was another factor in my choice of genre. Perhaps most directly relevant of these materials is the dossier submitted to UNESCO by the Vietnamese Ministry of Culture Sports and Tourism in 2009, nominating *ca trù* for inscription onto UNESCO's *Urgent Safeguarding List* (hereafter referred to as the "UNESCO nomination file"). It includes an 18-page report on the current state of the genre (Example 5.1 ◐) and an hour-long video documentary (Example 5.2 ◐). Two edited volumes on *ca trù* also emanated from preparations for the nomination. All these sources should be understood in the context of the rise of heritage and identity politics in Vietnam over the past couple of decades (discussed later), and with the consideration that one of their primary functions was to promote *ca trù* to local and foreign agents.

In carrying out this MVEF assessment, I also draw on interviews with *ca trù* musicians and Vietnamese and non-Vietnamese scholars with an expertise in either *ca trù* or Vietnamese traditional music. I conducted several of these interviews in 2010, including one with Phạm Thị Huệ, leader of the *ca trù* group Giáo Phường Ca Trù Thăng Long, who I had met in Brisbane a couple of years earlier in the context of the *Sustainable Futures for Music Cultures* project (QCRC, 2013). The remaining interviews were conducted in 2007 and 2010 by *Sustainable Futures* researchers Huib Schippers and Esbjörn Wettermark (and my thanks to them for providing me access to the raw materials). I also draw on my experiences from a field visit to Hanoi in July–August 2010, where I attended *ca trù* rehearsals and performances and met informally with several *ca trù* performers, students, teachers, and researchers.

In the last 10–15 years, much published research on *ca trù* has been written in, or translated into, English. All documentation for the 2009 nomination of *ca trù* to UNESCO's *Urgent Safeguarding List* was required to be in English or French (the working languages of the UNESCO Intergovernmental Committee); a considerable amount of recent scholarship on the genre has been associated in one way or other with the initiatives or enterprises of non-Vietnamese agencies, who mostly report on their projects in English (such as the Ford Foundation, Swedish International Development Agency, and Queensland Conservatorium Research Centre); and *ca trù* seems to have garnered somewhat greater research interest among outsiders than among Vietnamese scholars. The bias on English-language published sources in this case study is therefore partly mitigated by these circumstances, as well as by the fact that several of the interviews drawn on here represent a Vietnamese perspective.

Since Phạm Thị Huệ was my primary link with the *ca trù* community, this chapter places some emphasis on her and her group Giáo Phường Ca Trù Thăng Long. I suggest that this is not necessarily a deficiency: Giáo Phường Ca Trù Thăng Long displays striking leadership in the *ca trù* revival, and in many ways the group illustrates important features of the current and shifting vitality of the genre. Further research on other parts of the *ca trù* community, particularly those in non-urban areas of northern Vietnam and in Hồ Chí Minh City, where some *ca trù* activity is also found, would bring further breadth to future assessments of the genre.

In an essay on "insiders and outsiders" in ethnomusicological research, Nettl raises the concern of ethnocentrism, citing in particular the perception of certain Asian scholars and musicians that much research by Europeans and Americans is "thus flawed" (2005, p. 158). If this is a charge to which one must plead guilty or not, I plead guilty. The strictures of my MVEF framework, the parameters it measures, and the way it measures them are no doubt markedly Western, markedly different from the way the local Vietnamese community might approach or perceive its own tradition. But I would also argue that the perspective I present in this chapter, while not insider, is nevertheless valid, even putting to one side any philosophical arguments to that end. My reasoning is pragmatic: as long as major international cultural organizations operate their support schemes principally on Western paradigms (and after all, it is typically the Western organizations with the most money), Eurocentric perspectives on endangered cultures will be important for those communities wishing to access the funding and support these organizations provide. By dint of their engagement with organizations like these (including UNESCO, Ford Foundation, and others), the *ca trù* community, or at least parts of it, has indicated that it is one such group. I may be guilty of some ethnocentrism in fact, then, but less so in feeling.

5.3 A VITALITY ASSESSMENT OF CA TRÙ

This section addresses each of the twelve vitality factors of the *Music Vitality and Endangerment Framework* in turn, in relation to *ca trù*. For factors that relate to change over time, the 5–10 years to 2010 serves as the period for assessment. Where possible, for each factor I also indicate the likely short-term (5–10 year) outlook for *ca trù* in relation to that factor.

Factor 1: Intergenerational Transmission

This factor relates to the current strength of the transmission of *ca trù* from generation to generation. Before the decline of *ca trù* in the mid-twentieth century, learning *ca trù* had typically involved an apprenticeship of some years with a master musician, often a relative (a common practice in many genres from Asia and elsewhere). This method of transmission was broken during the decades of suppression of *ca trù* from the mid-twentieth century. The current middle generation (aged c.30–60) therefore grew up by and large without the opportunity to learn the genre in this way (though exceptions include instrumentalist Nguyễn Phan Khuê, b. 1962, and singer Nguyễn Thị Thúy Hò, b. 1973, who both belong to a family with ca trù lineage; Đặng, 2008, pp. 489, 499).

Thus, from the time the *ca trù* revival began in the early 1990s, some elderly *ca trù* masters have transmitted the genre directly to their grandchildren (or, at least, young people of that generation), skipping the middle generation altogether. Master singers Quách Thị Hồ and Phó Thị Kim Đức both passed on the art directly to their grandchildren (Lê, 2008, pp. 293, 296), and in 2008 Nguyễn Thị Chúc described her four *ca trù* students as "including a paternal grandchild, a maternal grandchild, and a great grandchild" (Vietnamese Institute for Musicology, 2008b). While the processes of transmission according to the old models of family lineage still exist, in the last two decades they have increasingly embraced anyone wishing to learn *ca trù*. Neither of two prominent middle-generation members of the *ca trù* community in Hanoi, for example, belongs to a family with *ca trù* lineage: both Lê Thị Bạch Vân (b. 1958) and Phạm Thị Huệ (b. 1973) learned the genre in their adulthood (Phạm with master artist teachers Nguyễn Thị Chúc and Nguyễn Phú Đẹ can be seen in Examples 5.3a and 5.3b respectively ◐ ◯).

Ca trù clubs currently represent the primary means for the intergenerational transmission of *ca trù* outside the traditional model of family apprenticeship. In 2002, a Ford Foundation grant enabled interested participants from several provinces to take intensive *ca trù* classes from members of the Thái Hà Ca Trù Club and singer Nguyễn Thị Chúc, over a two-month period. Returning to their localities, many participants began teaching the genre and establishing their own *ca trù* clubs. By 2004, over twenty clubs had sprung up across the cities and provinces of northern Vietnam, adding to several already in existence (see Đặng, 2008, pp. 535–536)—a striking success for Ford Foundation's limited investment. The clubs continue to act as infrastructure for workshops, performances, and training, particularly for young people from the ages of around 10 to 25. Since the establishment in 2006 of the Thăng Long Ca Trù Club (which later changed its identity from a club to "Giáo Phường," or "guild," for reasons described under Factor 7), Nguyễn Phú Đẹ (b. 1923) claims to have taught 30 singers and instrumentalists (Vietnamese Institute for Musicology, 2008b)—a feat that arguably would have been impossible without the infrastructure of the club. As of mid-2010, the group had around 15 students (both singers and instrumentalists) aged between 9 and 32 (Giáo Phường Ca Trù Thăng Long, 2010), one of whom is the daughter of director Phạm Thị Huệ (see Example 5.4 ◐ ◯).

According to the UNESCO nomination file, by early 2009 around 180 young people were engaged in learning *ca trù* from elderly musicians at these and similar clubs across northern Vietnam (Ministry of Culture Sports and Tourism of Vietnam, 2009, p. 5). In Hanoi, the most prominent clubs are currently the Thái Hà Ca Trù Club (formerly the Thái Hà Ca Trù Ensemble) established by Nguyễn Văn Mùi, which engages with training initiatives but remains a family-based group; Giáo Phường Ca Trù Thăng Long run by Phạm Thị Huệ, which holds regular public performances; and the Hanoi Ca Trù Club led by Lê Thị Bạch Vân, which gives monthly performances and youth classes. The latter was the first of its kind, established in 1991 explicitly to promote viability of the genre: "All was aimed at restoring this art" (Lê, 2008, p. 288).

Emanating from the 2009 inscription of *ca trù* onto UNESCO's *Urgent Safeguarding List* are extensive plans to consolidate its intergenerational transmission processes, including through further intensive classes. The UNESCO nomination file expressed the expectation that "after three years folk artists will hand down their whole art resources to the youth" (Ministry of Culture Sports and Tourism of Vietnam, 2009, p. 2). Despite high ambitions, there remain several challenges to reestablishing intergenerational transmission of the genre. Foremost, perhaps, is the fact that the ill health of master musicians, many in their 80s and 90s, disallows many of them to teach or perform. Another challenge to transmission is the preservation of prerevolutionary conventions relating to it, which are now less viable due to the lack of proficient master musicians. For Phạm Thị Huệ, for example, a traditional musician and teacher at the National Academy of Music, a lack of familial connection to *ca trù* and the lasting custom that each master hands down the art to only one student brought her significant difficulties in finding a willing teacher. She waited four years before finally securing one in 2005 (personal interview, May 7, 2009). A third impediment to intergenerational transmission has been the residual association of the genre with immoral habits in the minds of some elderly masters (Bùi T. H., personal interview with E. Wettermark, June 25, 2010; Anisensel, 2008, p. 38).

For *ca trù*, this first factor of the MVEF needs to be assessed using the grade system for emergent genres (genres that have undergone some degree of revitalization), presented in Table 5.1. Grade 3 most closely represents the current situation for *ca trù*: there are some middle-generation learners, though the genre is being reestablished primarily among young people aged from around 10 to their early 20s, through the institution of the clubs.

Factor 2: Change in the Number of Proficient Musicians

This factor assesses the change in the number of proficient *ca trù* musicians over the 5–10 years up to 2010. Standards of proficiency are a point of

Table 5.1 INTERGENERATIONAL TRANSMISSION OF CA TRÙ

Grade	Intergenerational transmission
5	The music genre is performed by all appropriate ages and is transmitted intergenerationally in an unbroken chain from older to younger generations.
4	The music genre is performed by all appropriate ages, though is not (yet) transmitted intergenerationally in an unbroken chain from older to younger generations.
3	The music genre is being reestablished among more than one appropriate generation.
2	The music genre is being reestablished among only one generation.
1	The music genre is being reestablished among only one generation, and then only partially and infrequently.

contention within the *ca trù* community; high levels of knowledge and technical skill are required before a musician is considered accomplished. In the UNESCO nomination file, the attribution of *proficient* seems to be largely reserved for elderly artists who learned the genre through traditional transmission processes of apprenticeship during the prerevolutionary era. According to that file, in 2005 there were 21 such *ca trù* musicians—17 singers and four instrumentalists, most aged in their 80s and 90s. Some have since died, and others have become too infirm to perform or teach. More recent research revealed several more elderly *ca trù* masters able to transmit the heritage (Ministry of Culture Sports and Tourism of Vietnam, 2009, p. 13), but on balance the change in number of these proficient musicians (so-defined) in the 5–10 years up to 2010 was small.

Ca trù is not an easy genre to master. Phạm Thị Huệ recalls her first encounter with it in the early 1990s: "I couldn't understand the words, I couldn't understand the music, and also the rhythm. [I felt it was] complex, too complex for me, and I never thought that I could study [this] music" (personal interview, May 7, 2009). According to researcher Defrance, learning the *ca trù* melodies does require "a long and very difficult technical apprenticeship" (2008, p. 37). Vietnamese musicologist Bùi Trọng Hiền believes that to sing *ca trù* well needs at least 5–7 years of continuous study (personal interview with E. Wettermark, June 25, 2010), and Addiss wrote that *ca trù* "is expected to take ten years of study at a minimum; the best performers have given several decades of their lives to the art" (1973, p. 31). Based on these reckonings (and the probability that many of the elderly master musicians will die during the next decade), the expectation expressed in the UNESCO nomination file that the number of heritage practitioners will double from 2009 numbers by 2015 (Ministry of Culture Sports and Tourism of Vietnam, 2009, p. 2) seems ambitious, if "heritage practitioners" is taken to mean musicians with high levels of skill and knowledge.

From these considerations, Grade 3 ("little or no change in the numbers of proficient musicians") best describes the situation for *ca trù* (Table 5.2).

Factor 3: Change in the Number of People Engaged with the Genre

This factor assesses the change in the number of people involved with *ca trù* in the 5–10 years up to 2010, whether by joining a club, taking lessons, attending rehearsals or performances, or "consuming" *ca trù* in other ways.

In the decade 2001–2010, new *ca trù* clubs, classes, festivals, workshops, recordings, and public performances all provided ways for people

Table 5.2 CHANGE IN THE NUMBER OF PROFICIENT MUSICIANS OF CA TRÙ

Grade	Change in number of proficient musicians in the past 5 to 10 years
5	Significant increase in proficient musicians
4	Moderate increase in proficient musicians
3	Little or no change in numbers of proficient musicians
2	Moderate decrease in proficient musicians
1	Significant decrease in proficient musicians
0	No proficient musicians

to engage with *ca trù*, and the number of people involved with the genre grew significantly. Festivals (including the Hanoi Ca Trù Festival in 2000, a National Ca Trù Festival in 2005, National Ca Trù Show Night in 2006, and a National Ca Trù singing contest in 2007) drew attention and interest not only from the *ca trù* community but also, to some extent, from the public. Classes were organized with the aim not to create proficient musicians but rather "to popularise ca trù" (Ministry of Culture Sports and Tourism of Vietnam, 2009, p. 9). Many of these initiatives have targeted the transmission of knowledge (rather than high-level skills) to children and youth. Phạm Thị Huệ believes this is a vital way forward for preserving or revitalizing *ca trù*, because it ensures a future audience for the genre:

> First thing I think is with the children now from 4 to 10 years, because when they grow up, if we teach them how to listen to *ca trù* music, inside they will know about [that] music. When they grow up they can be the listeners. (personal interview with H. Schippers, January 14, 2007)

Ca trù clubs continue to represent the primary mechanism through which the public may become involved in learning, or learning about, the genre. Giáo Phường Ca Trù Thăng Long, founded (as the Thăng Long Ca Trù Club) by Phạm Thị Huệ with elderly artists Nguyễn Thị Chúc and Nguyễn Phú Đẹ, is one of the most dynamic this regard. In mid-2010 its members delivered a six-week extracurricular course for 15 students at FPT University in Hanoi (a finance- and technology-focused institution), with the aim to teach students how to appreciate *ca trù* as audience members (Phạm T. H., personal communication, July 29, 2010). For a couple of years the club ran free weekly audience appreciation classes, and now continues its commitment to audience education in other ways, such as by holding regular open rehearsals and by including an educational aspect to its regular concerts. At one audience-appreciation class in December 2009, researcher Esbjörn Wettermark took the opportunity to talk to Thang,

> a young man who works at a bank in Hanoi. He said that he wanted to learn to appreciate *ca trù* because he saw it as a symbol of Hanoi, and wanted to be able to show his friends, from other parts of Vietnam, that part of Hanoian culture. Thang has no intention of learning to play *ca trù* himself, other than beating the *trong chau* [praise drum], and at home he prefers to listen to Vietnamese pop music. (2010b, pp. 76–77)

Ca trù remains a niche interest in Vietnam: the vast majority of Vietnamese people have only a superficial knowledge of it. Yet even over a three-year period up to 2010, Wettermark noted a marked change in the audience of Giáo Phường Ca Trù Thăng Long, "the present audience being much younger, and bigger, than the audience I encountered at my first performance in 2007" (2010a, p. 36). In addition to the significant increase in the number of people engaged with *ca trù* over the 5–10 years up to 2010 (indicating Grade 5 for this factor; see Table 5.3), optimism may also be warranted for the future. Initiatives emanating from inscription to UNESCO's *Urgent Safeguarding List*—including more regional and national festivals, and a plan to "disseminate and popularise" *ca trù* in high schools and universities by building extra-curricular activities, organizing talks at schools, and producing *ca trù*-related resources suitable for those students (Ministry of Culture Sports and Tourism of Vietnam, 2009, pp. 9–10)—may further grow the number of people engaged with the genre.

Table 5.3 CHANGE IN THE NUMBER OF PEOPLE ENGAGED WITH CA TRÙ

Grade	Change in number of people engaged with the genre in the past 5 to 10 years
5	Significant increase in people engaged with the genre
4	Moderate increase in people engaged with the genre
3	Little or no change in people engaged with the genre
2	Moderate decrease in people engaged with the genre
1	Significant decrease in people engaged with the genre
0	No people engaged with the genre

Factor 4: Change in the Music and Music Practices

This factor assesses change in *ca trù* over a 5–10 year period up to 2010 in three main loci: the repertoire itself; teaching and learning practices; and performance practices. A discussion of the changes in performance contexts and functions is reserved for the next factor of the MVEF, and the knowledge and skills needed for the creation, transmission and performance of *ca trù* is dealt with in Factor 8. The teaching and learning element of this factor is closely related to Factor 1, which assessed the *level* of intergenerational transmission taking place for *ca trù*. This factor incorporates an assessment of *change* in its transmission and transmission practices over time.

With regard to repertoire, *ca trù* is considered "closed": its musical melodies or "forms" (*thể*) are seen as fixed in number—though knowledge of many of them have been lost, as described in Factor 8—so the dearth of newly composed *thể* in the last decade does not represent stagnation (B. Norton, personal interview, July 26, 2010). Recent change in the *ca trù* repertoire has primarily manifested through new song texts (with concomitant adjustments to the *thể* to cater to the tonal inflections of the Vietnamese language). Many of these have been written in the free poetic form *hát nói*. In the last few years, new *hát nói* have been especially written for specific contemporary events; a striking example is *Chào Ông Bill Gates* ("To Mr. Bill Gates"), a *ca trù hát nói* composed on the occasion of Gates' visit to Vietnam (N. Nguyễn, 2008, pp. 218–220). Newly composed song texts hold greater potential to "speak" to people than prerevolution texts, which may not readily resonate with the younger generations in modern Vietnam.

With regard to methods of learning and teaching *ca trù*, the greatest innovation in recent times is certainly the continued growth of the club phenomenon, enabling, for example, several students to be taught simultaneously. In other respects, changes to transmission processes over the past decade have been relatively modest. Learning remains primarily aural, although some teachers have devised new pedagogical systems to facilitate and expedite the process (see Factor 12), and recording technology is now sometimes used for the same reasons.

During the decline of *ca trù* following the decades from 1945 on, many mechanisms for the transmission and performance of *ca trù* dissolved, such as the prerevolutionary expectation that musically talented members of families with *ca trù* lineage would continue the practice, or the social structures that allowed *ca trù* artists to live off the income from their performances. Mechanisms for systematic transmission and performance of *ca trù* have not yet been fully restored, though some efforts are being made to reclaim them. Giáo Phường Ca Trù Thăng Long, for example, has revived the prerevolutionary tradition of a graduation (*mở xiêm áo*) ceremony for students who, after three or four years of training, have reached a certain level of proficiency. Graduates are then permitted to teach in the club. In this way, with a growing number of teachers, the club hopes to be able to accept a growing number of students in coming years.

Ca trù has not yet penetrated the conservatory environment, though moves to that end have been made. As a musician and teacher working across the two contexts, Phạm Thị Huệ expresses concern about the different systems of transmission within and outside of the conservatorium, including the institutional preference for teaching through notation and the pressure on students who are required to take many subjects (personal interview, May 9, 2009). She declined an offer to teach *đàn đáy* at the National Academy of Music as she felt it was "an attempt by the academy to make ca trù into just another part of the revolutionary academy repertoire and hence tak[e] away its emotional and personal essence" (Wettermark, 2010a, p. 35). It is difficult to judge whether the institutionalization of *ca trù* would serve its viability well or ill. The institution would likely provide a more secure platform for teaching than clubs, with their minimal nonsubstantive funding and relatively limited resources. However, as Phạm clearly perceives, institutionalization holds the risk of making static a living tradition. These issues of the role music institutions play in musical transmissions are far wider and deeper than the case of *ca trù*.

Recent changes to *ca trù* performance practices have been more diverse, perhaps, than those to either repertoire or transmission processes. In 2010, a DVD was released (Norton, 2010) of music performed by Dai Lam Minh, a contemporary expanded *ca trù* ensemble situating piano, electric guitar, and electric bass alongside the *đàn đáy*, percussion, and female singers. On the matter of innovation and experimentation in performance practices, Phạm believes it important to "keep the ways the musicians were doing in the past and at the same time create something new to make the audience understand and like *ca trù*" (in Wettermark, 2010b, p. 75).

The fourth anniversary performance of Giáo Phường Ca Trù Thăng Long in Hanoi in July 2010 (at which I was present) indicates some of the new directions of the genre. Phạm and one of her younger female students performed on the *đàn đáy*, an instrument traditionally played by men. Some *ca trù* pieces featured four to six alternating solo singers, rather than the single soloist associated with *ca trù* since the early 20th century. Several *ca trù* pieces involved an expanded instrumental ensemble; others were accompanied by a reconstruction of *ca trù* dances; and yet others were from

Table 5.4 CHANGE IN THE MUSIC AND MUSIC PRACTICES OF CA TRÙ

Grade	Pace and direction of change in the music and the music practices in the last 5 to 10 years
5	Pace and direction of change in the music and associated music practices reflect significantly increased strength of the genre.
4	Pace and direction of change reflect moderately increased strength.
3	Pace and direction of change reflect little or no change in strength.
2	Pace and direction of change reflect moderately decreased strength.
1	Pace and direction of change reflect significantly decreased strength.
0	Pace and direction of change reflect no or almost no strength.

the *bát âm* repertoire, a ceremonial instrumental genre historically associated with *hát cửa đình* (Example 5.5 ◐ ◯).

It remains to be seen whether on balance the recent changes to repertoire, transmission processes, and performance practices auger well for the long-term viability of *ca trù*. The modest changes in repertoire (especially new song texts) and transmission processes (especially the infrastructure of the clubs) over the 5–10 years up to 2010, along with the innovations in performance practices during this time, may be seen to indicate the genre's ability to adapt to the changing reality of modern Vietnam, thereby indicating a moderate increase in the strength of the genre over this time (Grade 4 in Table 5.4).

Factor 5: Change in Performance Contexts and Functions

This factor looks at the changes in the social functions and performance contexts of *ca trù*, with emphasis on the 5–10 years up to 2010.

In 2005, the Hanoi Ca Trù Club was the only organization that regularly gave *ca trù* performances in Hanoi (Norton, 2005, p. 34). By 2010, the opportunities to hear *ca trù* publicly had grown considerably, with several clubs offering regular or semi-regular small-scale performances in venues ranging from private homes to *đình* (village communal houses). Schippers encountered a performance "in a small record shop where the displays were covered with black cloth to create the atmosphere of a performance space, with low tables and cushions for the audience to evoke traditional settings" (2009, p. 201). In late 2011, Giáo Phường Ca Trù Thăng Long officially launched the ongoing concert series "Ca trù comes back," comprising performances at a traditional-style house in the old quarter of Hanoi every evening of the week.

Ca trù clubs are also occasionally hired to perform at anniversary celebrations, longevity celebrations, or commemorations to honor ancestors, filling another modern socioeconomic niche for the genre. *Hát thờ* (worship singing for the ancestors of *ca trù*) still takes place in certain communities, and in recent years certain clubs in Hanoi, Lỗ Khê, and Cổ Đạm have made efforts to reestablish *hát cửa đình* in village communal houses (Văn, 2008, pp. 193–194).

Ca trù has also increasingly found a place within larger coordinated events such as festivals, competitions, and conferences. Urban and village-based festivals in particular (such as the 2005 National Ca Trù Festival in Hà Tĩnh and Hanoi) have formed a new context for the *hát chơi* repertoire. A *ca trù* competition held in Hải Dương city in 2007 drew the participation of up to twenty *ca trù* clubs, and the Hanoi Opera House has served as the venue for more than one *ca trù* related event, including the National Ca Trù Night in June 2006, in the context of an international conference on *ca trù* (Vietnamese Institute for Musicology, 2008a). Recontextualizations like these (as well as those achieved through commercial recordings and the Internet; see Factor 5) inevitably raise questions about authenticity, tradition, and innovation—issues discussed at more length in other factors of the MVEF (especially Factors 4 and 10), and more generally in earlier chapters of this book.

Another significant recent trend in context and function for *ca trù* is the expansion into the tourist market, though these ventures have not always been successful. In mid-2009 the Thăng Long Ca Trù Theatre was founded at the Museum of Vietnam Revolution by 28-year-old businesswoman Nguyen Lan Huong, in her belief that Hanoi's *ca trù* clubs were not attractive to foreigners (as reported in the local tourist paper VietnamNet Bridge). For a time the museum doubled both as the venue for the group's daily performances and as an exhibition space where visitors could learn more about *ca trù* through photos, documents, and artifacts. During a field visit in mid-2010 I heard that the theatre may have closed down; by early 2011 its website had not been updated with new events or news items for over six months, and my attempts at contact (through their over- quota web mailbox and by email) were unsuccessful. By July 2011, their website URL was defunct. Another (apparently) short-lived tourist-related enterprise was the nightly performances given by the Giáo Phường Ca Trù Thăng Long in early 2010 in a restaurant in Hanoi; this venture was discontinued at least partly due to leader Phạm Thị Huệ's discomfort at restaurant patrons eating and talking during the performances (Phạm T. H., personal communication, July 29, 2010). More successful are the group's concerts that aspire to reestablish *hát chơi* in a restored guild heritage house in the old quarter of Hanoi (the Hoàn Kiếm district). At the time of writing (mid-2013), these are taking place three times a week, and are ranked fourth out of 68 tourist attractions in Hanoi on the popular travel website TripAdvisor.

It seems probable that the expansion of *ca trù* into new performance contexts and functions, and the reclamation of some of its former ones, will continue into the immediate future. One initiative associated with the UNESCO inscription aims to restore eighteen communal houses for *hát chơi* and *hát thờ*, and in the decade up to 2020, there are plans to restore several other tangible spaces for *ca trù* performance, including worshipping houses, a palace, and a temple (Ministry of Culture Sports and Tourism of Vietnam, 2009). If the tourist-related initiatives described above continue to gain momentum, the tourist industry may represent an important new locus of performance contexts and functions of *ca trù* in coming years.

Overall, then, performance contexts and functions for *ca trù* increased over the decade leading up to 2010, warranting Grade 4 in Table 5.5. The genre is now performed in a range of contexts and for a range of functions; public performances were more frequent in 2010 than five or ten years previously, though outside of Hanoi they remain "sporadic and infrequent" (Norton, 2009, June).

Table 5.5 CHANGE IN THE PERFORMANCE CONTEXTS AND FUNCTIONS FOR CA TRÙ

Degree of endangerment	Grade	Change in performance context(s) and function(s) in the last 5 to 10 years
integral contexts and functions	5	The music genre continues to be performed in one or more regular, well-established contexts and holds integral function(s) within the community.
expanding contexts or functions	4	The music genre has expanded to new context(s) and function(s), and is performed regularly or semi-regularly.
static contexts or functions	3	Context(s) and function(s) for the music genre have remained largely static, even in relation to changing environments. The genre is performed regularly or semi-regularly.
formulaic contexts and functions	2	The music genre is performed only in irregular formulaic contexts and functions.
highly limited formulaic contexts and functions	1	The music genre is performed only on exceptional occasions in formulaic contexts and functions.
inactive	0	The music genre is not performed in any context for any function.

Factor 6: Response to Mass Media and the Music Industry

This factor examines the way *ca trù* engages with and responds to the music industry and mass media—especially print media, radio, television, and the Internet—from the local to international levels. The genre's response to the tourist industry also falls under this factor.

During the decade leading to 2010, *ca trù* was increasingly profiled on local and national television and radio, in magazines and newspapers, and within the music industry. Mid-decade, Norton referred to an "explosion" in the number of media articles, recordings, and television documentaries on *ca trù* (2005, p. 49—though he is "extremely critical" about the latter, believing they do little to increase the general understanding of the genre; personal interview, July 26, 2010). His own research on *ca trù* has been profiled through Vietnam Television's (VTV) documentary *A Westerner Loves Our Music*, aired on Vietnamese television several times since 1999 (2005, p. 49). Media cameras were plenty during the fourth anniversary performance of Giáo Phường Ca Trù Thăng Long in July 2010 (see Example 5.5 ⭕). Ducking out for a breath from the hot and crowded *đình* during the evening performance, I was an easy target for an interviewer and cameraman from a local English-language television station: "What do you think about *ca trù* music? Would you like to hear more *ca trù*?" English-language media like VietNamNet, Look at Vietnam, and the Hanoi Times have recently published dozens of articles on *ca trù*.

Several commercial *ca trù* recordings exist, including by members of the Thái Hà Ca Trù Club (e.g. *Ca Tru: The Music of North Vietnam*, 2001, and *Vietnam: Vocal Music From the Northern Plains*, 2006). While some of the labels are well distributed, the CDs in question remain a niche market and are not always readily available, even within Vietnam. Trying my luck on a street of stores selling CDs and DVDs in Hanoi in 2010, I emerged from five stores with a total of two *ca trù* CDs (invariably being first led to the shops' cartoon sections—a combined result, I suspect, of my imperfect pronunciation and the improbability of my request). From appearance, both these CDs were illegally copied; the Vietnamese music industry involves a good deal of bootlegging.

Some *ca trù* clubs are beginning to actively engage with the tourist industry, particularly in Hanoi (as described in Factor 5); this engagement is still in the experimental stages, and it is the cause of divided views within the community. Audience members at Giáo Phường Ca Trù Thăng Long's fourth anniversary performance in 2010 were invited to mark down and submit their "favorite tunes" for the evening, with a view toward helping future planning of performances. A risk in changing *ca trù* performances based on such data is that doing so may conform the genre into a tourist taste, homogenizing its style and repertoire. Expressing concern about "cheapening" the genre in this way, folklorist Tô Ngọc Thanh believes that *ca trù*'s engagement with tourism may in any case find itself restricted due to the "difficult-to-understand" nature of the genre (personal interview with H. Schippers, July 31, 2010). *Ca trù* arguably "remains an art independent of mass consumption, requiring a certain integrative knowledge" (Jähnichen, 2011, p. 152).

At the international level, the Internet is almost certainly the most powerful medium for the dissemination and promotion of *ca trù*. In 2010, a broadcast on Public Radio International's news magazine, *The World*, featured *ca trù* in popular terms ("*ca trù* songs are often full of pathos and longing about life and love, kind of like ancient Vietnamese blues") (Magistad, 2010); it was aired on over 200 radio stations in the United States and subsequently podcast (Example 5.6 ●). Perhaps the best testament to the power of the Internet to promote *ca trù* is the "Ca Trù Thăng Long" Facebook page, which has been "liked" by over 5000 people. The group also maintains its own YouTube channel (Giáo Phường Ca Trù Thăng Long, 2012a) and an extensive website with information on upcoming events, past performances, photos, and audio and video clips from their performances (Giáo Phường Ca Trù Thăng Long, 2012b). Members of at least two *ca trù* clubs have also traveled and performed abroad (the Thái Hà group to the UK, France, Belgium, the Netherlands, Japan, and Switzerland; and members of the Thăng Long Ca Trù group to Sweden and Australia), where they have been profiled in local press and media.

Beyond the challenges already described, other circumstances place some strain on *ca trù*'s engagement with media and industry. Widespread access to information and communication technology in Vietnam since the country's entry into a market economy in the late 1980s has created conditions for a young and curious public to enjoy a wide variety of mass-mediated music, but this has also been viewed as a "big barrier and a challenge to Ca trù art" (Ministry of Culture Sports and Tourism of Vietnam, 2009, p. 6), perhaps exacerbated by the fact that *ca trù* is "largely an acquired taste" offering "little satisfaction to listeners who cannot understand the poetry" (Miller, 2008, p. 192). Also, *ca trù* has struggled at times to retain a positive representation in the media. One particular instance of bad press was the reportage over a conflict that emerged in 2009 between the leaders of the Thăng Long Ca Trù Club (later Giáo Phường) and the Thăng Long Ca Trù Theatre over the similarity in names (e.g. Nguyễn Y., 2009).

On balance, though, *ca trù* demonstrates relatively constructive interaction with a range of mass media at the local and national levels; it has some representation in the music industry through commercial recordings and

Table 5.6 RESPONSE OF CA TRÙ TO MASS MEDIA AND THE MUSIC INDUSTRY

Degree of endangerment	Grade	Response to mass media and the music industry
robust	5	The genre displays significant strength in its engagement with and response to mass media and the music industry.
strong	4	The genre displays strength in its engagement with and response to mass media and the music industry.
coping	3	The genre displays an ability to cope in its engagement with and response to mass media and the music industry.
weak	2	The genre displays weakness in its engagement with and response to mass media and the music industry.
very weak	1	The genre displays significant weakness in its engagement with and response to mass media and the music industry.
unable to cope	0	The genre displays an inability to cope in its engagement with and response to mass media and the music industry.

the Internet; and its engagement with the tourist market is relatively small and experimental, but growing. Grade 3 represents the most appropriate grade level for this factor, indicating the ability of *ca trù* to cope in its engagement with, and response to, the media and music industry (see Table 5.6).

Factor 7: Infrastructure and Resources for Music Practices

This factor relates to the current infrastructure and tangible resources for the transmission and performance of *ca trù*, including professional opportunities and financial support for musicians.

One aim of Giáo Phường Ca Trù Thăng Long has been to enable *ca trù* musicians to make a living from their art—a difficult mission, not least since like most clubs it receives no government funding. To this end, in 2010 the club changed its name from Thăng Long Ca Trù Club to Giáo Phường Ca Trù Thăng Long, referring to the prerevolutionary organization of *ca trù* family lines into guilds (*giáo phường*) that managed processes of transmission and performance, set tenets for maintaining good social relations among its members, and attended to their professional interests and living conditions (Bùi T. H., 2008). For the group,

> the meaning in *giáo phường* is to care about the old masters who cannot go and perform themselves anymore, the younger musicians, who can earn money by

their singing, should give back some of that money to their masters and in turn the old masters can stay at home and teach children how to play and sing, and in this way they will develop a very tight relationship with their students. (Phạm T. H., in Wettermark, 2010b, p. 80)

Acting on this ethos, Giáo Phường Ca Trù Thăng Long returns some of the profits of its concerts to its elderly master artists Nguyễn Thị Chúc and Nguyễn Phú Đẹ (Wettermark, 2010b, p. 80). The conferral of state titles of honor like "People's Artist" is also an infrastructural mechanism in support of master artists, though as yet this scheme seems to have made little headway to this end (a circumstance discussed more under Factor 9).

While the 60-odd *ca trù* clubs (Ministry of Culture Sports and Tourism of Vietnam, 2009, p. 13) represent the primary infrastructure for teaching and learning *ca trù*, many operate without the substantive funding that would, in many cases, facilitate their sustainability. In early 2011, the leader of Giáo Phường Ca Trù Thăng Long described to me the financial status of the group as "terrible." Bùi believes those clubs without family association are particularly at risk of folding without sufficient funds (personal interview with E. Wettermark, June 25, 2010). Although the clubs may be a "great innovation" for *ca trù*,

> there has been so far no one who can think of the way to maintain activities of the clubs, to obtain the funds to support the clubs' operation and learning of the members, and to work out the schedule and the target for the members to learn. The questions have not found the answers. (Đặng, 2008, p. 539)

Further, the quality of the clubs remains variable and, unconnected now by any guild-like system, they remain relatively isolated entities with limited exchange of experience and ideas.

Potentially exacerbating the inadequacies of the club system is a lack of public and institutional recognition and support of musicians trained outside institutional contexts: "Only graduates of the conservatory system have access to the resources needed to promote their careers, including publicity, a venue to perform, and money for costumes and equipment" (Bùi T. H., in Arana, 1999, p. 120). *Ca trù* students are obliged to earn an income in other ways, leaving little time for learning the genre; many of them are also consumed with the demands of learning Western or other Vietnamese traditional genres in the conservatory environment. A lack of ensuing professional and commercial opportunities also leaves minimal incentive for people to learn *ca trù*. For these reasons, as well as the limited teaching and learning materials for *ca trù*, the genre's absence in the school education system, and a lack of the "preferential regulations and policies" that might attract students to a nonlucrative profession as *ca trù* artists (Nguyễn T. T., 2008, p. 307), the present educational-training model for *ca trù* arguably remains deficient.

Access to tangible resources has also sometimes presented a challenge for *ca trù*. In particular, appropriate performance and rehearsal venues have proven difficult for some clubs to secure at reasonable cost. Giáo Phường Ca Trù Thăng Long is one example: Time and again the club's rehearsal spaces have become unavailable, and finding new venues has sometimes been a considerable challenge. For periods at a time the group has resorted to using the private homes of its members or their relatives or friends for rehearsals and performances. Along with finances, performance space was a key factor in the dissolution after a year or two of *Am Sac Viet*, a group set up by *ca trù* singer Nguyễn Thuy Hoa, a member of the Ca Trù Thai Ha Ensemble (B. Norton, personal interview, July 26, 2010). In his examination report for the 2009 UNESCO nomination file, Norton observes that the difficulties *ca trù* clubs have had in finding appropriate venues for performance and training have hampered their efforts to teach and perform.

Access to musical instruments is another consideration in the vitality of *ca trù*. Jähnichen's observations from 1997 on the *dàn đáy* (p. 291) still remain largely true: the instrument is relatively expensive, perhaps prohibitively so for some people living in rural areas, and instrument makers are relatively few (B. Norton, personal interview, July 26, 2010). In 2008, a single *dàn đáy* in the house of an 85-year-old musician in Văn Vật village was the only remaining instrument in Nghệ An province (Nguyễn N. N., 2008, p. 232). Đặng recounts a poignant episode from his fieldwork preparing the UNESCO nomination file, during which he encountered an elderly *dàn đáy* player (b. 1923) in Bán Thạch village whose instrument had been taken from him some time earlier by another musician:

> Since then he became the instrumentalist without the instrument. In the talk with us, when he was in high spirit[s], he played the instrument with his mouth.... When we said goodbye to him, he still asked us: "if you meet Mr. Lê Thanh B. please tell him to pay me back the instrument." (Đặng, 2008, pp. 494–495)

The inscription of *ca trù* on the UNESCO safeguarding list brings some hope of improved infrastructure and resources in the next decade, with various measures planned to support musical practices, including restoration of venues for *ca trù* performance. The various tourist and music industry ventures described in Factor 5, if they gain momentum, may also help make

Table 5.7 INFRASTRUCTURE AND RESOURCES FOR CA TRÙ

Grade	Accessibility of infrastructure and resources for music practices
5	All infrastructure and resources required for creating, performing, rehearsing, and transmitting the music genre are easily available and accessible.
4	All infrastructure and resources required for creating, performing, rehearsing, and transmitting the music genre are accessible, but not necessarily easily.
3	Most but not all required infrastructure/resources are accessible.
2	Some but not all required infrastructure/resources are accessible.
1	Some required infrastructure/resources are only accessed with great difficulty.
0	Some required infrastructure/resources are completely inaccessible.

professionalism for *ca trù* musicians a more achievable goal. Nevertheless, infrastructure mechanisms for professionalism and transmission are still weak and lack substantive funding, and some of the tangible resources needed for rehearsing and transmitting *ca trù* (especially rehearsal venues and, in rural areas, *đàn đáy* instruments) remain very difficult for some sectors of the *ca trù* community to access (Grade 1 in Table 5.7).

Factor 8: Knowledge and Skills for Music Practices

This factor relates to the existence, extent, accessibility and availability of the sociocultural and musical knowledge and skills required for creating, transmitting, and performing *ca trù*—in particular, how these interrelate with knowledge of the *ca trù* repertoire, composition of new song texts, and pedagogical systems.

Relative to the repertoire of *ca trù* in the era before 1945, knowledge within the *ca trù* community of the repertoire is considerably depleted. Quantitative data on the number of *thể* ("forms" or melodies) varies, with cited figures ranging from 11 or 12 extant *thể* out of an entire repertoire of 46, to 16 out of a total of 65, to about 20 out of 56. What is clear is that the current knowledge of the full repertoire is considerably limited, though some parts of it continue to be "rediscovered through living memory of old musicians" (B. Norton, personal interview, July 26, 2010). Knowledge of the dances that once accompanied *hát cửa đình* (in the village communal houses) and *hát thờ* also remains partial and weak; some of what does remain has been used as the basis for reconstructing some of the dances.

The composition of new song texts notwithstanding (see Factor 4), obstacles exist for *ca trù* poets, musicians, and audiences in relation to the knowledge of texts. While *hát nói* composition is relatively common, few people have the skills to compose *ca trù* texts in other stricter and more elaborate poetic patterns. The *hán nôm* script in which *ca trù* texts were formerly written employs words or phrases that are difficult for modern-day native speakers to understand. Phạm reflects on the sometimes vague understanding of texts: "With *ca trù* music, sometimes I ask [my teachers] for the meaning of a song, sometimes they remember. Sometimes they know the meaning of the song—not each word exactly but the [overall] meaning" (personal interview with H. Schippers, January 17, 2007).

For *ca trù* especially, musical knowledge and skills are not only demanded of performers, learners, and teachers, but also of the audience, whose appreciation and involvement with a performance (for example by playing the praise drum) relies on an ability to understand the music and poetry. The contemporary audience typically has a limited understanding of *ca trù*; Jähnichen even believes that for the future of the genre, "the most dangerous development seems to be the growing incompetence of the audience" (2011, p. 170), which leads to changed musical practices and meanings. The drum, for example, is nowadays generally no longer performed by a *quan viên cầm chầu*—an audience member with a high social position, mastery in the *hán nôm* script, and thorough knowledge of text, music and repertoire—but rather by a member of the ensemble. Some *ca trù* musicians believe audience education, particularly about how to play the drum, may be an important way forward for vitality of the genre. Master artist Nguyễn Thị Chúc suggests the following:

> Teach the audience how to play the drum. When the people can sing in the right way . . ., the audience will like it much, but if they sing in the wrong way, then the audience will not like it. Because when they understand about *ca trù* music, they know how it's different. And when [the audience] understands about poem, about rhythm, about how to play the drum, then they will enjoy . . . *ca trù* music. (personal interview with H. Schippers [trans. Phạm T. H.], January 11, 2007)

Giáo Phường Ca Trù Thăng Long places considerable emphasis on educating the audience. Among other initiatives to this end (like the free audience education classes described in Factor 3), the group encourages audience participation during its performances, for example by playing the praise drum or adopting the historical practice of throwing wooden *trù* ("tally cards") into a metal bowl to signal enjoyment of the performance.

Theoretical knowledge of *ca trù* is limited, but this does not represent a radical change from the prerevolutionary era. Since at least the mid-20th century, knowledge of the five *cung* ("modes") used in *ca trù* has not been made explicit through research or transmission processes, and so the

Table 5.8 KNOWLEDGE AND SKILLS FOR MUSIC PRACTICES OF CA TRÙ

Grade	Accessibility of knowledge and skills for music practices
5	The community holds all knowledge and skills required for creating, performing, and transmitting the music genre, and these are easily available and accessible.
4	The community holds all required knowledge and skills, but these may not be easily available or accessible.
3	The community holds most but not all required knowledge and skills.
2	The community holds only some of the required knowledge and skills.
1	The community holds only a little of the required knowledge and skills.
0	Required knowledge and skills are almost or completely absent in the community.

current lack of conscious knowledge of them does not necessarily signal weakening vitality (Norton, 2005, p. 37). Phạm Thị Huệ observes the lack of explicit theory in the pedagogy of her teachers; she believes that making known a theory of *ca trù* may be beneficial for the genre (personal interview with H. Schippers, January 14, 2007).

In sum, the *ca trù* community has access to only some of the knowledge and skills that would indicate a fully vital genre (Grade 2 in Table 5.8). Specifically, knowledge of the repertoire is depleted, the skills needed for the creation of a diversity of song texts are rare, and audiences lack close acquaintance with the genre.

Factor 9: Governmental and Institutional Policies Affecting Music Practices

This factor assesses the impact of current government and institutional policies and attitudes relating to Vietnamese cultural heritage, traditional music genres, and *ca trù* in particular.

The Law on Cultural Heritage (National Assembly of the Socialist Republic of Vietnam, 2001) was the first explicit legal framework in Vietnam that articulated the responsibilities of the government, institutions, and individuals in protecting and promoting intangible cultural heritage. Around the same time as the Law was implemented, the attitudes of Vietnamese governmental bodies to *ca trù* began to shift, from no or limited interest in the mid-1990s to moderate or strong ideological support of the genre by the mid-2000s. In the UNESCO nomination file for *ca trù*, the Law on Cultural Heritage is invoked as the foundation on which communities, local authorities, and government agencies should construct and execute strategies toward safeguarding the genre (Ministry of Culture Sports and Tourism of Vietnam, 2009, p. 10).

In 2005, Vietnam ratified the 2003 UNESCO *Convention for the Safeguarding of Intangible Cultural Heritage*, providing a further scaffold for efforts to protect and promote traditional Vietnamese music. Both pre- and post-ratification, several traditional genres were inscribed onto UNESCO's list of *Masterpieces of Oral and Intangible Cultural Heritage in Urgent Need of Safeguarding*, including the court music of Huế (2003), the space of Central Highland's gong culture (2005), and *quan họ* folk songs (2009). *Ca trù* was successfully inscribed in late 2009. Norton (2010, July) argues that the demonstrated governmental concern for safeguarding intangible cultural heritage is inextricably linked with political ideology, propelled on the one hand by a concern for national identity, and on the other by an anxiety about the erosion of Vietnamese tradition due to the forces of globalization.

Various government and institutional bodies, operating both at a national level and within provinces that regard *ca trù* as a part of local heritage, support and nurture the genre in various ways—for example, by financing instruments and equipment, creating performance opportunities through cultural activities and festivals, and encouraging the foundation of clubs and groups. The central governmental body responsible for developing and implementing strategies to support *ca trù* and other forms of intangible cultural heritage is the national Ministry of Culture, Sports, and Tourism (formerly the Ministry of Culture and Information). This ministry is represented at the provincial level by Departments of Culture, Sports, and Tourism. The Vietnamese Institute for Musicology supports the Ministry in its strategies and initiatives for *ca trù* and other traditional genres.

Other agencies that have engaged with *ca trù* through documentation, research, or activism include the Vietnamese Institute for Hán-Nôm Studies, the Vietnam Cultural Heritage Association, and the Association of Vietnamese Folklorists. The latter is responsible for conferring the title "Master of Folklore" on highly skilled *ca trù* artists (*nghệ nhân*). By the time of the nomination of *ca trù* to UNESCO's *Urgent Safeguarding List* in 2009, no fewer than 19 artists had been honored in this way (Ministry of Culture Sports and Tourism of Vietnam, 2009, p. 11), in theory providing national recognition, financial assistance, material support, and other preferences to encourage and enable those artists to perpetuate their art and transmit their skills to the younger generation. However, some members of the *ca trù* community remain skeptical that these awards hold any real value for the master artists on whom they are conferred.

Despite what seems to be extensive government support of *ca trù*, some disquiet surrounds its involvement in the genre. One cause is the lack of deep government understanding about the best ways to approach protecting and promoting Vietnamese traditional music genres, including *ca trù* (a politically sensitive concern raised by more than one interviewee in this research). Another is the ongoing need for effective policy measures to support traditional Vietnamese music—for example, by helping traditional musicians earn their own living. A third concern relates to the limited extent of governmental consultation with the *ca trù* community about approaches for safeguarding the genre, despite heavy rhetoric in the UNESCO nomination file about the government's close community consultation.

The impact of the very inscription of *ca trù* onto UNESCO's *Urgent Safeguarding List* has also been brought into question. In relation to *ca trù*, Norton (2010, July) identifies a number of "thorny issues" concerning the unintended consequences of such top–down cultural heritage policy and plans: issues about ownership, control, and stewardship of the tradition, which sometimes fuel tensions and rivalry within the community; the fact that tradition is being reinvented "in a way that is designed to impress Vietnamese and international audiences of the value of *ca trù* as world heritage"; the concomitant risk that "deep appreciation" of the genre could be overshadowed by an emphasis on it as a Vietnamese cultural symbol; and in turn, the risk that this emphasis on cultural identity could "overshadow different points of view, which potentially limits the proliferation of diverse approaches to revival." The potentially harmful effect on music genres of international proclamations like UNESCO's is a real concern, and one that has been noted both generally and in relation to other specific genres, as described earlier in this book.

The limited freedom of expression in Vietnam in relation to traditional music practices, safeguarding mechanisms, and the quality and nature of government intervention should also be raised here. The restrictiveness was mentioned to me as a matter of concern by at least one local musician. An incident reported in the local media in relation to the traditional folk song genre *quan họ* indicates how this situation might impact on safeguarding approaches: in late 2009, researcher and employee of the Vietnam Culture and Art Institute Bùi Trọng Hiền was sanctioned for publicly expressing his belief that *quan họ* was becoming increasingly commercialized, and that the few remaining *quan họ* artists were viewed as "'natural resources' to be exploited by the *quan họ* society." His view was "severely opposed" by officials from his Institute and those from the provincial Bắc Ninh Ministry of Culture, Sports, and Tourism, who dispatched a request to the national cultural ministry that Bùi be disciplined and compelled to publicly apologize to *quan họ* artists for the offense caused by his comments (VietNamNet/Dat Viet, 2009).

Overall, governmental and institutional attitudes are presently ideologically favorable toward traditional (prerevolutionary) Vietnamese music genres like *ca trù*:

> As with many other cultural traditions that were condemned in Party documents and by officials during the revolutionary period, ca trù is no longer at odds with Party policy but is instead being aligned with it. Ca trù is increasingly being promoted as a cultural activity that contributes to the Party's aim of developing Vietnamese culture, which is "rich in national colour" (*dam da ban sac dan toc*). (Norton, 2005, p. 48)

Yet the policies that flow from that ideological support seem to be largely founded on the overarching aspiration to consolidate a national identity rather than concern about each music genre and its community, and these policies are manifest, by and large, without meaningful community consultation or significant policy differentiation between genres. Grade 4 best describes this situation (see Table 5.9).

Table 5.9 GOVERNMENTAL AND INSTITUTIONAL ATTITUDES TOWARD CA TRÙ

Degree of support	Grade	Official attitudes toward the music genre
differentiated support	5	The music genre is supported through specific cultural policies developed and implemented in consultation with culture bearers.
blanket support	4	The genre is supported through overarching policies supporting cultural expressions, without differentiation and without consultation with culture bearers.
passive assimilation	3	No explicit policy exists for supporting (or hindering) diverse cultural expressions, such as the music genre.
active assimilation	2	Implicitly or explicitly, the government encourages the abandonment of "small" or nonmainstream cultural expressions, for example by providing education only in the language and culture of the majority group.
forced assimilation	1	Government policy explicitly declares the majority group to represent the only recognized culture. "Small" or nonmainstream cultural expressions are neither recognized nor supported.
prohibition	0	Performance of the music genre is prohibited. It may be tolerated in private social contexts.

Factor 10: Community Members' Attitudes Toward the Genre

This factor relates to the attitudes toward *ca trù* of members of the *ca trù* community (in the sense of a "community of practice"). This community includes elderly masters, younger professional musicians, teachers and students, as well as audience members and locally based researchers.

In many revival movements, individuals play a critical role in driving revitalization initiatives and stimulating wider interest in the genre, and *ca trù* is no exception. Two current leading forces in the *ca trù* revival are Lê Thị Bạch Vân, scholar, singer, and founding leader of the Hanoi Ca Trù Club, who completed her master's degree on *ca trù* in 2004; and Phạm Thị Huệ, who, above and beyond her role teaching *tỳ bà* at the National Academy of Music, invests considerable time and effort managing Giáo Phường Ca Trù Thăng Long, liaising with academic and industry stakeholders, and actively generating media and public interest in *ca trù*. While Lê, Phạm, and others have personally contributed enormously to reviving *ca trù*, the central role of individuals in driving grassroots-level initiatives raises questions about the medium- to long-term sustainability of these efforts.

In principle, many members of the *ca trù* community harbor strong and enthusiastic commitment to the maintenance and revitalization of the genre. According to the UNESCO nomination file, all communities where *ca trù* is found committed their ideological support to the safeguarding measures entailed by its nomination to UNESCO's *Urgent Safeguarding List*. Also according to that file, communities called for a concrete governmental policy to support *ca trù* master artists, the organization of festivals to honor and promote the genre, the development of books and reference learning materials for *ca trù*, and "investment and guidance" from the ministries and local authorities to restore *ca trù* to former contexts. One of the examination reports for the nomination makes the observation that the number of *ca trù* musicians supporting the nomination is nearly identical with the number of *ca trù* musicians in general (International Council for Traditional Music, 2009, p. 226).

Despite the ideological commitment to the cause (perhaps also partly deriving from feelings of compulsion to comply with government decrees), community opinions about how *ca trù* should be perpetuated are by no means cohesive. The ideology of Giáo Phường Ca Trù Thăng Long—that only through wide dissemination and publicity will the genre's viability be secured—contrasts with, for example, that of the Thái Hà Ca Trù Club, which prefers to perpetuate the genre within its own close-knit family group. Quality is a major bone of contention, which may to some degree be attributed to rivalry and antagonism between the various *ca trù* groups.

Many squabbles within the community appear petty, like the copyright conflict between the Thăng Long Ca Trù Theatre and Club described in Factor 6. Following a difficult interview, Wettermark's translator suggested to him that the unwillingness of one *ca trù* musician to talk on record about how she learned or taught *ca trù* may have been due to a "fear of others stealing her methods" (E. Wettermark, personal communication, January 24, 2010). Another example of conflict within the *ca trù* community is the considerable criticism Phạm Thị Huệ has attracted for her quick transition from student to teacher, her playing the traditionally male *đàn đáy*, and the popularity of her club with the media (Wettermark, 2010b, p. 81). She has had her proficiency called into question by other *ca trù* artists on several occasions, including in a public manner at the 2010 Applied Ethnomusicology Study Group meeting of the International Council for Traditional Music in Hanoi (at which I was present), and her reinterpretation and reinstatement of terms like *hát cửa đình* and *giáo phường* have also proven provocative (Wettermark, 2010c). Arana positions the proneness of the *ca trù* community to "gossip, rumours and indignation" (Wettermark, 2010a, p. 6) within a wider political and social context in this way:

> I found their attempts [musicians and music scholars] to discredit other musicians and scholars to be revealing of how much is at stake: underlying the controversy about traditional music is a struggle for social, political, and economic power and recognition, one that is directly related to the larger political and economic forces that have affected Vietnamese society. (1999, p. 109)

Authenticity is another key locus of debate and dispute (as is often the case in music preservation and revival). Anxiety about preserving a "pure tradition" generates some conservative views on what is "authentic." Nguyễn Thế Thanh, director of the Thai Binh Culture and Information Department, has called for scholarly care to be taken "to accurately define original Ca trù tunes, to sort out borrowed ones, and to bravely reject the mixed tunes that have negative effects on Ca trù's artistic quality" (2008, pp. 305–306). Nguyễn Quảng Tuân, member of the Scientific Council of the Centre of National Culture Research, believes the audience size for *ca trù* performances should be limited to "a small group, and they must be absolutely silent for co-enjoyment" (2008, p. 115). Folklorist Tô Ngọc Thanh, urging for retention of "the authenticity of the past," laments the fact that some members of the *ca trù* community are composing new pieces: "Music

Table 5.10 COMMUNITY MEMBERS' ATTITUDES TOWARD CA TRÙ

Grade	Community members' attitudes toward the music genre
5	Community support for the maintenance of the music genre is very strong.
4	Community support for the maintenance of the music genre is strong.
3	Community support for the maintenance of the music genre is moderate.
2	Community support for the maintenance of the music genre is weak.
1	Community support for the maintenance of the music genre is minimal.
0	No community members support the maintenance of the genre.

à đào is something stable; [a] stable form. If now you modify [it], in fact it damages" (personal interview with H. Schippers, July 31, 2010).

These kinds of views conflict with the approach of certain other sectors of the *ca trù* community, which are more ready to experiment and adapt *ca trù* practices to suit contemporary Vietnamese audiences and society (see Factor 4). Phó Đức Phương, deputy president of Vietnam Hanoi Composers Association, apparently holds a considerably flexible view on authenticity and tradition: a YouTube video of singer Ngọc Hạ performing his composition *Tren Dinh Phu Van* ("On the mountain peak full of cloud") is an astonishingly eclectic mix of contemporary styles, theatrical dance, Tibetan chant, and *ca trù*, replete with backdrop and colored lighting effects (Ngọc, 2012). Similar examples of experimentation and adaptation are numerous.

In general, community attitudes to *ca trù* and its revitalization are in principle very strong, but the community is disempowered by its lack of solidarity. Overall, then, while ideological support for the maintenance of *ca trù* might be assigned a Grade 5, the splintering of community attitudes with respect to the genre and its future means that Grade 4 may more accurately represent the state of *ca trù* for this factor (see Table 5.10).

Factor 11: Relevant Outsiders' Attitudes Toward the Genre

This factor examines the attitudes of researchers, academics, students, fieldworkers, commercial agencies, funding bodies, and nongovernmental organizations located outside of the *ca trù* community toward *ca trù*, the way they interact and engage with the genre, and the effect this has on its vitality and viability. For purposes of this assessment, the focus lies on engagement with *ca trù* from outside Vietnam, given that Vietnamese-based association with the genre largely falls either under the realm of the *ca trù* community

(Factor 10), or of government and institutions (Factor 9). For this reason too, this factor does not address UNESCO's support of the genre, which is a direct consequence of community and government activism.

Individual foreign researchers have played a significant role in promoting and disseminating information about *ca trù* especially since the mid- to late-1990s, when Barley Norton (UK) completed a master's thesis on the genre (subsequently published, 1996) and Gisa Jähnichen (Germany), a *Habilitationsschrift* (1997). Both these researchers subsequently served on the examination panel for the UNESCO nomination of *ca trù* (Jähnichen in the capacity of representative of the International Council for Traditional Music). In the last decade, several postgraduate research students have investigated *ca trù*, including Aliénor Anisensel (France), Esbjörn Wettermark (Sweden/United Kingdom), and Bretton Dimick (United States). Like American ethnomusicologist Stephen Addiss some decades earlier (who found the *đàn đáy* "a fascinating if difficult instrument"; 1973, p. 19), Anisensel, Jähnichen, and Norton all learned and performed *ca trù* during their research. The latter has described himself as adopting an "unashamedly interventionist stance" in the *ca trù* revival (2008, p. 188).

Expatriate musicologist Trần Văn Khê played an activist role at the start of the *ca trù* revival era in the early 1990s, convincing authorities "that *hát à đào* represents a vital part of Vietnamese culture, that it is appreciated abroad, and that it has an important role to play in present and future Vietnamese musical performance" (Addiss, 1992, p. 205). Trần Văn Khê also played a key role bringing *ca trù* to wider international attention in the 1970s (as described in Section 6.1), and acted as an advisor in the preparatory stages of the UNESCO nomination. Other notable externally based researchers of *ca trù* have included former president of the French Ethnology Association Yves Defrance, and director of Queensland Conservatorium Research Centre Huib Schippers, whose first encounters with *ca trù* in 2006 partly inspired the *Sustainable Futures for Music Cultures* research project.

At an organizational level, various funding agencies have gone a long distance in supporting the *ca trù* community to achieve their short- and medium- term goals in relation to the transmission and promulgation of the genre. From 2006, the Centre of Educational Exchange with Vietnam sponsored a two-year youth training program for *ca trù*; in 2009 the Odon Vallet Scholarship Fund (founded by the France-based *Rencontres du Vietnam*) granted 10 scholarships to students of Giáo Phường Ca Trù Thăng Long to support their living expenses and music studies (Phạm T. H., personal communication, December 23, 2010); and the Ford Foundation sponsored both the 2002 *ca trù* transmission program (described under Factor 1) and the 2005 national *ca trù* festival. Back in 1996, the Ford Foundation had established a grant scheme supporting documentation and preservation of Vietnamese cultural traditions, but as a result of the global economic downturn, it closed its operations in Vietnam, including the grant scheme, in 2009.

Two nongovernmental organizations in particular display a level of commitment to *ca trù* that moves beyond financial support. Through its program *Supporting Vietnamese Culture for Sustainable Development*, the Swedish International Development Cooperation Agency (SIDA) has supported collaboration and exchange between Vietnam National Academy of Music/Vietnamese Institute for Musicology and the Malmö Academy of Music (University of Lund, Sweden), which has included international exchanges, research collaborations, workshops and classes, and promotional projects for *ca trù*. Another organizational interest in *ca trù* is that of Queensland Conservatorium Research Centre (Griffith University, Brisbane, Australia) which investigated the genre as a case study for its *Sustainable Futures* project.

The attitudes to the genre of relevant outsiders—individuals, funding bodies, and research institutes and other nongovernment organizations—are generally positive. In a circular way, outside interest (both individual and organizational) has been a source of pride and curiosity for the *ca trù* community, stimulating local interest in the genre (see Norton, 2009, pp. 13–14). However, the number of organizations that have demonstrated genuine and ongoing commitment to the viability of the genre is still relatively small, and most funding is granted on a non-substantive basis. Potential remains for more, and better, outsider support. Taking this into account, *ca trù* may be assigned a Grade 4 for this factor (see Table 5.11).

Table 5.11 RELEVANT OUTSIDERS' ATTITUDES TOWARD CA TRÙ

Grade	Relevant outsiders' attitudes toward the music genre
5	Support of the music genre by relevant outsiders is very strong.
4	Support of the music genre by relevant outsiders is strong.
3	Support of the music genre by relevant outsiders is moderate.
2	Support of the music genre by relevant outsiders is weak.
1	Support of the music genre by relevant outsiders is minimal.
0	Support of the music genre by relevant outsiders is absent altogether, or attitudes to the genre are adverse.

Factor 12: Amount and Quality of Documentation

This factor relates to the extent and quality of documentation and research on *ca trù*, including written materials and recordings, as well as the accessibility of archived materials. As a form of documentation, the issue of notation is also addressed here.

The groundswell of interest in *ca trù* since the early 2000s and the intention to nominate *ca trù* to UNESCO's *Urgent Safeguarding List* led to a flurry of documentation and research initiatives on the genre. Recent research into *ca trù* has drawn on temple engravings, epitaphs, family annals, stele, poetry compilations, instruments, guild contracts, and photographs to try to reconstruct a history of the genre. In collaboration with researchers, provincial cultural government departments, and the local communities where *ca trù* exists, the Vietnamese Institute for Musicology now compiles and manages an annual inventory of *ca trù* heritage (including artists, dances, *ca trù* activities, "vestiges," objects, and written documentation). Đặng, Phạm, and Hồ list 70 books, articles, and other resources relating to *ca trù* held at the library of the Institute in Hanoi (2008, pp. 657–662).

Nevertheless, knowledge about the history, repertoire, and musical practices of *ca trù* from the era before economic reform in the late 1980s remains relatively limited. Associated dance forms are poorly documented, and many of them have been lost altogether (notwithstanding some limited reconstruction based on the existing documentation). Some published research attempts a comprehensive account of aspects of existing knowledge, like Vũ Nhật Thăng's musicological "grammar" of *ca trù* and his itemization and classification of its repertoire (2008). Some knowledge of the historical anecdotes and legends surrounding *ca trù* enrich understanding of the genre (outlined, for example, in Nguyễn X. D., 2008). Archival *ca trù* recordings exist from as long ago as 1935 (Norton, 2005, p. 53), though in the early 1970s Addiss observed that the only one available was half an LP he himself made (1973, p. 28), and in the late 1990s Jähnichen lamented the lack of access to *ca trù* recordings older than 30 years (1997, p. 101).

Aside from the shortcomings of the historical documentation available on *ca trù*, researchers have also expressed concern over the imprecision and inaccuracy of recent research on the genre. Nguyễn Thụy Loan (2008) calls for great care when basing research on existing documentation, and even suggests a reappraisal of sources. She singles out the dubious quality of research in two 2005 issues of the Vietnamese Institute for Musicology bulletin, special issues on *ca trù* that Wettermark describes as "at the best vague but in many cases contradictory and at times next to incomprehensible" (2010a, p. 24). Nguyễn pleads:

> A person can be wrong. Many people can be wrong. However, in capacity of a government's research organization, the *Bulletin,* and the *Special issues on Ca trù* of an Institute majoring in music researches, they should try to minimize the untrue informations [sic]. [This] is because when a national-level Institute gives information in such above special issues, many researchers will think that those have been appraised and are reliable informations. As a result, it will be good if those given informations are correct and vice versa. (2008, p. 280)

The very volume in which Nguyễn's paper is published (Ministry of Culture Sports and Tourism of Vietnam et al., 2008) arguably exemplifies her concerns about the quality of documentation on *ca trù*. Many of its papers lack reference lists; important information, such as names of the musicians in photographs, is missing; and the English translation is often unclear or dubious (witness one author's hope that *ca trù* be recognized as "immaterial heritage"; p. 242).

According to Norton (1996), the only "indigenous" written notation for *ca trù* is the characters (and their roman-script equivalents) for the vocal mnemonic system that exists for the *đàn đáy*, as well as a verbal mnemonic system for the drum strokes; both are used in teaching. Although *ca trù* remains orally transmitted, several musicians and scholars have devised or explored ways to notate it, most to a pedagogical end, like *ca trù* singer Phó Thị Kim Đức—"so in the future if we need to teach we have something" (Phó T. K. D., personal interview with E. Wettermark, July 5, 2010). Phạm Thị Huệ found sol-fa notation of *ca trù* helpful in her own learning (personal interview with H. Schippers, January 17, 2007). Both Norton (1996, 2005) and Addiss (1992) employ an adaptation of Western staff notation in their musical analyses, and in collaboration with *ca trù* musicians, Jähnichen (1997) worked out her own system of notation for practical and pedagogical purposes. No standardized way to notate *ca trù* exists, and no single system has been used to document the repertoire.

Plans to document what remains of *ca trù* are extensive. The UNESCO nomination file states an ambition to audio- and video-record "30 different musical forms of singing and 8 dances in Ca trù performed by 12 senior folk artists from 14 cities and provinces" in the coming years, with the support of the Vietnamese Institute for Musicology (Ministry of Culture Sports and Tourism of Vietnam, 2009, p. 7). Funds will also be put toward researching and publishing resources on *ca trù*, including educational textbooks,

Table 5.12 AMOUNT AND QUALITY OF DOCUMENTATION OF CA TRÙ

Nature of documentation	Grade	Documentation of the music genre
superlative	5	Abundant high-quality documentation exists in a range of formats, including audiovisual.
good	4	Adequate high-quality documentation exists.
fair	3	Adequate documentation exists in varying quality.
fragmentary	2	Limited documentation exists in varying quality.
inadequate	1	Documentation is very limited or is of unusable quality.
undocumented	0	Documentation is nonexistent.

musicological analyses, translation of prior research, a collection of *ca trù* songs, and a DVD.

In short, while the situation seems poised to improve in the short-term future, current documentation of *ca trù* is of variable quality, and relative to the complete repertoire, history, and social practices of *ca trù*, its quantity is limited (Grade 2 in Table 5.12).

5.4 CONCLUSIONS

Overall, this case study assessment of *ca trù* according to the Music Vitality and Endangerment Framework (MVEF) points to a genre very strong in some ways, but considerably weak in others. Figure 5.1 synthesizes the findings of this chapter.

According to the MVEF assessment, *ca trù* performs well or very well in six out of the twelve factors in the vitality of a music genre. A very strong factor in its vitality is the change in the proportion of people engaged with it in recent years. *Ca trù* also displays strength in its development of new performance contexts, functions, and music practices over the last decade or so, and through the changes in the music itself. The attitudes held toward it—by government and institutions, by outsiders, and by its own community—are also generally positive for its vitality.

While *ca trù* displays moderate vitality through the strength of its intergenerational transmission, through its response to media and industry, and through the change in number of proficient musicians in the past five to ten years, it rates relatively poorly in two other factors: the accessibility of required knowledge and skills for creating, learning, teaching, and performing; and the amount and quality of its documentation. The single

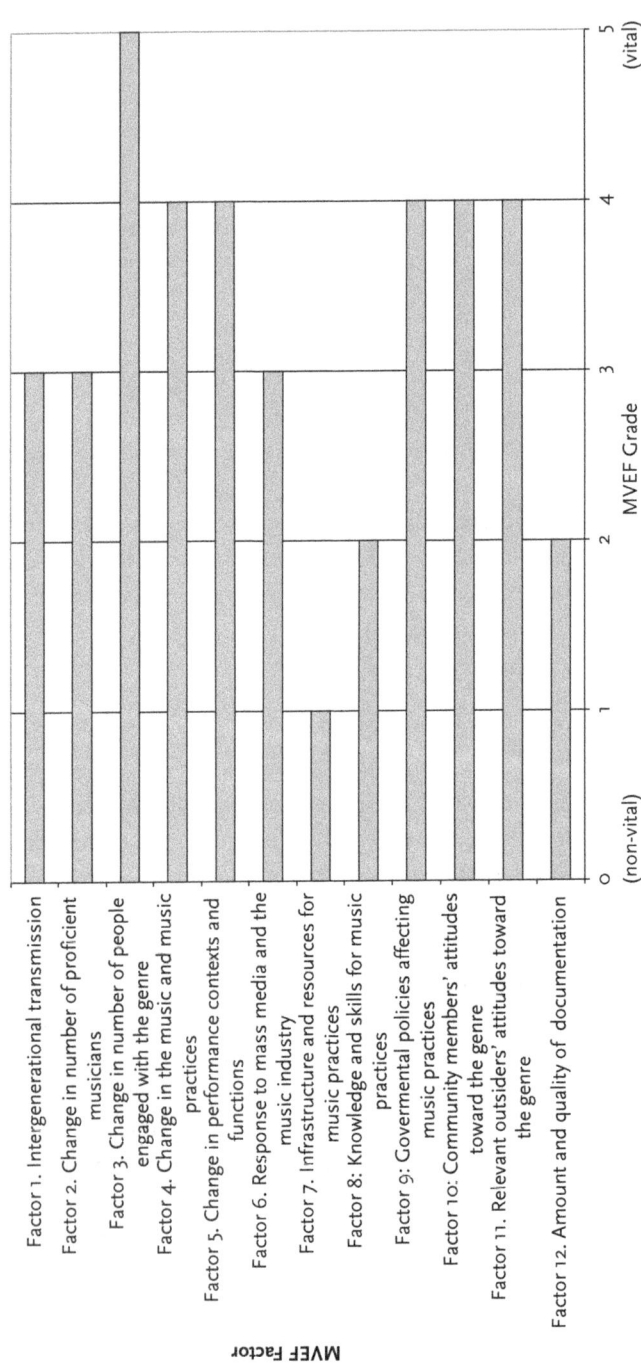

Figure 5.1 Summative assessment of ca trù according to the MVEF

factor for which *ca trù* rated very poorly relates to the availability and accessibility of infrastructure and tangible resources. On none of the factors was *ca trù* completely nonvital.

Approaches suggested by researchers, officials, and activists to boost the vitality and viability of *ca trù* diverge vastly in nature, from those directed toward better organization and management of *ca trù* activities, to greater media and public profiling of the genre, annual festivals, further research, supportive governmental regulations and policies, and professional music education and training. It stands to reason (though should not be uncritically assumed) that sustainability initiatives might most appropriately target the factors in musical vitality where the genre is weakest (that is, Factors 7, 8, and 12). It is beyond my intention here to determine whether that is currently the case, or to what extent, though this could be relatively easily done by cross-mapping the aims of those sustainability initiatives against the twelve factors of the MVEF, and inspecting the correlation.

The primary purpose of this chapter has been to demonstrate how the MVEF might work in practice and to implicitly uncover some of the challenges of applying a preexisting evaluative tool onto a distinct sociocultural, economic, and political environment. Although it by no means explores all the nuanced dynamics of *ca trù*, this case study underscores how the vitality of the genre interrelates in complex ways with modern-day realities in Vietnam. In the concluding chapter, I reflect in general terms on the process of mapping these case study data onto the 12 preexisting factors of the MVEF, and I suggest in more depth how assessments like the one presented in this chapter might provide a knowledge base on which appropriate strategies supporting the sustainability of music genres like *ca trù* may be built.

CHAPTER 6

Where to From Here?

In some ways, the prospects for fostering vibrant, viable music genres do not appear especially encouraging. Despite the extent of the threat to intangible expressions of culture across the world, public awareness of music endangerment remains limited, meaning that ideological and practical support for sustainability initiatives is not as readily available as it might otherwise be. Scholarly understanding of the issues, though growing, is incipient. The evidence presented in the Introduction to this book suggests that meanwhile, many music genres, like many languages, continue to undergo rapid decline. Some of them are already lost altogether, despite (or sometimes without) their communities' efforts to maintain them. The fast-changing global environment continues to present constant challenges and threats to the sustainability of particular music genres, and efforts to support them.

On the other hand, there are many indications that a positive shift is afoot. The body of research on music sustainability is growing, redolent of the surge of research into language endangerment and maintenance in the early 1990s. Local projects and initiatives are demonstrably bolstering the vitality of specific music genres around the world. Importantly too, many ethnomusicologists are keenly aware of the urgent need to actively support communities to keep their music strong. In a post to the Society for Ethnomusicology e-list, one scholar observed: "There are countless cultural traditions around the world—and close to home—that are dying with each passing minute. Let us agree to get 'out there' and do our part to keep them alive" (H. Chami, June 12, 2011). Another list member directly responded: "If there's anything we have lost sight of, perhaps it is just this" (J. Cohen, June 15, 2011).

The role of ethnomusicologists in music sustainability has run as a recurring, but often implicit, theme throughout this book. One of the key dilemmas facing ethnomusicologists in relation to sustainability seems to be how to resolve the tension (real or perceived) between local and global approaches. On the one hand, it makes sense for researchers to foreground the local in their work on music sustainability, since arguably "we can only really be knowledgeable about those places in which we're doing our research.... Those are the spaces where there might be potential for us as researchers to be concerned about what's challenging the musical environment" (T. Ramnarine, personal interview, March 16, 2011). If this is so, ethnomusicologists engaging in the cause of music sustainability "can only really operate at a community level, because that enables close contact and really responding to what any particular musician wants at a particular moment in time" (T. Ramnarine, personal interview, March 16, 2011).

Yet a strong case can be made for ethnomusicologists to approach sustainability from a wider perspective than the local. The issue of limited human and financial resources for sustainability efforts has arisen at several points in these pages, including the unlikelihood that ethnomusicologists will be able to work with each and every endangered-music community that wishes for, and might benefit from, outsider support. The problem of resources is compounded by the fact that it is marginalized and disadvantaged communities that are most likely to be facing cultural pressures, yet also most likely to lack the resources or knowledge to be able to take matters into their own hands. The Australian context is an egregious example, where the few remaining Aboriginal ceremonial traditions are in such a critical state that they may not survive for more than another generation or two (Marett, 2010, p. 253). The combination of these two factors—the extent of the problem and the limited resources available to remedy it—may lead some to believe that, at the wide-scale at least, "sustainability is just too hard, because there's too few of us to do it" (M. Kartomi, personal interview, October 21, 2010).

This is only true in the most general sense, however, and it does not mean that nothing can or should be done to support endangered music genres. One argument that runs as a thread throughout this book is that a strategic, coordinated approach to sustainability efforts may maximize outcomes. Rather than working on a reactive basis, adopting a proactive, coordinated approach to sustainability is more likely to strengthen the collective visibility and impact of local efforts, while minimizing the adverse effect of limited resources. In this way, sustainability efforts may be carried forward *simultaneously* at the grassroots and the wider regional, transnational, or even international levels. Various possibilities for communicating widely the experiences gained from grassroots initiatives, for collaborating and sharing ideas, and for supporting "good practice" in music sustainability initiatives have been explored in earlier chapters, such as the ethical guidelines and models, research hubs, and resource networks presented in Chapter 3. Some of these arise again in the recommendations for action later in this chapter. In this way, I hope this book points to the benefit of a new, integrated approach to music sustainability that holds the greatest promise for the future of endangered music genres.

6.1 TAKING STOCK: A BRIEF SUMMARY

The overarching aim of this book was to suggest ways in which language maintenance might inform efforts to support music sustainability. In the Introduction, I identified four objectives as stepping-stones along the way. Revisiting each of these objectives helps take stock of earlier chapters of this book.

> Objective 1: To identify and appraise the range of current theory and practice relating to the vitality and viability of music genres.

In the first chapter, I identified four areas of ethnomusicological research that relate closely to theory of music sustainability: globalization and musical diversity, musical transculturation and change, music revivals, and ecological models for sustainability. I also described a range of practical sustainability initiatives, grouped into five categories: documentation and preservation, recognition and celebration, transmission and dissemination, policy and enterprise, and coordination and evaluation mechanisms.

In the discussion, I proposed that the field of music sustainability displays a number of strengths at both the theoretical and practical levels. Theoretical frameworks exist to describe processes of musical transculturation, change, and revival, as well as musical diversity and the effect of globalization on small music genres. Ecological models give insight into the dynamics of cultural sustainability. Ethical principles in undertaking applied ethnomusicological research are keenly understood and foregrounded within the discipline. Recent projects on music sustainability signal a disciplinary readiness to actively engage with the issues. A number of successful strategies hold promise to inform future sustainability efforts (particularly in relation to documentation and archiving, festivals, and transmission). Finally, a number of nonmusic-specific mechanisms help coordinate and monitor sustainability efforts, such as UNESCO's various schemes in support of safeguarding cultural heritage.

I also identified five areas of current theory and practice of music sustainability that would benefit substantially from further development: (1) the need for a systematic way to identify and assess endangerment; (2) the need to develop advocacy arguments for music sustainability efforts; (3) the need to develop understanding of effective approaches to maintenance and revitalization; (4) the need to critically reflect on possible unexpected or equivocal outcomes of sustainability efforts; and (5) the need to develop music-specific measures that coordinate and carry forward music sustainability efforts. Many of these areas already have some basis in the ethnomusicological literature and practice. I also suggested in Chapter 1 that an understanding of the threats to the viability of specific music genres would be crucial in order to develop appropriate and feasible sustainability strategies for those genres. These threats include some that are likely to fall beyond the immediate control of researchers or communities, such as the potentially adverse impact on community music practices of mass media or commercial enterprises, overpowering political or legislative forces, and limited funding and resources for cultural maintenance initiatives.

> Objective 2: To identify the similarities and differences between music and languages in relation to their vitality and viability.

Founded on an analysis of the synergies and disjunctions between languages and music in relation to factors in their vitality and viability, Chapter 2 resulted in a *Comparative Framework* relating the two (summarized in Table 2.1). The framework revealed many parallels between language and music in relation to their vitality and viability. A close relationship exists, for example, between the vitality of both a music genre and a language and the attitudes of the community toward it. For both languages and music, the effect of socioeconomic and political circumstances on vitality can be substantial, and sustainability efforts themselves can sometimes have a profound impact on their vitality (whether adverse or beneficial). Language and music also share certain core characteristics in relation to the processes of their transmission.

The *Comparative Framework* also highlighted a number of areas where language maintenance is less likely to be able to appropriately inform research into music sustainability. Considerable differences between the sustainability of languages and music genres include the social functions each serves, the social contexts within which each is typically located, and the role of industry and commerce in their vitality. These dissimilarities need to be taken into account, since, as Nettl has observed:

> Uncritical attempts to use methods from linguistics at random on music often fail; the similarities between music and language are important, but the two differ in essence and at many levels.... [T]aking what is helpful...and leaving what is not seems more hopeful than the insistence on analogy. (2005, pp. 310–311)

By identifying the similarities and disconnects between language and music sustainability, the *Comparative Framework* forms a foundation for understanding the theoretical and pragmatic ways in which language maintenance may—and probably cannot—inform approaches to maintaining and revitalizing music genres.

> Objective 3: To propose ways in which theoretical and practical approaches to language maintenance and revitalization may help repair the key gaps and weaknesses of current approaches for music.

In Chapter 3, I proposed several concrete ways in which theory and practice of language maintenance may help inform ways to address a number of key gaps and weaknesses of current approaches to music sustainability. First, a range of tools from language maintenance were explored that might serve as models for assessing music endangerment, including UNESCO's *Language Vitality and Endangerment* framework. Second, I presented a number of approaches to (and arguments from) advocacy for language maintenance, and I suggested how recourse to these may be useful for music sustainability. Third, I offered some examples of linguists' theories about successful language maintenance strategies, argued that further development of theory by ethnomusicologists would refine knowledge about the desirable preconditions for successful music sustainability strategies, and proposed some likely preconditions based on theory from language maintenance. Fourth, I explored how linguists approach the dilemmas of the inefficacy and unexpected outcomes of language maintenance strategies, and I suggested that their approaches may help ethnomusicologists define realistic aims and outcomes of music sustainability strategies. Finally, I argued that specific coordinating mechanisms for language maintenance represent potentially valuable prototypes and infrastructure for music-specific coordinating mechanisms. Language maintenance thus demonstrated potential to inform all five issues in music sustainability under consideration.

In that chapter I also suggested that ethnomusicology might benefit not only from dialogue with the theoretical, philosophical, and practical experience of linguists, but also from the ethical discourse surrounding language maintenance. Ethical issues presenting to the researcher in situations of endangerment, the role of outsiders in sustainability and sustainability efforts, approaches to community attitudes toward tradition and authenticity, and perspectives on the various "failures" and unexpected outcomes of language maintenance activities all provide road maps for those working to support music sustainability. Also instructive is the vigor and commitment of linguists (and culture bearers themselves) in the face of the significant challenges—suggesting that efforts to sustain endangered music genres might need to be approached with a similar "pessimism of the intellect and optimism of the will" (to echo Antonio Gramsci's famous words).

> Objective 4: To provide a concrete example of how theory from the field of language maintenance could be adapted for use with music.

The later chapters of this book developed and illustrated a methodology for assessing musical vitality, based on an existing methodology for assessing language vitality. They therefore provide a concrete example of how language maintenance theory may be adapted for use with music. The *Music Vitality and Endangerment Framework* (MVEF) presented in Chapter 4 is a systematic, replicable means of identifying and assessing the vitality of any music genre. Assessing a genre according to the twelve factors of the MVEF leads to an understanding of the genre's overall vitality, as well as specific factors that may be contributing to its endangerment. Deploying this single methodology will enable vitality comparisons to be made between genres, which until now have been difficult. The MVEF also provides a way to measure trends in music vitality over time.

In Chapter 5, I employed the MVEF to assess the level of vitality of a specific music genre, Vietnamese *ca trù*, by appraising its strength against each of the MVEF's twelve factors. While the representation of the vitality of *ca trù* generated by the case study indicates potential for employing the MVEF in other contexts, the process of applying a single evaluative framework to a diversity of cultural, social, economic, political, and geographic circumstances is likely to generate challenges. With this in mind, in the next section I make some specific recommendations for further implementing the MVEF.

6.2 NEXT STEPS IN PRACTICAL TERMS

Despite the existence of many local projects aiming to support the vitality of specific music genres, the limited coordinated response to musical endangerment heightens the risk of reinventing the wheel, with a concomitant waste of energy, knowledge, and resources. For this reason, the recommendations I make here for future efforts in music sustainability emphasize *consolidated response* to music endangerment, particularly creating synergies between stakeholders across the world (including communities themselves). By consolidated response, I certainly do not mean that responses to situations of endangerment should be the same the world over; indeed, a diversity of responses is both warranted and necessary. I am referring rather to a coordinated, systematic way to determine which response is most appropriate in a given case, and how to go about implementing it.

All six recommendations I make here flow directly from the discussion in previous chapters; implementing them over the next few years would seem a worthwhile investment in the cause of endangered music genres.

1. **Develop a tool** that permits systematic identification and assessment of situations of music endangerment, suitable for use across the range of global contexts. The need for such a tool has already been described: it could help identify endangered genres, help determine the extent of global musical endangerment, increase knowledge of the factors contributing to endangerment, enable appropriate response strategies to be developed and evaluated, and enable better monitoring of changes in vitality. Chapter 4 of this book presents one possible realization of this recommendation—the *Music Vitality and Endangerment Framework* (MVEF).
2. **Undertake a scoping study** to advance knowledge of the extent of musical endangerment globally (using a vitality assessment tool like the MVEF, and a methodology such as a survey-questionnaire), realized with the input of experienced ethnomusicologists with strong regional expertise and networks. This recommendation arises from the observation that existing knowledge about music endangerment remains relatively piecemeal.
3. **Implement a public advocacy initiative** on a continuing basis, with the aim of promoting general awareness of the extent, causes, and consequences of musical endangerment. This recommendation is based on the proposition that public awareness and support for the cause of music sustainability will play an important role in the success of efforts to counter endangerment.

4. **Within the discipline of ethnomusicology, promote the need for consolidated response** to the situation of musical endangerment, for example through training and education, conferences, workshops, and published research. This recommendation stems from the understanding that scholarly action and activism has been a critical part of language maintenance successes, and that the same is likely to hold for music.
5. **Establish a music-specific resource network** to act as an international hub for knowledge and resources about strategies and approaches that support endangered music genres. This initiative is already planned as an outcome of the *Sustainable Futures for Music Cultures* project (QCRC, 2013), and a number of resource networks relating to cultural and linguistic sustainability already exist. A music-specific resource network would help maximize effective use of energy, resources, and experience in music sustainability.
6. **Develop an independent, international nonprofit foundation** to support the sustainability of endangered music genres, building on and consolidating (for music) the work already carried out in this area by organizations such as UNESCO. This recommendation arises from the suggestion that a music-specific body for sustainability could serve to monitor, evaluate, coordinate and carry forward music sustainability efforts at an international level.

These recommendations flow into each other; in fact, all six could be implemented progressively. As each step is implemented, its processes and outcomes will inform approaches to implementing later steps. The order presented is not the only possibility: Recommendations 3 and 4, on advocacy and consolidated response, may be undertaken simultaneously, for example, and the resource network listed as Recommendation 5 could be set up at any time.

I wish to comment at more length specifically on Recommendation 2, which suggests undertaking a scoping study on music endangerment, using an assessment tool like the MVEF. I elaborate on this recommendation here partly because it is the logical next step for implementation, but also because the previous two chapters of this book raised, but did not respond to, certain fundamental questions relating to it.

As described in Chapter 4, the MVEF is based on the UNESCO *Language Vitality and Endangerment* framework. To make this framework operational, UNESCO developed a questionnaire based on it (UNESCO, 2006; Example 6.1 ⦿), which was then disseminated online and through various networks, inviting responses from linguists and community members.

Over a three-year period (2006–2009), 300 surveys were collected (105 of them from China). While data obtained in this way have somewhat progressed understanding of the situation of these languages (informing updates to UNESCO's landmark *Atlas of the World's Languages in Danger of Disappearing*, for example), linguists have expressed various reservations about the questionnaire. Some of these are detailed in the subsequent background paper released by UNESCO that reflected on the success of the *Language Vitality and Endangerment* methodology and associated data collection (UNESCO Culture Sector, 2011).

Apart from its length (24 questions plus sub-questions) and "a certain degree of ambiguity" in definitions of terms and phrasing of questions (UNESCO Culture Sector, 2011, p. 9), one criticism that has been raised about the questionnaire is that its very format does not allow for the true complexity of a situation to be revealed. It ignores (for example) that respondents' own claims about their language reflect "the ideological and political positions that players in the language game are playing" (P. Austin, personal interview, June 16, 2010), and it leaves open the risk of respondents overestimating, or underestimating, their own language skills or usage. A third potential concern (raised by Ramnarine in relation to music) is that it is difficult for outsiders to gauge the changes in vitality of a music genre based on data gathered at any one point in time:

> I think it's very difficult for a researcher to enter a music scene at a particular moment and then talk about whether or not it needs to be sustained, or what the situation of the tradition is—because researchers don't necessarily have that longer-term perspective.... [W]hat you determine might be happening might not be what's happening at all. (personal interview, March 16, 2011)

There are at least two possible responses to these concerns about method in undertaking vitality assessments. One is for a researcher to spend an extended period of time with a community to come to a thorough understanding of the situation at hand, including political, ideological, and other noncultural dimensions. In the words of one linguist,

> you have to work with the community for a long time...to really know what's happening with the language. If you take peoples' reports, self-reports, other reports, at face value, you might not have an accurate [assessment]. (J. Sallabank, personal interview, June 17, 2010)

While long-term ethnographic work may yield accurate data on sustainability, a considerable disadvantage of this approach is that it demands the focused and extended devotion of one researcher within a single community. Given the extent of cultural endangerment, the urgency to remedy it, and the limited human and financial resources to do so, this is a significant drawback. This again underscores the importance of collaboration, as well as of lobbying governments, funding agencies, and other stakeholders for support to undertake high-quality research on music sustainability.

In situations where a community wishes to engage in coordinated sustainability efforts but lacks a researcher to work with, an alternative approach would be to empower the community to undertake its own assessments of musical vitality—an arguably preferable approach in any case. The training that may be needed for communities to carry out assessments using a questionnaire methodology (and to ensure data are comparable across contexts) might be realized in a number of ways: by running local or regional workshops and/or providing online guidance, for example. Building the capacity of communities to undertake their own music vitality assessments is likely to cost significantly less than the alternative of researchers carrying out extensive fieldwork within individual communities. It is also likely to expand the possible depth of research by obviating the need for scholarly expertise to gather data: after all, it is the culture bearers themselves who are most likely to have the deepest understanding of the vitality or endangerment of their music. Perhaps most importantly of all, this approach prioritizes the ethical principle of the "First Voice" (Galla, 2008) and draws on the community's own human resources and skills to undertake the assessment.

In Recommendation 2, I proposed that such a scoping study assessing music endangerment be realized with the involvement of experienced researchers with strong regional expertise and networks. In relation to this community-driven methodology, the possible roles of ethnomusicologists (or other scholars) include informing communities of the nature and extent of the study; encouraging participation; organizing and facilitating community access to training and resources; training local mediators; ensuring access (taking into account levels of literacy and technological proficiency among community members); and receiving back the questionnaire data, which would then feed back into the wider scoping study at a regional and eventually international level. Other relevant entities, such as government departments and NGOs, may also be involved in these tasks.

One of the challenges of carrying out a survey in this way (that is, where the community undertakes its own assessments) will be gauging and ensuring, as far as possible, the accuracy, coherence, and reliability of the responses. Even with careful guidance, communities are likely to interpret the questionnaire in different ways, and responses may represent political or ideological stances as well as cultural ones. To minimize anomalous responses and maximize the reliability of the survey, it may be advisable for both communities *and* outsiders to carry out the questionnaire where possible—outsiders (ethnomusicologists, anthropologists, or others with a deep knowledge of the social and cultural context) basing their responses on their understanding of the situation combined with data gathered through any other means (e.g., literature survey, participant observation, interviews). This dual-survey method may be particularly important in the preliminary phases of a scoping study: the moderation it would permit between the data gathered by "insiders" and "outsiders" could help identify significant divergences between responses, and allow for subsequent adjustments to the survey methodology, as necessary. In describing the implementation of an inventorying project for the intangible cultural heritage of Portugal, Cabral (2011) describes a possible model: When enough community members and other stakeholders had completed questionnaires about a particular intangible heritage element, the researchers then merged them "into one single inventory sheet and the information concerning the ICH element [was] systematized, completed and validated through fieldwork" (p. 37).

Example 6.2 ⭕ provides an exemplar survey questionnaire on music vitality and endangerment, based on the *Music Vitality and Endangerment Framework* and UNESCO's languages questionnaire.

6.3 NEXT STEPS IN RESEARCH TERMS

According to Rice, developing ethnomusicological theory involves conversations—at a minimum, conversations among ethnomusicologists (2010, p. 106). He argues in favor of critically engaging with prior research, applying it in new ways, adapting and expanding it, believing that "it is through conversations of this sort (theorizing in this manner, that is) that we build the intellectual capacity of ethnomusicology to make powerful, provocative, memorable, and insightful statements about the particular musical traditions we study and about music in general" (p. 106). It is in Rice's spirit of sustained argumentation and interdisciplinary conversation that I wish this book to be positioned and understood, and I suggest that future research into music sustainability consider also deploying a spirit of dialogue.

A number of specific recommendations for further research flow from the discussion in previous chapters. In Chapter 3, I briefly described certain language maintenance strategies that demonstrate high potential to act as models for specific music sustainability strategies, like language nests and master–apprentice programs. I argued that such models would need to be tailored to suit specific local conditions, and that a preliminary analysis of the possible ways to adapt these strategies for music is warranted. The *Comparative Framework* could assist in that analysis. This exercise would carry forward the outcomes of this present book, and may engender valuable new insights into ways to approach music sustainability.

Also in Chapter 3, I examined how language maintenance might advance five salient issues in music sustainability (namely, those I earlier identified as requiring particular consideration). Given the demonstrated relevance of language maintenance to these issues, it seems likely that language maintenance may be able to inform music sustainability in other ways too. Theoretical frameworks from language maintenance, for example, might help advance knowledge of the interrelationship between people's music-related practices, beliefs, and ideologies; ecolinguistic models may help elucidate the relationship between music, people, and the natural environment; and experience from language maintenance may shed light on possible ways to negotiate political or social challenges when implementing maintenance strategies. These are just three examples. Further investigation of the possibilities is strongly indicated.

This research has examined only those potential efforts toward music sustainability that have precedent in language maintenance (successful or unsuccessful, direct or indirect). As such, it has explored only a subset of the possible ways forward for supporting endangered music genres. Language maintenance is not the only field of inquiry that may inform music sustainability, and future studies might consider challenging other interdisciplinary boundaries. Rice regrets that "ethnomusicologists often reference theory from outside the discipline for the authority and interdisciplinarity it appears to give to their work, but it is rarely the object of sustained argumentation" (2010, p. 101), and Svanibor Pettan suggests that ethnomusicologists "should keep being open toward various disciplines for other concepts or ideas that can help us to work with more theoretical, more founded, bases" (personal interview, July 30, 2010). From the early chapters of this book, it seems that biocultural diversity and ecology are two fields of study holding particular promise to inform research into music sustainability. There may be high return on investment in examining these and other fields for their relevance to music.

As music-related investigations grow, ethnomusicological research into sustainability may reciprocally feed back to inform the field of language maintenance. In Chapter 1, for example, I suggested that substantial research already exists into the interactions between music genres and the mass media and industry. While the *Comparative Framework* underscored the fact that these entities play a more critical part in the sustainability of music than of languages, music-related research on this aspect of sustainability may signal their important functions in cultural, or specifically linguistic, sustainability. More generally, new applied strategies to support music sustainability may in turn lead to new perspectives on language maintenance efforts. This is another argument in favor of cultivating ongoing interdisciplinary dialogue between ethnomusicologists and linguists.

One final recommendation relates to neither language nor music directly. I have argued in this book that language maintenance holds strong potential to inform music-related efforts toward sustainability. If this is so, it is not unreasonable to suspect that language maintenance may be able to inform ways to sustain other cultural expressions too. Theatre, dance, ceremony, oral storytelling, and other intangible cultural expressions all may benefit from the experience and knowledge in that field. Each of these cultural expressions is unique with regard to the dynamics of their vitality and viability. Yet if the time is ripe for an exchange of knowledge on this matter from language to music, it may also be ready for exchanges of knowledge about sustainability across the range of intangible expressions of culture. These kinds of exchanges could advance knowledge of cultural sustainability at large, as well as acknowledge and do justice to the interdependence of the manifold forms of intangible cultural expressions.

6.4 CLOSING WORDS

Our track record in stewardship of cultures and cultural expressions has been less than ideal.

> The truth is, the twentieth century three hundred years from now is not going to be remembered for its wars or its technological innovations, but rather as the era in which we stood by and either actively endorsed or passively accepted the massive destruction of both biological and cultural diversity on the planet. (Davis, 2003, 14:31–14:46)

If the twenty-first century is to signal a marked change, the time for action is now. Linguists and biocultural diversity researchers are fully aware of the urgency of counteracting endangerment, and they recognize that "the need for more research in the future should not be a deterrent for taking action in the present" (Maffi & Woodley, 2010, p. 178). Since for many music genres the predicament is similarly pressing, the action-based recommendations

I have presented in this chapter should ideally be explored in tandem with, or even in advance of, the various avenues for research.

I hope this book provides impetus for developing a new direction in music sustainability research, a direction that finds inspiration in drawing from outside of itself, in challenging and expanding its existing boundaries, and in continually reassessing what this implies for the music it aims to support. In this way, I hope it might also contribute to action, driven by equitable and respectful collaborations between communities and other stakeholders, that fully embraces the range of possibilities for maintaining and strengthening endangered music genres. In short, by helping communities and individuals reap the benefits that flow from vibrant musical expressions, I hope this book might ultimately—however modestly—help make a difference.

BIBLIOGRAPHY

Abley, M. (2003). *Spoken here: Travels among threatened languages.* Boston, MA: Houghton Mifflin.

Addiss, S. (1973). Hat a dao, the sung poetry of North Vietnam. *Journal of the American Oriental Society, 93*(1), 18–31.

Addiss, S. (1992). Text and context in Vietnamese sung poetry: The art of *hat a dao*. *Selected Reports in Ethnomusicology, 9*, 203–224.

Afghanistan National Institute of Music (2013). Website. Retrieved May 11, 2013, from http://www.afghanistannationalinstituteofmusic.org/

Alliance for Linguistic Diversity (2012). Endangered languages project [Website]. Retrieved October 27, 2013, from http://www.endangeredlanguages.com/about/

Amery, R. (2002). *Indigenous language programs in South Australian schools: Issues, dilemmas and solutions* (Report commissioned by Office of the Board of Studies). Adelaide: Unaipon School, University of South Australia.

Anisensel, A. (2008). Surveys on ca trù in Vietnam. In Ministry of Culture Sports and Tourism of Vietnam, Vietnam National Academy of Music & Vietnamese Institute for Musicology (Eds.), *Proceedings of the International Scientific Conference "Ca trù singing of the Việt people"* (pp. 235–242). Hanoi: Vietnamese Institute for Musicology.

Appadurai, A. (1996). *Modernity at large: Cultural dimensions of globalization.* Minneapolis: University of Minnesota Press.

Arana, M. (1999). *Neotraditional music in Vietnam.* Kent, Ohio: International Association for Research in Vietnamese Music.

Archer, W. K. (1964). On the ecology of music. *Ethnomusicology* 8(1), 28–33.

Asia-Pacific Cultural Centre for UNESCO (2013). Website. Retrieved May 11, 2013, from http://www.accu.or.jp/en/

Assembly of the World Conference on Linguistic Rights (1996). *Universal declaration of linguistic rights.* Retrieved May 11, 2013, from http://www.linguistic-declaration.org/index-gb.htm

Aubert, L. (2007). *Music of the other: New challenges for ethnomusicology in a global age* (C. Ribiero, Trans.). Aldershot, UK: Ashgate.

Austin, P. (2006). Survival of languages. *Twentyfirst Annual Darwin College Lecture Series*, 1–14. Retrieved May 11, 2013, from http://www.hrelp.org/aboutus/staff/peter_austin/AustinDarwinLecture.pdf

Austin, P. (2008). Survival of language. In E. Shuckburgh (Ed.), *Survival: The survival of the human race.* New York: Cambridge University Press.

Australian Institute of Aboriginal and Torres Strait Islander Studies (2005). *National Indigenous Languages Survey Report*. Canberra: Australian Department of Communications Information Technology and the Arts, Federation of Aboriginal and Torres Strait Islander Languages.

Barwick, L., & Thieberger, N. (Eds.). (2006). *Sustainable data from digital fieldwork. Proceedings from the conference at the University of Sydney*. Sydney, Australia: Sydney University Press.

Baumann, M. P. (1992). Safeguarding of musical traditions: Towards the "rehabilitation of the alien." In M. P. Bauman (Ed.), *World music, musics of the world: Aspects of documentation, mass media and acculturation* (pp. 151–176). Wilhelmshaven, Germany: Florian Noetzel.

Berez, A., & Holton, G. (2006). Finding the locus of best practice: Technology training in an Alaskan language community. In L. Barwick & N. Thieberger (Eds.), *Sustainable data from digital fieldwork: Proceedings from the conference at the University of Sydney* (pp. 69–86). Sydney, Australia: Sydney University Press.

Bilby, K. (1999). "Roots explosion": Indigenization and cosmopolitanism in contemporary Surinamese popular music. *Ethnomusicology*, 43(2), 256–296.

Bithell, C. (2011). Desperately seeking impact. *Ethnomusicology Forum*, 20(2), 233–244.

Blacking, J. (1973). *How musical is man?* Seattle: University of Washington Press.

Blake, J. (2009). UNESCO's 2003 Convention on Intangible Cultural Heritage: The implications of community involvement in "safeguarding." In L. Smith & N. Akagawa (Eds.), *Intangible heritage* (pp. 45–73). London: Routledge.

Blaukopf, K. (1990). Legal policies for the safeguarding of traditional music: Are they utopian? *World of Music*, 32(1), 125–133.

Blaukopf, K. (1992). Mediamorphisis and secondary orality: A challenge to cultural policy. In M. P. Bauman (Ed.), *World music, musics of the world: Aspects of documentation, mass media, and acculturation* (pp. 19–36). Wilhelmshaven, Germany: Florian Noetzel Verlag.

Bohlman, P. V. (2002). *World music: A very short introduction*. New York, NY: Oxford University Press.

Bojórquez, F. S. (2010). Noam Chomsky and Indigenous education in Oaxaca, Mexico. In L. Meyer & B. Maldonado Alvarado (Eds.), *New world of Indigenous resistance: Noam Chomsky and voices from North, South, and Central America* (pp. 101–113). San Francisco, CA: City Lights.

Bowern, C., & James, B. (2010). Yan-nhanu language documentation and revitalisation. In J. Hobson, K. Lowe, S. Poetsch, & M. Walsh (Eds.), *Re-awakening languages: Theory & practice in the revitalisation of Australia's Indigenous languages* (pp. 361–371). Sydney, Australia: Sydney University Press.

Bradley, D., & Bradley, M. (2002). *Language endangerment and language maintenance*. London: Routledge Curzon.

Bùi, T. H. (2008). Culture: Social cultural functions and manifestation forms of Ca trù arts. In H. L. Đặng, M. H. Phạm, & H. D. Hồ (Eds.), *Monograph on Vietnamese ca trù* (pp. 65–119). Hanoi: Vietnamese Institute for Musicology, Hanoi National Conservatory of Music.

Cabral, C. B. (2011). Collaborative internet-mediated ICH inventories. *International Journal of Intangible Heritage*, 6, 36–43.

Cambodian Living Arts (2013). Website. Retrieved May 11, 2013, from http://www.cambodianlivingarts.org/

Campbell, G. (2012). *Ngariwanajirri*, the Tiwi "strong kids' song": Using repatriated song recordings in a contemporary music project. *Yearbook for Traditional Music, 44*, 1–23.

Campbell, P. S., Drummond, J., Dunbar-Hall, P., Howard, K., Schippers, H., & Wiggins, T. (Eds.). (2005). *Cultural diversity in music education: Directions and challenges for the 21st century*. Bowen Hills: Australian Academic Press.

Carnie, A. (1996). Modern Irish: A case study in language revival failure. In J. D. Bobaljik, R. Pensalfini, & L. Storto (Eds.), *Papers on language endangerment and the maintenance of linguistic diversity* (pp. 99–114). Cambridge, MA: MITWPL.

Centre of Educational Exchange with Vietnam (n.d.). Website. Retrieved May 11, 2013, from http://ceevn.acls.org/

Chaudhuri, S. (1992). Preservation of the world's music. In H. Myers (Ed.), *Ethnomusicology: An introduction* (Vol. 1, pp. 365–374). London: Macmillan.

Christensen, D. (1992). Music worlds and music of the world: The case of Oman. In M. P. Bauman (Ed.), *World music, musics of the world: Aspects of documentation, mass media, and acculturation* (pp. 107–122). Wilhelmshaven, Germany: Florian Noetzel.

Cohen, J. M. (2009). Music institutions and the transmission of tradition. *Ethnomusicology, 53*(2), 308–325.

Consortium on Training in Language Documentation and Conservation (2012). Website. Retrieved May 11, 2013, from http://www.ctldc.org/

Corn, A. (2011). National Recording Project for Indigenous Music in Australia. Retrieved May 11, 2013, from http://www.aboriginalartists.com.au/NRP.htm

Corn, A. (2012). Now and in the future: The role of the National Recording Project for Indigenous Music in Australia in sustaining Indigenous music and dance traditions. *MUSICultures 39*(1), 231–250.

Cottrell, S. (2010). Ethnomusicology and the music industries: An overview. *Ethnomusicology Forum, 19*(1), 3–25.

Cottrell, S. (2011). The impact of ethnomusicology [Impact roundtable]. *Ethnomusicology Forum, 20*(2), 229–232.

Coulter, N. R. (2007). *Music shift: Evaluating the vitality and viability of music styles among the Alamblak of Papua New Guinea*. Unpublished doctoral dissertation. Kent, OH: Kent State University.

Coulter, Neil R. (2011). Assessing music shift: Adapting EGIDS for a Papua New Guinea community. *Language Documentation and Description 10*, 61–81.

Crystal, D. (2000). *Language death*. New York, NY: Cambridge University Press.

Cultures in Harmony (2013). Website. Retrieved May 11, 2013, from http://culturesinharmony.org

Dalby, A. (2003). *Language in danger: The loss of linguistic diversity and the threat to our future*. New York: Columbia University Press.

Đặng, H. L. (2008). Ca trù: The remaining traces. In H. L. Đặng, M. H. Phạm, & H. D. Hồ (Eds.), *Monograph on Vietnamese ca trù* (pp. 455–608). Hanoi: Vietnamese Institute for Musicology, Hanoi National Conservatory of Music.

Đặng, H. L., Phạm, M. H., & Hồ, H. D. (Eds.). (2008). *Monograph on Vietnamese ca trù*. Hanoi: Vietnamese Institute for Musicology, Hanoi National Conservatory of Music.

Davis, W. (2003). [Presentation delivered at TED Conference.] Retrieved October 28, 2013, from http://www.ted.com/talks/lang/eng/wade_davis_on_endangered_cultures.html

Dauenhauer, N. M., & Dauenhauer, R. (1998). Technical, emotional, and ideological issues in reversing language shift: Examples from Southeast Alaska. In L. A. Grenoble & L. J. Whaley (Eds.), *Endangered languages: Current issues and future prospects* (pp. 57–99). Cambridge, UK: Cambridge University Press.

De Ferranti, H. (2009). *The last Biwa singer: A blind musician in history, imagination, and performance*. Ithaca, NY: Cornell University East Asia Program.

Defrance, Y. (2008). Ca trù singing, a unique music phenomenon in the world. In Ministry of Culture Sports and Tourism of Vietnam, Vietnam National Academy of Music & Vietnamese Institute for Musicology (Eds.), *Proceedings of the International Scientific Conference "Ca trù singing of the Việt people"* (pp. 36–43). Hanoi: Vietnamese Institute for Musicology.

Digital Himalaya (2013). Website. Retrieved May 11, 2013, from http://www.digitalhimalaya.com/

Dixon, R. M. W. (1991). The endangered languages of Australia, Indonesia and Oceania. In R. Robins & E. M. Uhlenbeck (Eds.), *Endangered languages* (pp. 229–255). Oxford, UK: Berg.

Dixon, R. M. W. (1997). *The rise and fall of languages*. Cambridge, UK: Cambridge University Press.

Dunbar-Hall, P., & Adnyana, I. W. T. (2004). Expectations and outcomes of intercultural music education: A case study in teaching and learning a Balinese gamelan instrument. In M. Chaseling (Ed.), *Australian Association for Research in Music Education: Proceedings of the XXVIth Annual Conference* (pp. 144–151). Melbourne: Australian Association for Research in Music Education.

Durán, L. (2011). Music production as a tool of research, and impact. *Ethnomusicology Forum, 20*(2), 245–253.

Dutta, S. (1999). North American Dhrupad Association (NADA) [Website]. Retrieved May 11, 2013, from http://www.raga.com/text/221dhrupad_text.html

E-MELD (2006). E-MELD School of Best Practices in Digital Language Documentation. Retrieved May 11, 2013, from http://emeld.org/school/

Edwards, J. (1992). Sociopolitical aspects of language maintenance and loss: Towards a typology of minority language situations. In W. Fase, K. Jaspaert, & S. Kroon (Eds.), *Maintenance and loss of minority languages* (pp. 37–54). Amsterdam, The Netherlands: John Benjamins.

Ellingson, T. (1992a). Notation. In H. Myers (Ed.), *Ethnomusicology: An introduction* (Vol. 1, pp. 153–164). London: Macmillan Press.

Ellingson, T. (1992b). Transcription. In H. Myers (Ed.), *Ethnomusicology: An introduction* (Vol. 1, pp. 110–152). London: Macmillan Press.

Ellis, C. J. (1992). Documentation as disintegration: Aboriginal Australians in the modern world. In M. P. Bauman (Ed.), *World music, musics of the world: Aspects of documentation, mass media, and acculturation* (pp. 259–280). Wilhelmshaven, Germany: Florian Noetzel.

Erlmann, V. (1993). The politics and aesthetics of transnational musics. *World of Music, 35*(2), 3–15.

Evans, N. (2001). The last speaker is dead—long live the last speaker! In P. Newman & M. Ratliff (Eds.), *Linguistic fieldwork* (pp. 250–281). Cambridge, UK: Cambridge University Press.

Feintuch, B. (1993). Musical revival as musical transformation. In N. V. Rosenberg (Ed.), *Transforming tradition: Folk music revivals examined* (pp. 183–193). Urbana: University of Illinois Press.

Feintuch, B. (2006). Revivals on the edge: Northumberland and Cape Breton. *Yearbook for Traditional Music, 38*, 1–17.

Feld, S. (1974). Linguistic models in ethnomusicology. *Ethnomusicology, 18*(2), 197–217.

Feld, S. (1990). *Sound and sentiment: Birds, weeping, poetics, and song in Kaluli expression* (2nd ed.). Philadelphia: University of Pennsylvania Press.

Feld, S., & Fox, A. A. (1994). Music and language. *Annual Review of Anthropology, 23*, 25–53.

First People's Cultural Foundation (2011). FirstVoices: Language legacies celebrating indigenous cultures. Retrieved May 12, 2013, from http://www.firstvoices.com/

Fishman, J. A. (1991). *Reversing language shift: Theoretical and empirical foundations of assistance to threatened languages*. Bristol, UK: Multilingual Matters.

Fishman, J. A. (Ed.). (2001). *Can threatened languages be saved? Reversing language shift, revisited: A 21st century perspective*. Clevedon, UK: Multilingual Matters.

Ford Foundation Vietnam (n.d.). [Brochure.] Retrieved May 12, 2013, from http://www.fordfoundation.org/pdfs/library/regional_vietnam.pdf

Foundation for Endangered Languages (1995). Allied societies and activities. Retrieved May 12, 2013, from http://www.ogmios.org/ogmios_files/44.htm

Foundation for Endangered Languages (2013). Website. Retrieved May 12, 2013, from http://www.ogmios.org/home.htm

Freemuse (2013). Freemuse: Freedom of musical expression. Retrieved May 19, 2013, from http://www.freemuse.org/

Frigyesi, J. (1996). The aesthetic of the Hungarian revival movement. In M. Slobin (Ed.), *Returning culture: Musical changes in Central and Eastern Europe* (pp. 54–75). Durham, NC: Duke University Press.

Frith S. (2000). The discourse of world music. In G. Born & D. Hesmondhalgh (Eds.), *Western music and its others: Difference, representation, and appropriation in music.* (pp. 305–322). Berkeley: University of California Press.

Future of Music Coalition (2013). Website. Retrieved May 12, 2013, from http://futureofmusic.org/about

Galla, A. (2008). The First Voice in heritage conservation. *International Journal of Intangible Heritage, 3*, 10–25.

Garza-Cuarón, B., & Lastra, Y. (1991). Endangered languages in Mexico. In R. Robins & E. M. Uhlenbeck (Eds.), *Endangered languages* (pp. 93–134). Oxford, UK: Berg.

Giáo Phường Ca Trù Thăng Long (2010). Promotional brochure. Hanoi, Vietnam: Author.

Giáo Phường Ca Trù Thăng Long (2012a). Ca Trù Thăng Long YouTube Channel. Retrieved May 12, 2013, from http://www.youtube.com/user/catruthanglong

Giáo Phường Ca Trù Thăng Long (2012b). Website. Retrieved May 12, 2013, from http://www.catruthanglong.com/

Gibson, C., & Connell, J. (2005). *Music and tourism: On the road again*. Clevedon, UK: Channel View.

Giddens, A. (1990). *The consequences of modernity*. Redwood City, CA: Stanford University Press.

Global Voices (2009). Peru: Traditional music takes on internet love. Retrieved May 12, 2013, from http://globalvoicesonline.org/2009/04/14/peru-traditional-music-takes-on-internet-love/

Government of Canada (2012). International Network on Cultural Policy [Website]. Retrieved October 27, 2013, from http://www.pch.gc.ca/eng/1332873737001/1332874414115

Gramsci, A. (1929/1989). *Letters from prison* (L. Lawner, Trans.). New York: Noonday Press.
Grant, C. (2010). The links between safeguarding language and safeguarding musical heritage. *International Journal of Intangible Heritage 5*, 44–59. Retrieved October 27, 2013, from http://www.ijih.org/volumeMgr.ijih?cmd=volumeView&volNo=5&manuType=02
Grant, C. (2011). Key factors in the sustainability of language and music: A comparative study. *Musicology Australia 33*(1), 95–113.
Grant, C. (2012a). Analogies and links between cultural and biological diversity. *Journal of Cultural Heritage Management and Sustainable Development 2*(2), 153–163.
Grant, C. (2012b). Rethinking safeguarding: Objections and responses to protecting and promoting endangered musical heritage. *Ethnomusicology Forum 21*(1), 39–59.
Graves, J. B. (2005). *Cultural democracy: The arts, community, and the public purpose.* Urbana: University of Illinois Press.
Gray, J. (1996). Returning music to the makers: The Library of Congress, American Indians, and the Federal Cylinder Project. *Cultural Survival Quarterly, 20*(4). Retrieved May 12, 2013, from http://www.culturalsurvival.org/ourpublications/csq/article/returning-music-makers-the-library-congress-american-indians-and-federal
Green, L. (2001). *How popular musicians learn: A way ahead for music education.* London: Ashgate.
Green, R. (2010). Reclamation process for Dharug in Sydney using song. In J. Hobson, K. Lowe, S. Poetsch, & M. Walsh (Eds.), *Re-awakening languages: Theory & practice in the revitalisation of Australia's Indigenous languages* (pp. 181–187). Sydney, Australia: Sydney University Press.
Grenoble, L. A., & Whaley, L. J. (1998). Toward a typology of language endangerment. In L. A. Grenoble & L. J. Whaley (Eds.), *Endangered languages: Current issues and future prospects* (pp. 22–54). Cambridge, UK: Cambridge University Press.
Grenoble, L. A., & Whaley, L. J. (2006). *Saving languages: An introduction to language revitalization.* New York, NY: Cambridge University Press.
Hale, K. (1998). On endangered languages and the importance of linguistic diversity. In L. A. Grenoble & L. J. Whaley (Eds.), *Endangered languages: Current issues and future prospects* (pp. 192–216). Cambridge, UK: Cambridge University Press.
Hale, K. (2001). Linguistic aspects of language teaching and learning in immersion contexts. In L. Hinton & K. Hale (Eds.), *The green book of language revitalization in practice* (pp. 227–235). San Diego, CA: Academic Press.
Hale, K., Krauss, M., Watahomigie, L. J., Yamamoto, A. Y., Craig, C., Jeanne, L. M., & England, N.C. (1992). Endangered languages. *Language, 68*(1), 1–42.
Harmon, D., & Loh, J. (2010). The Index of Linguistic Diversity: A new quantitative measure of trends in the status of the world's languages. *Language Documentation and Conservation*, 97–151. Retrieved May 12, 2013, from http://nflrc.hawaii.edu/ldc/2010/
Harrison, K., & Pettan, S. (2010). Introduction. In K. Harrison, E. Mackinlay, & S. Pettan (Eds.), *Applied ethnomusicology: Historical and contemporary approaches* (pp. 1–20). Newcastle Upon Tyne, UK: Cambridge Scholars.
Hayward, P. (2005). Culturally engaged research and facilitation: Active development projects with small island cultures. In M. Evans (Ed.), *Proceedings of the First International Small Island Cultures Conference* (pp. 55–60). Sydney, Australia: Small Islands Cultures Research Initiative.

Heritage Foundation of Newfoundland and Labrador (n.d.). Intangible Cultural Heritage: *Newfoundland, Labrador*. Retrieved May 12, 2013, from http://www.mun.ca/ich/ichstrategy.pdf

Heritage Languages in America (2009). Indigenous Language Institute. Retrieved May 12, 2013, from http://www.cal.org/heritage/profiles/programs/Indigenous_Language_Institute.html

Hesselink, N. (2004). Samul nori as traditional: Preservation and innovation in a South Korean contemporary percussion genre. *Ethnomusicology, 48*(3), 405–439.

Higgins, A. (2011, August 11). A showdown over traditional throat singing divides China and Mongolia. *Washington Post*. Retrieved May 12, 2013, from http://www.washingtonpost.com/world/asia-pacific/a-showdown-over-traditional-throat-singing-divides-china-and-mongolia/2011/06/24/gIQASaZS7I_story.html?hpid=z9

Hinton, L. (1997). Survival of endangered languages: The California master-apprentice program. *International Journal of the Sociology of Language, 123*, 177–191.

Hinton, L. (2001). Audio-video documentation. In L. Hinton & K. L. Hale (Eds.), *The green book of language revitalization in practice* (pp. 265–271). San Diego, CA: Academic Press.

Hinton, L. (2002). *How to keep your language alive: A commonsense approach to one-on-one language learning*. Berkeley, CA: Heyday Books.

Hinton, L. (2003). Language revitalization. *Annual Review of Applied Linguistics, 23*, 44–57.

Hinton, L., & Hale, K. L. (Eds.). (2001). *The green book of language revitalization in practice*. San Diego, CA: Academic Press.

Hobsbawm, E., & Ranger, T. (Eds.). (1983). *The invention of tradition*. Cambridge, UK: Cambridge University Press.

Hobson, J., Lowe, K., Poetsch, S., & Walsh, M. (Eds.). (2010). *Re-awakening languages: Theory & practice in the revitalisation of Australia's indigenous languages*. Sydney, Australia: Sydney University Press.

Hood, M. (1960). The challenge of "bi-musicality." *Ethnomusicology, 4*(2), 55–59.

Hood, M. M. (2010). Gamelan gong gede: Negotiating musical diversity in Bali's highlands. *Musicology Australia, 32*(1), 69–93.

Howard, K. (2006). *Preserving Korean music: Intangible Cultural Properties as icons of identity* (Vol. 1). Aldershot, UK: Ashgate.

International Council for Traditional Music (2009, June). *Examination report for the nomination for inscription on the Urgent Safeguarding List in 2009: Ca trù singing*. Retrieved May 12, 2013, from http://www.unesco.org/culture/ich/index.php?pg=00246

International Federation of Coalitions for Cultural Diversity (2013). About us. Retrieved May 12, 2013, from http://www.ficdc.org/A-propos-de-nous?lang=en

International Network for Cultural Diversity (2003). Website. Retrieved May 12, 2013, from http://www.incd.net/incden.html

International Network of Lawyers for the Diversity of Cultural Expressions (2011). Website. Retrieved May 12, 2013, from http://www.fd.ulaval.ca/rijdec

International Society for Music Education (2006). ISME vision and mission. Retrieved May 12, 2013, from http://www.isme.org/index.php?option=com_content&view=article&id=29:isme-vision-and-mission&catid=1:general-information&Itemid=5

International Telecommunications Union (2013). The world in 2013: ICT facts and figures. Retrieved November 2, 2013, from http://www.itu.int/en/ITU-D/Statistics/Pages/facts/default.aspx

Jähnichen, G. (1997). *Studien zu traditionellen Vietnamesischen Instrumentalpraktiken des hát a đào und des ca vọng cô [Studies of traditional Vietnamese instrumental-praxis in hát a đào and ca vọng cô]*. [Habilitationsschrift.] Berlin: Verlag der Deutsch-Vietnamesische Gesellschaft.

Jähnichen, G. (2008). Cultural diversity and preservation strategies within modern Vietnamese society: Can we save the *hát a đào*? In Ministry of Culture Sports and Tourism of Vietnam, Vietnam National Academy of Music & Vietnamese Institute for Musicology (Eds.), *Proceedings of the International Scientific Conference "Ca trù singing of the Việt people"* (pp. 154–164). Hanoi: Vietnamese Institute for Musicology.

Jähnichen, G. (2011). Uniqueness re-examined: The Vietnamese lute *đàn đáy*. *Yearbook for Traditional Music, 43*, 147–179.

Janse, M., & Tol, S. (Eds.). (2003). *Language death and language maintenance: Theoretical, practical and descriptive approaches*. Amsterdam, The Netherlands: John Benjamins.

Johnson, H. (2005). Maintaining and creating heritage: Music and language on Jersey. In M. Evans (Ed.), *Proceedings of the First International Small Island Cultures Conference* (pp. 73–84). Sydney, Australia: Small Islands Cultures Research Initiative.

Johnson, H. (2013). "The Group from the West": Song, endangered language and sonic activism on Guernsey. *Journal of Marine and Island Cultures 1*(2), 99–112.

Jovanović, J. (2005). The power of recently revitalized Serbian rural folk music in urban settings. In A. J. Randall (Ed.), *Music, power, politics* (pp. 133–142). New York: Routledge.

Kaeppler, A. L. (2004, December). *Safeguarding intangible cultural heritage. The Tongan lakalaka: Sung speeches with choreographed movements*. Paper presented at the regional meeting on the promotion of the Convention for the Safeguarding of the Intangible Cultural Heritage for countries of Europe and Northern America.

Karpeles, M. (1973). *An introduction to English folk song*. Oxford, UK: Oxford University Press.

Kartomi, M. J. (1981). The processes and results of musical culture contact: A discussion of terminology and concepts. *Ethnomusicology, 25*(2), 227–249.

Kartomi, M. J., & Blum, S. (Eds.). (1994). *Music-cultures in contact: Convergences and collisions*. Sydney, Australia: Currency Press.

King, J. (2001). Te Kohanga Reo: Maori language revitalization. In L. Hinton & K. Hale (Eds.), *The green book of language revitalization in practice* (pp. 129–132). San Diego, CA: Academic Press.

Kinkade, M. D. (1991). The decline of native languages in Canada. In R. H. Robins & E. M. Uhlenbeck (Eds.), *Endangered languages* (pp. 157–176). Oxford, UK: Berg.

Krauss, M. (1992). The world's languages in crisis. *Language, 68*(1), 4–10.

Krauss, M. (1998). The scope of the language endangerment crisis and recent response to it. In K. Matsumura (Ed.), *Studies in Endangered Languages: Papers from the International Symposium on Endangered Languages, Tokyo, November 18–20, 1995* (pp. 101–113). Tokyo, Japan: Hituzi Syobo.

Krauss, M. (2007). Mass language extinction and documentation: The race against time. In O. Miyaoka, O. Sakiyama, & M. Krauss (Eds.), *The vanishing languages of the Pacific rim* (pp. 3–24). Oxford, UK: Oxford University Press.

Ladefoged, P. (1992). Another view of endangered languages. *Language, 68*(4), 809–811.

Langton, M. (1994). *Valuing cultures: Recognising Indigenous cultures as a valued part of Australian heritage*. Canberra: Australian Government Publishing Service.

Lê, T. B. V. (2008). Ca trù in Hà Nội: Reality and some solutions. In Ministry of Culture Sports and Tourism of Vietnam, Vietnam National Academy of Music & Vietnamese Institute for Musicology (Eds.), *Proceedings of the International Scientific Conference "Ca trù singing of the Việt people"* (pp. 281–301). Hanoi: Vietnamese Institute for Musicology.

Lê, T. H. (1998). *Đàn tranh music of Vietnam: Traditions and innovations*. Melbourne: Australia Asia Foundation.

León, J. F. (2007). The *"Danza de las Canas"*: Music, theatre and Afroperuvian modernity. In T. K. Ramnarine (Ed.), *Musical performance in the diaspora* (pp. 127–155). London: Routledge.

Letts, R. (2003). *The effects of globalisation on music in five contrasting countries: Australia, Germany, Nigeria, the Philippines and Uruguay*. Retrieved May 12, 2013, from http://www.mca.org.au/research/research-reports/research-reports/638-the-effects-of-globalisation-on-music-in-five-contrasting-countries-australia-germany-nigeria-the-philippines-and-uruguay

Letts, R. (2006). *The protection and promotion of musical diversity*: Study carried out for UNESCO by the International Music Council. Retrieved May 12, 2013, from http://www.mca.org.au/research/research-reports/research-reports/640-the-protection-and-promotion-of-musical-diversity

Lewis, M. P. (2006). *Towards a categorization of endangerment of the world's languages*. SIL Working Paper. Retrieved May 12, 2013, from http://www.sil.org/resources/publications/entry/7869

Lewis, M. P., & Simons, G. F. (2010). Assessing endangerment: Expanding Fishman's GIDS. *Revue Roumaine de Linguistique* [Special issue: *Language Endangerment and Language Death*], *55*(2), 103–120.

Lewis, M. P., Simons, G. F., & Fennig, C.D. (Eds.). (2013). *Ethnologue: Languages of the world* (17th ed.). Dallas, TX: SIL International. Online version: http://www.ethnologue.com

Livingston, T. E. (1999). Music revivals: Towards a general theory. *Ethnomusicology*, *43*(1), 66–85.

Lo Bianco, J., & Rhydwen, M. (2001). Is the extinction of Australia's indigenous languages inevitable? In J. A. Fishman (Ed.), *Can threatened languages be saved? Reversing language shift, revisited: A 21st century perspective* (pp. 391–422). Clevedon, UK: Multilingual Matters.

Lomax, A. (1968). *Folk song style and culture*. Washington, DC: American Association for the Advancement of Science.

Lomax, A. (1977). Appeal for cultural equity. *Journal of Communication*, *27*(2), 125–138.

Mackey, W. F. (2003). Forecasting the fate of languages. In J. Maurais & M. A. Morris (Eds.), *Languages in a globalising world* (pp. 64–81). Cambridge, UK: Cambridge University Press.

Maffi, L. (2003). The "business" of language endangerment: Saving languages or helping people keep them alive? In H. Tonkin & T. Reagan (Eds.), *Language in the twenty-first century: Selected papers of the millenial conferences of the Center for Research and Documentation on World Language Problems* (pp. 67–86). Amsterdam, The Netherlands: John Benjamins.

Maffi, L. (2005). Linguistic, cultural, and biological diversity. *Annual Review of Anthropology*, *34*, 599–617.

Maffi, L., & Woodley, E. (2010). *Biocultural diversity conservation: A global source book.* London: Earthscan.

Magistad, M. K. (2010, January 26) Global hit: Ca tru [Podcast]. *PRI's "The World."* Retrieved May 12, 2013, from http://pri.org/stories/2010-01-26/ca-tru

Malm, K. (1992). Local, national and international musics: A changing scene of interaction. In M. P. Bauman (Ed.), *World music, musics of the world: Aspects of documentation, mass media and acculturation* (pp. 211–217). Wilhelmshaven, Germany: Florian Noetzel.

Malm, K. (1993). Music on the move: Traditions and mass media. *Ethnomusicology*, 37(3), 339–352.

Marett, A. (2005). *Songs, dreamings, and ghosts: The Wangga of North Australia.* Middletown, CT: Wesleyan University Press.

Marett, A. (2010). Vanishing songs: How musical extinctions threaten the planet. Laurence Picken Memorial Lecture 2009. *Ethnomusicology Forum*, 19(2), 249–262.

Marett, A., & Barwick, L. (2003). Endangered songs and endangered languages. In R. M. Brown & J. Blythe (Eds.), *Maintaining the links: Language, identity and the land. Proceedings of Seventh FEL Conference, Broome, Western Australia* (pp. 144–151). Bath, UK: Foundation for Endangered Languages.

McCloskey, J. (2001). *Voices silenced: Has Irish a future?* Dublin, Ireland: Cois Life Teoranta.

McConvell, P., & Thieberger, N. (2001). *State of indigenous languages in Australia—2001.* Australia State of the Environment Second Technical Paper Series (Natural and Cultural Heritage). Retrieved May 12, 2013, from http://www.environment.gov.au/soe/2001/publications/technical/indigenous-languages.html

McKay, G. (1996). *The land still speaks: Review of Aboriginal and Torres Strait Islander language maintenance and development needs and activities.* Canberra: Australian Government Publishing Service.

McLaren, A. E. (2010). Revitalisation of the folk epics of the Lower Yangzi Delta: An example of China's intangible cultural heritage. *International Journal of Intangible Heritage*, 5, 28–43.

McLaren, A. E., English, A., Ingram, C., & Xinhuan, H. (Eds). (2013). *Environmental preservation and cultural heritage in China.* Champaign, IL: Common Ground.

McLean, M. (1996). *Maori music.* Auckland, New Zealand: Auckland University Press.

Merriam, A. (1964). *The anthropology of music.* Evanston, IL: Northwestern University Press.

Miller, T. E. (2008). Vietnam: Musiques vocales des plaines du nord/Vietnam: Vocal music from the Northern plains (Ca Trù, Hát Chèo, Quan Ho) [CD Review]. *Yearbook for Traditional Music*, 40, 192–193.

Ministry of Culture Sports and Tourism of Vietnam (2009). *Nomination for inscription on the Urgent Safeguarding List in 2009: Ca trù singing.* Document submitted to the Intergovernmental Committee for the Safeguarding of the Intangible Cultural Heritage, Abu Dhabi, United Arab Emirates.

Ministry of Culture Sports and Tourism of Vietnam, Vietnam National Academy of Music, & Vietnamese Institute for Musicology (Eds.). (2008). *Proceedings of the International Scientific Conference "Ca trù singing of the Việt people," Hanoi, June 20, 2006.* Hanoi: Vietnamese Institute for Musicology.

Mithun, M. (1998). The significance of diversity in language endangerment and preservation. In L. A. Grenoble & L. J. Whaley (Eds.), *Endangered languages: Current issues and future prospects* (pp. 163–191). Cambridge, UK: Cambridge University Press.

Moseley, C. (Ed.). (2009). *UNESCO interactive atlas of the world's languages in danger* (online ed.). Paris, France: UNESCO.

Moyle, R. M. (1997). *Balgo: The musical life of a desert community*. Perth: Callaway International Resource Centre for Music Education, University of Western Australia.

Moyle, R. M. (2007). *Songs from the second float: A musical ethnography of Takū Atoll, Papua New Guinea* (N. Nake & L. Tekaso, Trans.). Honolulu: University of Hawai'i Press.

Mundy, S. (2001). *Music and globalisation: A guide to the issues*. Paris, France: International Music Council.

Myers, H. (1992). Fieldwork. In H. Myers (Ed.), *Ethnomusicology: An introduction* (Vol. 1, pp. 21–49). London: Macmillan.

Nahir, M. (1998). Micro language planning and the revival of Hebrew: A schematic framework. *Language and Society, 27*(3), 335–357.

Nathan, D. (2006). Proficient, permanent, or pertinent: Aiming for sustainability. In L. Barwick & N. Thieberger (Eds.), *Sustainable data from digital fieldwork. Proceedings from the conference at the University of Sydney* (pp. 57–68). Sydney: Australia: Sydney University Press.

National Assembly of the Socialist Republic of Vietnam (2001). *Law on Cultural Heritage*. Retrieved May 12, 2013, from http://www.thuvienphapluat.vn/archive/Luat/Law-No-28-2001-QH10-of-June-29-2001-on-Cultural-Heritage-vb71739t10.aspx

NeSmith, R. K. (2009). Tūtū's Hawaiian and the emergence of a neo Hawaiian language. *'Ōiwi Journal, 3*, 1–15. Retrieved May 13, 2013, from http://www.traditionalhawaiian.com/Oiwi-Journal-_3-1-09_.pdf

Nettl, B. (1978). Some aspects of the history of world music in the twentieth century: Questions, problems and concepts. *Ethnomusicology, 22*(1), 123–136.

Nettl, B. (2005). *The study of ethnomusicology: Thirty-one issues and concepts*. Urbana: University of Illinois Press.

Nettl, B. (2010). *Nettl's elephant: On the history of ethnomusicology*. Urbana: University of Illinois Press.

Nettle, D. (1999). *Linguistic diversity*. Oxford, UK: Oxford University Press.

Neuman, D. M. (1980). *The life of music in North India: The organization of an artistic tradition*. Chicago, IL: University of Chicago Press.

Newman, P. (1998). "We have seen the enemy and it is us": The endangered languages issue as a hopeless cause. *Studies in the Linguistic Sciences, 28*(2), 11–20.

Newman, P. (2003). The endangered language issue as a hopeless cause. In M. Janse & S. Tol (Eds.), *Language death and language maintenance: Theoretical, practical and descriptive approaches* (pp. 1–13). Amsterdam, The Netherlands: John Benjamins.

Ngapartji Ngapartji (2013). Ninti Ngapartji. Retrieved May 12, 2013, from http://ninti.ngapartji.org/index.php

Ngọc, H. [performer] (2012). Tren Dinh Phu Van ["On the mountain peak full of cloud"]. Retrieved May 12, 2013, from http://www.youtube.com/watch?v=2Dzj4okH6fw

Nguyễn, N. (2008). Ca trù in the past and at present in Sài Gòn: A spring of traditional ca trù. In Ministry of Culture Sports and Tourism of Vietnam, Vietnam National Academy of Music & Vietnamese Institute for Musicology (Eds.), *Proceedings of the International Scientific Conference "Ca trù singing of the Việt people"* (pp. 207–221). Hanoi: Vietnamese Institute for Musicology.

Nguyễn, N. N. (2008). Ca trù singing of the Việt people in Nghệ An. In Ministry of Culture Sports and Tourism of Vietnam, Vietnam National Academy of Music & Vietnamese Institute for Musicology (Eds.), *Proceedings of the International Scientific Conference "Ca trù singing of the Việt people"* (pp. 222–234). Hanoi: Vietnamese Institute for Musicology.

Nguyễn, P. T. (1991a). Ethno-historical perspectives on the traditional genres of Vietnamese music. In P. T. Nguyen (Ed.), *New perspectives on Vietnamese music: Six essays* (pp. 1–19). New Haven, CT: Council on Southeast Asia Studies, Yale Center for International and Area Studies.

Nguyễn, Q. T. (2008). Live Ca trù in Lạc Việt Club in Saigon. In Ministry of Culture Sports and Tourism of Vietnam, Vietnam National Academy of Music & Vietnamese Institute for Musicology (Eds.), *Proceedings of the International Scientific Conference "Ca trù singing of the Việt people"* (pp. 114–124). Hanoi: Vietnamese Institute for Musicology.

Nguyễn, T. L. (2008). Exchange: Some issues relating to Ca trù. In Ministry of Culture Sports and Tourism of Vietnam, Vietnam National Academy of Music & Vietnamese Institute for Musicology (Eds.), *Proceedings of the International Scientific Conference "Ca trù singing of the Việt people"* (pp. 257–280). Hanoi: Vietnamese Institute for Musicology.

Nguyễn, T. T. (2008). Ca trù in the south of Vietnam before and after 1975. In Ministry of Culture Sports and Tourism of Vietnam, Vietnam National Academy of Music & Vietnamese Institute for Musicology (Eds.), *Proceedings of the International Scientific Conference "Ca trù singing of the Việt people"* (pp. 302–308). Hanoi: Vietnamese Institute for Musicology.

Nguyễn, X. D. (2008). About history and development of Vietnamese Ca trù. In H. L. Đặng, M. H. Phạm, & H. D. Hồ (Eds.), *Monograph on Vietnamese ca trù* (pp. 13–37). Hanoi: Vietnamese Institute for Musicology, Hanoi National Conservatory of Music.

Nguyễn, Y. (2009, May 25). Ca tru artists spar over name of center. *Thanh Nien Daily*. Retrieved May 12, 2013, from http://www.thanhniennews.com/2009/Pages/200949104125047836.aspx

Norton, B. (1996). Ca trù: A Vietnamese chamber music genre. *Nhac Viêt: The Journal of Vietnamese Music* [Special issue], 5(1), 1–103. Kent, OH: International Association for Research in Vietnamese Music.

Norton, B. (2005). Singing the past: Vietnamese ca tru, memory, and mode. *Asian Music*, 36(2), 27–56.

Norton, B. (2008). Ca trù restoration: Issues and challenges. In Ministry of Culture Sports and Tourism of Vietnam, Vietnam National Academy of Music & Vietnamese Institute for Musicology (Eds.), *Proceedings of the International Scientific Conference "Ca trù singing of the Việt people"* (pp. 187–192). Hanoi: Vietnamese Institute for Musicology.

Norton, B. (2009). *Songs for the spirits: Music and mediums in modern Vietnam*. Urbana: University of Illinois.

Norton, B. (2009, June). *Examination report for the nomination for inscription on the Urgent Safeguarding List in 2009: Ca trù singing*. Retrieved May 12, 2013, from http://www.unesco.org/culture/ich/index.php?pg=00246

Norton, B. (2010, July). *Cultural heritage, music revivalism and Vietnamese ca tru*. Paper presented at the Second Symposium of the ICTM Study Group on Applied Ethnomusicology, Hanoi, Vietnam.

Norton, B. (Producer). (2010). Hanoi Eclipse: The music of Dai Lam Linh [DVD]. Watertown, MA: Documentary Educational Resources.

Osamu, Y. (2001). Proposal for a tripartite theory (transformation/transcontextualization/transposition) and its application to the empowerment of an East Asian Court Music Network, with emphasis on the Vietnamese case. In P. Seitel (Ed.), *Safeguarding traditional cultures: A global assessment* (pp. 178–181). Washington DC: Center for Folklife and Cultural Heritage, Smithsonian Institution.

PARADISEC (2013). Endangered languages and cultures [Blog]. Retrieved May 13, 2013, from http://www.paradisec.org.au/blog/

Phạm, D. (Ed.). (1975). *Musics of Vietnam*. Carbondale: Southern Illinois University Press.

Phipps, P. (2009). Globalization, indigeneity, and performing culture. *Local-Global: Identity, Security, Community, 6*, 28–48.

Playing for Change (2011). Episode 39: Music School in Kirina, Mali. Retrieved May 13, 2013, from http://www.playingforchange.com/episodes/39/Music_School_in_Kirina_Mali

QCRC (2008a). Deborah Wong: On applied ethnomusicology [Video recording]. Retrieved October 29, 2013, from http://musecology.griffith.edu.au/videos/Deborah_Wong.mp4/view

QCRC (2008b). Phil Hayward: On engaged ethnomusicology [Video recording]. Retrieved October 28, 2013, from http://musecology.griffith.edu.au/videos/Phil_Hayward.mp4/view

QCRC (2013). Sustainable futures: Towards an ecology of musical diversity. Retrieved May 13, 2013, from http://musecology.griffith.edu.au/

Ramnarine, T. K. (2003). *Ilmater's inspiration: Nationalism, globalization, and the changing soundscapes of Finnish folk music*. Chicago, IL: University of Chicago Press.

Resource Network for Linguistic Diversity (2013). Resource Network for Linguistic Diversity Retrieved May 13, 2013, from http://www.rnld.org/

Reyhner, J., Cantoni, G., St. Clair, R. N., & Parsons Yazzie, E. (Eds.). (1999). *Revitalizing indigenous languages*. Flagstaff: North Arizona University.

Reyhner, J., & Lockard, L. (Eds.). (2009). *Indigenous language revitalization: Encouragement, guidance, and lessons learned*. Flagstaff: North Arizona University.

Rice, T. (2010). Ethnomusicological theory. *Yearbook for Traditional Music, 42*, 100–134.

Romaine, S. (2007). Preserving endangered languages. *Language and Linguistic Compass, 1*(1–2), 115–132.

Romero, R. R. (1992). Preservation, the mass media, and dissemination of traditional musics: The case of the Peruvian Andes. In M. P. Bauman (Ed.), *World music, musics of the world: Aspects of documentation, mass media and acculturation* (pp. 191–208). Wilhelmshaven, Germany: Florian Noetzel.

Ronström, O. (1996). Revival reconsidered. *World of Music, 38*(3), 5–20.

Rosenberg, N. V. (Ed.). (1993b). *Transforming tradition: Folk music revivals examined*. Urbana: University of Illinois Press.

Sanyal, R., & Widdess, R. (2004). *Dhrupad: Tradition and performance in Indian music*. Aldershot, UK: Ashgate.

Saurman, T. W. (2013). Singing for survival in the highlands of Cambodia: Tampuan revitalization of music as cultural reflexivity. [Unpublished doctoral dissertation.] Chiang Mai University, Thailand.

Schippers, H. (2007). The guru recontextualized? Perspectives on learning North Indian classical music in shifting environments for professional training. *Asian Music, 38*(1), 123–138.

Schippers, H. (2009). From *ca tru* to the world: Understanding and facilitating musical sustainability. In B.-L. Bartleet & C. Ellis (Eds.), *Music autoethnographies: Making autoethnography sing, making music personal* (pp. 197–207). Bowen Hills: Australian Academic Press.

Schippers, H. (2010). *Facing the music: Shaping music education from a global perspective.* New York: Oxford University Press.

Schmidt, A. (1990). *The loss of Australia's Aboriginal language heritage.* Canberra, Australia: Aboriginal Studies Press.

Seeger, A. (2004). *Why Suyá sing: A musical anthropology of an Amazonian people* (2nd ed.). Urbana and Chicago: University of Illinois Press.

Seeger, A. (2009). Lessons learned from the ICTM (NGO) evaluation of nominations for the UNESCO Masterpieces of the Oral and Intangible Heritage of Humanity, 2001–5. In L. Smith & N. Akagawa (Eds.), *Intangible heritage* (pp. 112–128). London: Routledge.

Seeger, A., & Chaudhuri, S. (Eds.). (2004). *Archives for the future: Global perspectives on audiovisual archives in the 21st century.* Calcutta, India: Seagull Books.

Sethi, R. (2001). A seed is not shy of germination. In P. Seitel (Ed.), *Safeguarding traditional cultures: A global assessment* (pp. 83–86). Washington, DC: Center for Folklife and Cultural Heritage, Smithsonian Institution.

Sheehy, D. (1992). A few notions about philosophy and strategy in Applied Ethnomusicology. *Ethnomusicology, 36*(3), 323–336.

Sheehy, D. (2006). *Mariachi music in America: Experiencing music, expressing culture.* New York: Oxford University Press.

Slobin, M. (1993). *Subcultural sounds: Micromusics of the West.* Middletown, CT: Wesleyan University Press.

Smith, L., & Akagawa, N. (Eds.). (2009). *Intangible heritage.* London: Routledge.

Smithsonian Institution (2013). Smithsonian Folkways. Retrieved May 13, 2013, from http://www.folkways.si.edu/

Spolsky, B. (2003). Reassessing Maori regeneration. *Language in Society, 32*(4), 553–578.

Spolsky, B. (2005). Language policy. In J. Chohen, K. T. McAlister, K. Rolstad, & J. MacSwan (Eds.), *4th International Symposium on Bilingualism* (pp. 2152–2164). Somerville, MA: Cascadilla Press.

Spolsky, B., & Shohamy, E. (2001). Hebrew after a century of RLS efforts. In J. A. Fishman (Ed.), *Can threatened languages be saved? Reversing language shift, revisited: A 21st century perspective* (pp. 349–362). Clevedon, UK: Multilingual Matters.

Stepwise Heritage and Tourism (2008). Stepping stones for tourism. Retrieved May 13, 2013, from http://www.steppingstonesfortourism.net/

Stiles, D. B. (1997). Four successful Indigenous language programs. In J. Reyhner (Ed.), *Teaching Indigenous Languages.* (pp. 248–262). Flagstaff: Northern Arizona University.

Stobart, H. (2010). Rampant reproduction and digital democracy: Shifting landscapes of music production and "piracy" in Bolivia. *Ethnomusicology Forum, 19*(1), 27–56.

Stokes, M. (2004). Music and the global order. *Annual Review of Anthropology, 33*, 47–72.

Stubington, J. (1987). Preservation and conservation of Australian traditional musics: An environmental analogy. *Musicology Australia, 10*, 2–15.

Tan, S. B. (2008). Activism in Southeast Asian ethnomusicology: Empowering youths to revitalize traditions and bridge cultural barriers. *Musicological Annual, 44*(1), 69–83.

Taylor, T. (1997). *Global pop: World music, world markets*. New York: Routledge.

Terralingua (2013). Website. Retrieved May 12, 2013, from http://www.terralingua.org

Thieberger, N. (2002). Extinction in whose terms? Which parts of a language constitute a target for language maintenance programmes? In D. Bradley & M. Bradley (Eds.), *Language endangerment and language maintenance* (pp. 310–328). London: Routledge Curzon.

Thomason, S. G. (2001). *Language contact*. Edinburgh, Scotland: Edinburgh University Press.

Titon, J. T. (2009a). Economy, ecology, and music: An introduction. *World of Music*, *51*(1), 5–15.

Titon, J. T. (2009b). Music and sustainability: An ecological viewpoint. *World of Music*, *51*(1), 119–137.

Titon, J. T. (Ed.). (2009c). *World of Music* [Special issue: *Music and Sustainability*], *51*(1). Bamberg, Germany: Department of Ethnomusicology, Otto-Friedrich-University.

Titon, J. T. (2009d). The music-culture as a world of music. In J. T. Titon (Ed.), *Worlds of music: An introduction to the music of the world's peoples* (5th ed., pp. 1–32). Belmont, CA: Schirmer Cengage Learning.

Tonkin, H. (2003). The search for a global strategy. In J. Maurais & M. A. Morris (Eds.), *Languages in a globalising world* (pp. 319–333). Cambridge, UK: Cambridge University Press.

Tonkin, H., & Reagan, T. (2003). Introduction: Language and the pursuit of the millennium. In H. Tonkin & T. Reagan (Eds.), *Language in the Twenty-First Century: Selected papers of the millennial conferences of the Center for Research and Documentation on World Language Problems* (pp. 1–8). Amsterdam, The Netherlands: John Benjamins.

Trần, V. K., & Nguyen, T. P. (2007–2011). Vietnam. *Oxford Music Online*. Retrieved July 21, 2011, from http://www.oxfordmusiconline.com

Tsering Bum, T., & Roche, G. (2009). Plateau music project: Grass-roots preservation of the Tibetan Plateau's diverse musical heritage. Retrieved May 11, 2013, from http://www.scribd.com/doc/37276498/Plateau-Music-Project-English

Tunstill, G. (1987). Melody and rhythmic structure in Pitjantjatjara song. In M. Clunies Ross, T. Donaldson, & S. A. Wild (Eds.), *Songs of Aboriginal Australia* (pp. 121–141). Sydney, Australia: Oceania.

UNESCO (2001). *Universal declaration on cultural diversity*. Retrieved May 13, 2013, from www.unesco.org/education/imld_2002/unversal_decla.shtml

UNESCO (2003a). *Convention for the safeguarding of Intangible Cultural Heritage*. Retrieved May 13, 2013, from http://www.unesco.org/culture/ich/index.php?pg=00006

UNESCO (2003b). *A methodology for assessing language vitality and endangerment*. Retrieved May 13, 2013, from http://www.unesco.org/new/en/culture/themes/endangered-languages/language-vitality/

UNESCO (2003c). *Promotion and use of multilingualism and universal access to cyberspace*. Retrieved May 13, 2013, from http://www.unesco.org/new/en/communication-and-information/about-us/how-we-work/strategy-and-programme/promotion-and-use-of-multilingualism-and-universal-access-to-cyberspace/

UNESCO (2005). *Convention on the protection and promotion of the diversity of cultural expressions*. Retrieved May 13, 2013, from http://www.unesco.org/new/en/culture/themes/cultural-diversity/diversity-of-cultural-expressions/the-convention/convention-text/

UNESCO (2006). UNESCO survey: Linguistic vitality and diversity. Retrieved May 27, 2013, from http://www.unesco.org/new/en/culture/themes/endangered-languages/atlas-of-languages-in-danger/contribute-your-comments/

UNESCO (2007). *International days*. Retrieved May 13, 2013, from http://portal.unesco.org/culture/en/ev.php-URL_ID=15327&URL_DO=DO_TOPIC&URL_SECTION=201.html

UNESCO (2008). *Links between biological and cultural diversity: Report of the International Workshop 26–28 September 2007*. Paris, France: UNESCO.

UNESCO (2012a). Frequent [sic] asked questions on endangered languages. Retrieved July 27, 2011, from http://www.unesco.org/new/en/culture/themes/endangered-languages/faq-on-endangered-languages/

UNESCO (2012b). The traditional music of the Morin Khuur. Retrieved May 13, 2013, from http://www.unesco.org/culture/ich/index.php?RL=00068

UNESCO (2013). Intangible Cultural Heritage. Retrieved May 13, 2013, from http://www.unesco.org/culture/ich/

UNESCO/Norwegian Ministry of Foreign Affairs (2006). *Ethiopia: Traditional music, dance, and instruments*. Addis Abbaba, Ethiopia: UNESCO Cluster Office.

UNESCO Ad Hoc Expert Group on Endangered Languages (2003). *Language vitality and endangerment*. Retrieved May 13, 2013, from http://www.unesco.org/culture/ich/doc/src/00120-EN.pdf

UNESCO Culture Sector (2011). UNESCO's *Language Vitality and Endangerment* methodological guideline: Review of application and feedback since 2003 [background paper]. Retrieved May 26, 2013, from http://www.unesco.org/new/fileadmin/MULTIMEDIA/HQ/CI/CI/pdf/unesco_language_vitaly_and_endangerment_methodological_guideline.pdf

UNESCO Section of Intangible Heritage/Korean National Commission for UNESCO (2002). *Guidelines for the establishment of national "Living Human Treasures" systems* (Updated version). May 13, 2013, from http://unesdoc.unesco.org/images/0012/001295/129520eo.pdf

United Nations High Commission for Human Rights (2007). *Declaration on the rights of indigenous peoples*. Retrieved May 13, 2013, from http://social.un.org/index/IndigenousPeoples/DeclarationontheRightsofIndigenousPeoples.aspx

Vakhtin, N. (2013). Epilogue. In E. Kasten & T. de Graff (Eds.), *Sustaining Indigenous knowledge: Learning tools and community initiatives for preserving endangered languages and local cultural heritage* (pp. 259–268). Fürstenberg/Havel, Germany: Kulturstiftung Sibirien.

Văn, S. (2008). Ca trù activity in today's life. In H. L. Đặng, M. H. Phạm, & H. D. Hồ (Eds.), *Monograph on Vietnamese ca trù* (pp. 191–210). Hanoi: Vietnamese Institute for Musicology, Hanoi National Conservatory of Music.

van Zanten, W. (2009). UNESCO News: 2003 Convention. *Bulletin of the International Council for Traditional Music, 114*, 40–42.

Vietnamese Institute for Musicology (2008a). Ca trù singing [1-hour video documentary]. Retrieved May 13, 2013, from http://www.youtube.com/watch?v=Tz35icN-stA

Vietnamese Institute for Musicology (2008b). Ca trù singing [10-minute video documentary]. Retrieved May 13, 2013, from http://www.unesco.org/culture/ich/index.php?USL=00309

VietnamNet (2009, March 23). Thang Long Ca Tru Theatre opens for tourists. Retrieved May 13, 2013, from http://www.travelvietnam.org/tvn/vietnam-today/thang-long-ca-tru-theatre-opens-for-tourists-id2113.html

VietNamNet/Dat Viet (2009, November 12). Punishment requested for love duet dissenter. *Look at Vietnam*. Retrieved May 13, 2013, from http://www.lookatvietnam.com/2009/11/punishment-requested-for-love-duet-dissenter.html

Vũ, N. T. (2008). Music of ca trù singing. In H. L. Đặng, M. H. Phạm, & H. D. Hồ (Eds.), *Monograph on Vietnamese ca trù* (pp. 120–174). Hanoi: Vietnamese Institute for Musicology, Hanoi National Conservatory of Music.

Wachsmann, K. P. (1982). The changeability of musical experience. *Ethnomusicology*, 26(2), 197–215.

Walsh, M. (2002). *Teaching NSW's indigenous languages: Lessons from elsewhere* (Report commissioned by Office of the Board of Studies). Department of Linguistics, University of Sydney.

Walsh, M. (2005). Will Indigenous languages survive? *Annual Review of Anthropology*, 34, 293–315.

Walsh, M. (2009). The rise and fall of GIDS in accounts of language endangerment. In H. Elnazarov & N. Ostler (Eds.), *Endangered Languages and History: Proceedings of FEL XIII, Khorog, Tajikistan* (pp. 134–141). Bath, UK: Foundation for Endangered Languages.

Walsh, M. (2010). Why language revitalization sometimes works. In J. Hobson, K. Lowe, S. Poetsch, & M. Walsh (Eds.), *Re-awakening languages: Theory & practice in the revitalisation of Australia's Indigenous languages* (pp. 22–36). Sydney, Australia: Sydney University Press.

Wang, Y.-F. (2003). Amateur music clubs and state intervention: The case of nanguan music in postwar Taiwan. *Journal of Chinese Ritual, Theatre and Folklore*, 141, 95–167.

Warschauer, M., Donaghy, K., & Kuamoÿo, H. (1997). Leokï: A powerful voice of Hawaiian language revitalization. *Computer Assisted Language Learning*, 10(4), 349–361.

Welsh Assembly Government (2003). *I aith pawb: A national action plan for a bilingual Wales*. Retrieved May 13, 2013, from http://new.wales.gov.uk/depc/publications/welshlanguage/iaithpawb/iaithpawbe.pdf?lang=en

Wettermark, E. (2010a). *Shifting mindscapes in the Vietnamese historical consciousness and its impact on music revivalism: Ca trù and the Thăng Long Ca Trù Club*. [Unpublished masters dissertation.] Goldsmiths, University of London.

Wettermark, E. (2010b). Thăng Long Ca Trù Club: New ways for old music. *Finnish Journal of Music Education*, 13(1), 72–87.

Wettermark, E. (2010c, July). *Thang Long Ca Tru: New ways for old music*. Paper presented at the Second Symposium of the ICTM Study Group on Applied Ethnomusicology, Hanoi, Vietnam.

Whaley, L. J., & Stanford, J. N. (2013). The sustainability of languages. In F. E. Gebert & K. Gibson (Eds), *Sustaining living culture* (pp. 87–101). Champaign, IL: Common Ground.

Widdess, R. (1994). Festivals of dhrupad in Northern India: New contexts for an ancient art. *British Journal of Ethnomusicology*, 3, 89–109.

Wilson, G. N. (2008). The revitalization of the Manx language and culture in an era of global change. In I. Novaczek (Ed.), *Proceedings of the Third International Small Island Cultures Conference* (pp. 7481). Sydney, Australia: Small Islands Cultures Research Initiative.

Wiora, W. (1965). *The four ages of music*. New York: Norton.

Wood, G. S., & Judikis, J. C. (2002). *Conservations on community theory*. West Lafayette, IN: Purdue University Press.

World Intellectual Property Organization (n.d.). Traditional cultural expressions. Retrieved October 27, 2013, from http://www.wipo.int/tk/en/
World Oral Literature Project (2013a). Endangered languages database. Retrieved May 13, 2013, from http://www.oralliterature.org/research/databaseterms.html
World Oral Literature Project (2013b). Plateau Culture Heritage Protection Group: Collections from the Tibetan Plateau 2006–2012. Retrieved May 19, 2013, from http://www.oralliterature.org/collections/pchpgcollections.html
Wurm, S. A. (1998). Methods of language maintenance and revival, with selected cases of language endangerment in the world. In K. Matsumura (Ed.), *Studies in endangered languages: Papers from the International Symposium on Endangered Languages, Tokyo, November 18–20, 1995* (pp. 191–211). Tokyo, Japan: Hituzi Syobo.
Yamamoto, A. Y. (1998). Linguists and endangered language communities: Issues and approaches. In K. Matsumura (Ed.), *Studies in endangered languages: Papers from the International Symposium on Endangered Languages, Tokyo, November 18–20, 1995* (pp. 231–252). Tokyo Japan: Hituzi Syobo.
Zuckermann, G., & Walsh, M. (2011). Stop, revive, survive: Lessons from the Hebrew revival applicable to the reclamation, maintenance and empowerment of Aboriginal languages and cultures. *Australian Journal of Linguistics*, *31*(1), 111–127.

INDEX

Abley, M., 54, 94
Aceh, Sumatra (Indonesia), 53, 63
Addiss, S., 157, 160
advocacy, 79–84
Afghanistan, 32, 61
Afghanistan National Institute of Music, 32
Afroperuvian music, 22–23
aleke (Suriname), 94
All India Radio, 36
Alliance for Linguistic Diversity, 6
Am Sac Viet, 147
Anisensel, A., 157
The Anthropology of Music (Merriam), 53
Arana, M., 155
Archer, W. K., 19
Archive of Maori and Pacific Music (AMPM), 25
Asia-Pacific Cultural Centre for UNESCO (ACCU), 41–42
Association of Vietnamese Folklorists, 151
Atlas of the World's Languages in Danger (UNESCO), 5–6, 76, 81, 98–99, 107
Aubert, L., 24, 68
Austin, P., 60, 78, 94, 172
Australian Indigenous languages
 Australia's National Indigenous Languages Survey and, 79
 bilingual education and, 52
 language maintenance programs and, 93
 language vitality of, 75
 role of contexts and constructs in, 58–59
 technology and, 92
 terminology and, 107
 See also Kaurna (Aboriginal language)
Australian Indigenous music
 acquisition of musical skills and, 50–51
 cultural ownership and, 54
 documentation and, 24, 25
 festivals and, 30
 mass media and, 65
 performance traditions and, 2
 tourism and, 39
Australia's National Indigenous Languages Survey, 79
awareness, 80–81

bardic singing (Indonesia), 53
Baumann, M. P., 3, 7
biocultural diversity, 4
Blacking, J., 74
Blaukopf, K., 35, 43
Bohlman, P. V., 66
Bolivia, 36, 37
Bùi, T. H., 135, 146, 152–53

ca trù (Vietnam)
 change in performance contexts and functions of, 140–42, 142, *162*
 change in the music and music practices of, 138–140, 140, *162*
 change in the number of people engaged with, 135–37, 137, *162*
 change in the number of proficient musicians of, 134–35, 136, *162*
 community members' attitudes toward, 154–56, 156, *162*

ca trù (Cont.)
   documentation and, 25, 159–161, 161, *162*
   governmental and institutional policies and, 150–53, *153*
   history of, 127–130
   infrastructure and resources for, 145–48, 148, *162*
   intergenerational transmission and, 132–34, 134, *162*
   knowledge and skills for, 148–150, *150*, *162*
   learning and teaching of, 33, 138–39, 146–47
   outsiders' attitudes toward, 156–58, *158*, *162*
   purpose of sustainability strategies for, 97
   recognition and celebration of, 30
   response to mass media and the music industry, 143–45, *145*, 147–48, *162*
   revitalization and, 20, 129–30
   sources for vitality assessment of, 130–31
   summary of vitality assessment for, 161–63
   tourism and, 141–42, 143–44, 147–48
Ca Trù Thai Ha Ensemble, 147
Cabral, C. B., 174
cải biên nhạc tộc dân (Vietnam), 128
Cambodia, 13, 32, 37, 61
Cambodian Living Arts (CLA), 32
Campbell, G., 4
Campbell, P., 34–35
Canada, 29
Cape Breton fiddling (Canada), 29
Catalan language, 74
ceilidh dance tunes (Northumberland), 33–34
censorship, 61–62
Chami, H., 164
Chào Ông Bill Gates ("To Mr. Bill Gates"), 138
Charoensook, S., 94
chầu văn (Vietnam), 128
Chengdu Intangible Cultural Heritage Protection Center (China), 41
China Intangible Cultural Heritage Protection Center, 41

classical music (Thailand), 31–32, 94
Cohen, J. M., 164
community
   ca trù and, 154–56, *156*, *162*
   definitions of, 107
   importance of music for, 9
   MVEF and, 121–22, 123, 154–56, *156*, *162*
   role in language sustainability, 55–56, 58–60, 69, 88–89
   role in music sustainability, 52–56, 58–60, 69, 88–89
   use of term, 107
Consortium for Training in Language Documentation and Conservation, 99
Convention for the Safeguarding of the Intangible Cultural Heritage (UNESCO)
   ca trù and, 151
   definition of intangible cultural heritage in, 10
   on endangerment, 2, 3
   overview, 30, 36, 41
Convention on the Protection and Promotion of the Diversity of Cultural Expressions (UNESCO), 36, 42, 64
Cottrell, S., 19–20
Coulter, N. R., 28, 77
creolization, 54–55
Croatia, 37
Crystal, D., 5, 80, 86, 90
Cuba, 65
cultural diversity
   coordination and evaluation mechanisms of, 42–43
   importance of, 8
   UNESCO and, 7, 36, 42, 64
Cultural Diversity in Music Education (CDIME), 34, 48–49
cultural hegemony, 2
Cultures in Harmony, 61

Dai L. M., 139
đàn đáy (Vietnam), 127, 139, 147, 155, 160
Đang H. L., 146, 159
Danielou, A., 61
Dauenhauer, N. M., 67

Dauenhauer, R., 67
Davis, W., 176
De Ferranti, H., 75
Declaration on the Rights of Indigenous Peoples (United Nations High Commission for Human Rights), 36, 64
"deep ecology" movement, 20
Defrance, Y., 135, 157
DELEMAN (Digital Endangered Languages and Musics Archives Network), 25
dhrupad (India)
  ecological models and, 20
  festivals and, 28, 29, 68
  role of outsiders in musical vitality and, 61
  royal patronage and, 54
Digital Himalaya, 27
Dimick, B., 157
DISMARC (Discovering Music Archives), 25
diversity. *See* linguistic diversity; musical diversity
Dixon, R. M. W., 75, 83
documentation
  ca trù and, 25, 159–161, 161, *162*
  language vitality and, 105, 123–24
  music vitality and, *16*, 23–28
  MVEF and, 123–25, 124, 159, 161, *162*
Dokumentation der Bedrohte Sprachen ("Documentation of endangered languages," Germany), 102
Dunbar-Hall, P., 51

Edwards, J., 75, 77–78
Ellis, C. J., 24, 29, 71
E-MELD (Electronic Metastructure for Endangered Languages Data), 98
emergent languages, 108–9
emergent music genres, 108–9, 113
Endangered Language Fund, 5, 102
Endangered Languages and Cultures blog, 98
Endangered Languages Archive (ELAR), 25
Endangered Languages Project, 5–6
Endangered Languages Week, 81

endangerment. *See* language endangerment; music endangerment
enterprise, 38–39. *See also* tourism
Erlmann, V., 22, 65
Ethiopia: Traditional Music, Dance and Instruments (UNESCO), 27
ethnocentrism, 131
Ethnologue, 79, 80–81, 98–99
Evans, N., 54

Facebook, 144
fasıl (Ottoman Empire), 24
The Federal Cylinder Project, 26
Feintuch, B., 22, 23
festivals
  ca trù and, 129, 135–36, 141
  music vitality and, 28–30
  tourism and, 68
FirstVoices, 91–92
Fishman, J. A., 75, 77, 94, 108–9
folk music (Finland)
  documentation and, 23
  kantele and, 33, 59
  music education and, 33
  music revivals and, 22–23
  performance contexts for, 58
  role of community in vitality of, 89
  role of outsiders in vitality of, 61
  tourism and, 68
folk music (Hungary), 22–23, 89
folk music (Peru), 66
folk music (Serbia), 22–23, 94–95
Folk Music Institute (Kaustinen, Finland), 33
FolkWorks, 33
Ford Foundation, 33, 133, 157–58
Foundation for Endangered Languages, 6, 100, 102
Freemuse (Freedom of Musical Expression), 36, 61
Future of Music, 36

gamelan (Bali), 51
gamelan gong gede (Bali), 116, 120–21
gamelan kebyar (Bali), 116, 120
Garza-Cuarón, B., 74
genres (music)
  definition of, 106–7
  total number of, 3

Giáo Phường Ca Trù Thăng Long (Thăng Long Ca Trù Club)
    change in *ca trù* and, 139–140
    concert series "Ca trù comes back" and, 140
    education of the audience and, 149
    funding and, 157
    intergenerational transmission and, 133
    mass media and, 143, 144
    music tourism and, 141
    number of people engaged with *ca trù* and, 136–37
    resources for *ca trù* and, 145–46, 148
    role in vitality assessment of, 130, 131
    role in vitality of *ca trù*, 154–55
    teaching and, 139
Giddens, A., 17
GIDS (Graded Intergenerational Disruption Scale), 77, 108–9
globalization, 17–19
Graded Music Shift Scale (GMSS), 77
Gramsci, A., 169
Graves, J. B., 33–34, 39, 54–55, 59
Grenoble, L. A., 50, 76–77, 78
guqin (China), 37–38
guru-śisya-paramparā (India), 48

hán nôm script (Vietnam), 149
Hanoi Ca Trù Club, 30, 129, 133, 140, 154
Hans Rausing Endangered Languages Project (UK), 25, 81, 102
hát chơi (Vietnam), 127–28, 141–42
hát cửa đình (Vietnam), 128, 139–140, 141, 148
hát cửa quyền (Vietnam), 128
hát nói (Vietnam), 138, 148–49
hát thi (Vietnam), 127
hát thờ (Vietnam), 127, 141, 142, 148
Hawaiian language, 84, 92, 94, 95
Hayward, P., 19, 22
Hebrew language, 85, 94, 95
Hemetek, U., 25, 60–61
huaylarsh (Peru), 66

identity, 9
Index of Linguistic Diversity, 81
India, 36, 57–58, 68. See also *dhrupad* (India)

Indigenous Language Institute (ILI), 6
Indonesia, 53, 63
intangible cultural heritage, 1, 10, 12
Intangible Cultural Heritage in Need of Urgent Safeguarding (UNESCO)
    ca trù and, 130, 131, 133–34, 135, 137, 147, 150–51, 152, 154, 159, 160–61
    emergent music genres and, 109
    overview, 30
intergenerational transmission
    ca trù and, 132–34, 134
    language and music sustainability and, 48
    language vitality and, 105, 112
    MVEF and, 111–13, 112, 113, 132–34, 134
International Clearing House for Endangered Languages, 6
International Contest for Better Practices in Community Intangible Cultural Heritage Revitalization, 41–42
International Council for Traditional Music (ICTM), 11, 43
International Federation of Coalitions for Cultural Diversity, 42
International Mother Language Day, 81
International Music Council (IMC), 3, 43
International Music Day, 81
International Network for Cultural Diversity (INCD), 42
International Network of Lawyers for the Diversity of Cultural Expressions, 42–43
International Network on Cultural Policy, 42
International Society for Music Education (ISME), 43
Internet
    ca trù and, 144–45
    language sustainability and, 67
    music endangerment and, 2
    music sustainability and, 66–67
invented tradition, 22
Irish (language), 93

Jähnichen, G., 147, 149, 157, 160
joik (Finland), 23, 61

kantaoming (Cambodia), 13
kantele (Finland), 33, 59
Karpeles, M., 25
Kartomi, M. J., 21–22, 54, 55, 63, 165
Kaurna (Aboriginal language), 58, 89, 95–96
Kaustinen Festival of Folk Music, 68
kawina (Suriname), 94
kōhanga reo (New Zealand), 70
Khmer Rouge, 61
khöömei (China/Mongolia), 37
Kinkade, M. D., 75
Kit on Intangible Cultural Heritage (UNESCO), 41
Korea, 93–94
Kouyaté, B., 65
Krauss, M., 74, 109

Laitinen, H., 59
lakalaka (Tonga), 52, 53
Langton, M., 68
Language (journal), 5
Language Death (Crystal), 5
language endangerment, 5–6, 12, 102
language maintenance
  aims and outcomes of strategies, 93–97
  advocacy and, 80–84
  coordinating mechanisms for, 97–102
  ethical considerations on, 13
  identification and assessment of endangerment in, 74–79
  music and, 4–7
  strategies for, 84–92
  use of term, 11–12
language nests, 70, 84
language revitalization, 11. *See also* language maintenance
language shift, 4, 55, 77
  intergenerational transmission and, 48
  mass media and, 64–65, 67, 70
  role of community in, 55–56, 58–60, 69, 88–89
  role of contexts and constructs in, 56–62, 69
  role of infrastructure and regulations in, 62–64, 70
  systems of learning and, 48–52, 69, 90–91

  tourism and, 68
Language Vitality and Endangerment framework (UNESCO)
  absolute number of speakers and, 113–14
  assessment and, 108
  change and, 115–16
  documentation and, 123–24
  function of language and, 117
  music endangerment and, 103
  overview, 76–78, 105–6
  terminology and, 106–7
language vitality and viability
  intergenerational transmission and, 105, 112
  typologies and classifications of, 75–77, 76
The Last Biwa Singer (De Ferranti), 75
Lastra, Y., 74
Law on Cultural Heritage (Vietnam), 150
Lê, T. B. V., 133, 154
Leoki (computer-assisted Hawaiian-language learning project), 92
Letts, R., 19, 43
Lewis, M. P.
  GIDS and, 109
  on language endangerment, 75
  language vitality framework and, 77, 78, 112, 113–14, 124, 126
linguistic diversity, 81, 99
literacy, 49–50
Living National Treasures (Living Human Treasures, Intangible National Treasures), 30–31
Livingston, T. E., 22, 28, 38–39
Lomax, A., 7, 18

Maffi, L., 55
magazines, 143
Malaysia, 32
Mali, 32, 65
Malm, K., 19, 21, 38, 43–44
Malmö Academy of Music (University of Lund, Sweden), 158
Manx culture and language, 94
Maori language, 70, 84, 94
Maori songs, 56, 57–58
Marett, A., 8
mariachi (Mexico), 22–23, 34–35, 89

mass media
    ca trù and, 143–45, 145, 147–48, *162*
    festivals and, 29
    language sustainability and, 64–65, 67, 70
    music endangerment and, 18–19
    music sustainability and, 64–68, 70, 71
    music vitality and, 38
    MVEF and, 118–19, 119, 143–45, 145, *162*
master-apprentice model of language learning, 48, 84
master-disciple system of learning music, 48
Masterpieces of Oral and Intangible Cultural Heritage in Urgent Need of Safeguarding (UNESCO)
    ca trù and, 130, 151
    ill effects of, 37–38
    lakalaka and, 52
McCloskey, J., 93
McConvell, P., 75, 78
mediaization, 18–19
Merriam, A., 53
Mexico, 22–23, 34–35, 89
Millennium Development Goals, 10
Mongolia, 37
morin khurr (Mongolia), 57–58
Moyle, R. M., 20
Mundy, S.
    on commodification of music, 53
    on cross-fertilisation, 54
    on globalization, 17, 19
    IMC and, 43
    on mass media and music industry, 65
    on piracy, 67
music
    commodification of, 18–19, 53, 65
    language and, 4–7
    tourism and, 38–39, 68, 141–42, 143–44, 147–48
music culture, 106–7
music education
    ca trù and, 33, 138–39, 146–47
    music sustainability and, 48–52, 69
    music vitality and, 31–35
    See also intergenerational transmission
music endangerment
    ethical considerations on, 12–14, 26, 29
    identification and assessment of, 74–79
    introduction to, 1–4
    terminology and, 10–12
    use of term, 12
music genres
    definition of, 106–7
    total number of, 3
music industry
    ca trù and, 143–45, 145, 147–48, *162*
    music sustainability and, 64–68, 70
    MVEF and, 118–19, 119, 143–45, 145, *162*
music revivals
    documentation and, 24–25
    enterprise and, 38–39
    overview, 22–23
    use of term, 11
music shift, 55–56, 77
music sustainability
    advocacy for, 79–84
    aims and outcomes of strategies for, 93–97
    contexts and constructs of musical tradition and, 56–62, 69, 90
    coordinating mechanisms for, 97–102
    ecological models for, 19–21
    intergenerational transmission and, 48
    language sustainability and, 69–72, 69–70
    role of community in, 52–56, 58–60, 69, 88–89
    role of ethnomusicologists in, 3–4, 164–65
    role of infrastructure and regulations in, 62–64, 70, 90–91
    role of media and the music industry in, 64–68, 70, 71
    role of musicians and communities in, 52–56, 69
    strategies for, 84–92
    systems of learning music and, 48–52, 69
Music Vitality and Endangerment Framework (MVEF)
    assessment and, 108–10

[202]   Index

Language Vitality and Endangerment
  and, 106–7, 108, 109–11
 overview, 106, 125, 169
 terminology and, 106–7
 use of, 125–26
Music Vitality and Endangerment
  Framework (MVEF) factors
 amount and quality of documentation, 123–25, 124, 159, 161, *162*
 change in performance contexts and functions, 117–18, 118, 140–42, 142, *162*
 change in the music and music practices, 115–16, 117, 138–140, 140, *162*
 change in the number of people engaged with the genre, 115, 116, 135–37, 137, *162*
 change in the number of proficient musicians, 113–14, 114, 134–35, 136, *162*
 community members' attitudes toward the genre, 121–22, 123, 154–56, 156, *162*
 governmental and institutional policies affecting music practices, 121, 122, 150–53, 153
 infrastructure and resources for music practices, 119–120, 120, 145–48, 148, *162*
 intergenerational transmission, 111–13, 112, 113, 132–34, 134, *162*
 knowledge and skills for music practices, 120–21, 121, 148–150, 150, *162*
 relevant outsiders' attitudes toward the genre, 123, 124, 156–58, 158, *162*
 response to mass media and the music industry, 118–19, 119, 143–45, 145, *162*
 summary of vitality assessment for *ca trù* with, 161–63
music vitality and viability
 coordination and evaluation mechanisms of, *16*, 39–44, 40
 documentation and preservation of music and, *16*, 23–28
 importance of, 7–10
 outsiders' attitudes and, 60–61
 recognition and celebration of music and, *16*, 28–31
 role of policy and enterprise in, *16*, 35–39
 strengths, weaknesses, and gaps in current theory and practice of, 44–46, 73, 102–4
 theoretical foundations for, 15–23
 transmission and dissemination of music and, *16*, 31–35
musical diversity
 Cultural Diversity in Music Education and, 34, 48–49
 globalization and, 17–19
 importance of, 8
 technology and, 2
Musical Futures Foundation, 102
musical heritage, 12
musical transculturation, 21–22
Myers, H., 12

nanguan (Taiwan), 34, 36–37
Nanning International Folk Song Festival (China), 29
National Recording Project for Indigenous Performance in Australia, 24
nativistic revival, 21–22
Nettl, B.
 on documentation and preservation, 24, 25
 on ethnocentrism, 131
 on globalization, 17–18
 on "musical energy," 55
 on musical transculturation, 21
Neuman, D. M., 20, 59
new conservation ecology, 20–21
newspapers, 143
Ngọc, H., 156
ngoni (Mali), 65
Nguyen L. H., 141
Nguyễn P. Đ., 133, 136, 146
Nguyễn P. K., 132
Nguyễn Q. T., 155
Nguyễn T. C., 132, 133, 136, 146, 149
Nguyễn T. H., 147
Nguyễn T. L., 159–160
Nguyễn T. T., 155
Nguyễn T. T. H., 132
Nguyễn V. M., 133

nhạc lễ (Vietnam), 128
Ninti Ngapartji (website), 92
Norman language, 68
Norton, B.
　on *ca trù*, 143, 147, 153, 157, 160
　on documentation, 25
　on ecological models, 20
　on governmental policies, 151, 152, 153
notation
　ca trù and, 160
　music revivals and, 23
　music sustainability and, 49

"On the ecology of music" (Archer), 19
Oruro Carnival (Bolivia), 37

Pacific and Regional Archive for Digital Sources in Endangered Cultures (PARADISEC), 25, 27
p'ansori (Korea), 93–94
performance, 57
Peru, 22–23, 38, 66
Pettan, S., 37, 175
phách (Vietnam), 127
Phạm D., 128–29
Phạm T.H.
　on *ca trù*, 135
　criticism of, 155
　intergenerational transmission and, 133, 134
　music tourism and, 141
　on notation, 160
　role in vitality assessment of, 130, 131
　role in vitality of *ca trù*, 154
　on teaching, 136, 139
Phipps, P., 29, 30
Phó Đ. P., 156
Phó T. K. Đ., 132, 160
piping (Northumbria), 23, 25
piracy, 35–36, 67
Pitjantjatjara people (Australia), 50–51, 92
Plateau Cultural Heritage Protection Group, 27
Plateau Music Project, 27
Playing for Change Foundation, 32
poverty, 61
preservation, 16, 23–28

Proclamation of Masterpieces of the Oral and Intangible Heritage of Humanity (UNESCO), 30
p'ungmul (Korea), 94

Quách T. H., 129, 132
quan họ (Vietnam), 151, 152–53
Queensland Conservatorium Research Centre (Australia), 158

radio, 36, 143, 144
Ramnarine, T. K., 33, 37, 58, 165, 172
Recommendation on the Promotion and Use of Multilingualism and Universal Access to Cyberspace (UNESCO), 67
Recommendation on the Safeguarding of Traditional Culture and Folklore (conference), 97
Red Book of Endangered Languages of the World (UNESCO), 5–6
Register of Best Safeguarding Practices (UNESCO), 41, 98
Representative List of the Intangible Cultural Heritage of Humanity (UNESCO), 30, 37
Resource Network for Linguistic Diversity (RNLD), 99
Revival of Afghan Music, 32, 97
Rice, T., 174
Romero, R. R., 27, 38, 39, 66, 71
Royal Ballet of Cambodia, 37

safeguarding
　definition and use of term, 10, 12
　UNESCO and, 30–31, 41–42, 98
　See also *Intangible Cultural Heritage in Need of Urgent Safeguarding* (UNESCO)
Sallabank, J., 96–97, 172
Sámi joik traditions, 23, 61
Sámi language, 61
Sanyal, R., 20
Sarmast, A., 97
Schippers, H.
　ca trù and, 130, 140, 149, 157
　on ecological models for music sustainability, 19
　on five domains of music sustainability, 47, 48, 52, 56–57, 62, 63, 64, 69–70

Schmidt, A., 75
Seeger, A., 3, 37, 88–89
Sen, A., 11
Seng N., 13
Serbia, 94–95
Sethi, R., 97
shift (music shift; language shift), 4, 55–56, 77
Simons, G. F., 75, 77, 109, 112
Slobin, M., 19
Smithsonian Global Sounds, 25
Society for Ethnomusicology (SEM), 43
son (Cuba), 65
sound archives, 25–26
speech communities, 107
Stepping Stones for Tourism, 39
stewardship, 20–21
Stiles, D. B., 60
Stobart, H., 36
Stubington, J., 19, 25
Supporting Vietnamese Culture for Sustainable Development, 158
surbahār (India), 59
sustainability, 11, 12. *See also* language sustainability; music sustainability
Sustainable Futures for Music Cultures (Australia), 43, 100, 130
Sutherland, W., 98–99
Suyá people, 9
Swedish International Development Cooperation Agency (SIDA), 158

taboos, 54
Taiwan, 34, 36–37
Takū atoll (Polynesia), 20, 56, 59, 63
Taliban, 61
Tan, S. B., 32
tantric ritual music (India), 68
technology, 50, 91–92
television, 143
Terralingua, 7, 81, 100
Thái Hà Ca Trù Club (formerly Thái Hà Ca Trù Ensemble), 133, 143, 144, 154–55
Thailand, 31–32, 94
Thăng Long Ca Trù Club *see* Giáo Phường Ca Trù Thăng Long (Thăng Long Ca Trù Club)
Thăng Long Ca Trù Theatre, 141, 144
Thieberger, N., 75, 78, 94

Tibetan Endangered Music Project, 27
Tipiloura, L., 9
Titon, J. T., 10–11, 20, 31, 37–38, 42
Tô N. T., 144, 155–56
tourism
  ca trù and, 141–42, 143–44, 147–48
  music and, 38–39, 68
Toyota Foundation, 129
trade liberalization, 2
Trần V. K., 129, 157
transcriptions, 23, 49
trống chầu (Vietnam), 127
Tunstill, G., 50–51
Turkey, 61

umbrella networks, 25
UNESCO
  documentation and, 27
  on intangible cultural heritage, 1, 10
  language endangerment and, 5–6, 75
  safeguarding and, 30–31, 41–42, 98
  See also specific projects
United Nations, 10
Universal Declaration of Linguistic Rights (Assembly of the World Conference on Linguistic Rights, 1996), 64
Universal Declaration on Cultural Diversity (UNESCO), 7, 36
urgent anthropology, 3
Urgent Safeguarding List (UNESCO). *See Intangible Cultural Heritage in Need of Urgent Safeguarding* (UNESCO)

Vakhtin, N., 5
van Zanten, W., 42
Vietnam. *See ca trù* (Vietnam)
Vietnam Cultural Heritage Association, 151
Vietnam National Academy of Music/Vietnamese Institute for Musicology, 158
Vietnamese Court Music Revitalization Plan, 129
Vietnamese Institute for Hán-Nôm Studies, 151
Vũ, N. T., 159

Wachsmann, K. P., 9
Walsh, M.
  on community's attitudes, 59, 88
  on frameworks and classification, 78, 110–11
  on language revitalization programs, 86–87, 90, 92, 95, 96
Wang, Y.-F., 31
Welsh language, 59–60, 94
A Westerner Loves Our Music (documentary), 143
Wettermark, E.
  ca trù and, 130, 137, 146, 155, 157
  on documentation, 159–160
Whaley, L. J., 50, 76–77, 78

whirling dervish ceremony, 61
Widdess, R., 20
Wiora, W., 18
Wong, D., 94
The World (news magazine), 144
World Intellectual Property Organization (WIPO), 36
World Oral Literature Project, 27, 98–99
Wurm, S. A., 75

Yamamoto, A. Y., 86
Yan-nhaŋu language, 95
YouTube, 144

Zuckermann, G., 95